# THREE DEGREES
# ABOVE ZERO

# THREE DEGREES ABOVE ZERO

## BELL LABS
## IN THE
## INFORMATION AGE

### JEREMY
### BERNSTEIN

CHARLES SCRIBNER'S SONS · NEW YORK

Portions of this book originally appeared in *The New Yorker*
Copyright © 1984 Jeremy Bernstein

**Library of Congress Cataloging in Publication Data**

Bernstein, Jeremy, 1929–
   Three degrees above zero.

   Bibliography: p.
   Includes index.
   1. Bell Telephone Laboratories, inc.  I. Title.
T178.B45B47  1984       621.38′072073       84–5450
ISBN 0–684–18170–3

3 5 7 9 11 13 15 17 19  F/C  20 18 16 14 12 10 8 6 4

PRINTED IN THE UNITED STATES OF AMERICA.

All photos courtesy AT&T Bell Laboratories Public Relations Photo Service.

To B. B. — A foul-weather friend

# Preface

AS IS HAPPILY MY WONT, I spend a good deal of each summer in Aspen, Colorado, at the Aspen Center for Physics. Sometime in July 1982, while wandering in a field adjoining the center, I encountered a colleague, Philip W. Anderson. As the reader will learn, Anderson is a Nobel Prize-winning theoretical physicist who for over thirty years has been associated with Bell Laboratories, the research and development arm of the American Telephone and Telegraph Company. While we talked, Anderson asked if I had ever thought of writing anything about Bell Labs. I had to confess that I had not—for several reasons, not the least of which is the fact that those areas of physics for which Bell Labs is most noted are just the areas of physics with which I am least acquainted. The same argument applies *a fortiori* to the numerous branches of science and technology done at Bell Labs that are not physics at all. Another equally important reason was the practical question of how to write, in a meaningful and interesting way, about an institution that had some 25,000 employees, before the divestiture, working at thirteen locations in New Jersey and at seven other locations all over the country. (It now has 18,000 employees in ten New Jersey and six out-of-state locations.) Finally, there was the potential problem of writing about a world-famous industrial laboratory that might have its own strong views on how its story should be told to the public. In other words, would it be possible to have free access to such a laboratory and thereafter to let the literary chips fall where they may?

I explained all of these reservations to Anderson but agreed anyway to make at least a preliminary foray into the subject. He, in turn, spoke to people at the Laboratories. The first result was the arrival at *The New Yorker* of some gigantic parcels of reading material, including the proofs of a thousand-page volume produced at Bell Labs on the physics research done at the Labs since their founding in 1925. At the sight of it my heart sank. How would it be possible to translate something like this into literature for popular consumption? The material was, in turn, followed by an amiable letter from Anderson inviting me to visit Murray Hill, in New Jersey, the branch of Bell Labs most directly concerned with basic research. A daily car pool of theoretical physicists commuted from Greenwich Village, where I live, to Murray Hill, he told me. This gives me an opportunity to thank my fellow car poolers Susan Coppersmith, Daniel Fisher, Pierre Hohenberg, and Chandra Varma, theoretical physicists all, for a series of rides to, and discussions about, Bell that went on for the better part of a year. In any event, in September 1982 I accepted Anderson's invitation.

While I have spent much of my working life around scientific laboratories, I have never seen anything on the scale and complexity of the various Bell Laboratories and, in particular, of Murray Hill. Constructed in 1941, Murray Hill is essentially one gigantic building, housing some four thousand people, the majority of whom are engaged in research in almost every known discipline. The building has been partitioned into modules that can be moved to create various laboratory spaces. On the outer wall, at six-foot intervals, fourteen essential laboratory support services, including gases under pressure, electricity, and water, are duplicated. It has been estimated that by moving the partitions around an entirely new laboratory configuration is created once every seven years. Both the offices and the specific laboratories are kept as small as possible; space is at a premium, and there are very few frills. The whole thing at present resembles a gigantic technological warren within which, at least at first sight, everything resembles everything else. Until I got used to the place, I had a menacing fantasy that, in the process of going from one laboratory to another, I would take the wrong turn and never find my way out.

As it happened, the period of my visits coincided with the transition that the laboratories were making because of the breakup of AT&T.

On 24 August 1982 Federal District Judge Harold H. Greene signed a modified version of the consent agreement between the Justice Department and AT&T that split up the telephone company but allowed AT&T to retain Bell Labs. But even before the laboratories entered their new competitive mode, a security system within Bell made it mandatory for visitors to be escorted, so there was no chance of my getting lost. Escort or not, the place, at least initially, gave the impression of bewildering complexity. It did not seem to be something that I could readily compress into a usable piece of writing.

The fog began to lift sometime around noon of the day of my first visit. Anderson had organized a sandwich lunch to which he had invited a number of people. As the lunch progressed it became clear that many of the people there had never met each other—not surprising, considering the size of the place. It dawned on me that the way to write about Bell Labs was, in the first instance, to break the subject up into people; to construct a kind of mosaic of people that, when assembled, would make a coherent sample of the whole. That afternoon I began a series of tape-recorded interviews that went on for months and, in the end, produced several thousand pages of transcript. It later became clear that merely presenting a collection of barely related people could be as bewildering as presenting barely related ideas. Thus I divided up my people into four groups according to subject matter. While the four main sections can be read independently, the reader will, in my opinion, be better off to read them serially. The first section, entitled "Bits," contains profiles of people whose work is related to computers and computation. While Bell Laboratories has been in the business of computers and computation since the 1930's, AT&T was enjoined from competing in the open market in this area until the divestiture. Many things such as integrated circuits were not commercially pursued at Bell Labs because there was no way the parent company could exploit them. This has now changed, and this group of profiles may suggest the future direction of Bell Labs research in these now commercially available fields.

The second section is called "The Solid State." In some sense, this branch of physics has been the crown jewel of Bell Labs research. Four of the seven Nobel Prizes in physics awarded to Bell Labs scientists have gone to solid-state physicists—the most famous of whom are the three who were awarded the prize for the invention of the transistor. No discussion of Bell Labs would be valid without a complete account of the invention of the transistor, and so the reader will find what I hope is an accessible discussion of this history and of its aftermath. I have also attempted to bring this history up to date by including a section on the present state of the art—the latest in solid-state technology. The section concludes with a long profile of my mentor, Phil Anderson.

While basic research has given Bell Labs much of its international reputation, it constitutes, in terms of money and manpower, less than 10 percent of the laboratory effort. The other 90 percent has been devoted to development connected fairly directly to communications and, primarily, to what is known at Bell as *telephony*—the art and science of the telephone. Before I began visiting Bell Labs I had only the vaguest idea of how a modern telephone works and still less of how the modern telephone system works. In particular, I did not realize that much of what is now transmitted over telephone wires is digital information and the percentage keeps increasing. Furthermore, there is now a major effort to transmit this information not over the traditional copper wires but over glass fiber cables. I found these developments fascinating and describe them in the section called "Telephony." It gives an account of this evolution, largely in the voices of some of the people who have played a role in this work. While doing research on this section, I had the chance to visit a remarkable rural laboratory at Chester, New Jersey, that is devoted to the "outside plant"—things that actually go into the ground or are suspended above it. The reader may be surprised at the kind of attention to detail that is necessary to make the telephone system operate.

The final section of the book is called "Three Degrees Above Zero." This title, which may seem a bit arcane, refers to the average temperature of the universe, which is about three degrees above absolute zero—the coldest temperature there is. We know this temperature because of a remarkable series of discoveries that began with, and followed on the heels of, a serendipitous observation in 1964 by two Bell radio astronomers, Arno A. Penzias and Robert W. Wilson, of the cosmic static that is caused by the bath of low-energy light quanta in which we are all immersed. (An interesting and related question, which

I also will discuss, is why Bell Labs has radio astronomers on its staff at all.) These quanta are "souvenirs" left over from the so-called Big Bang which occurred some 12 billion years ago and heralded the creation of our universe. Penzias and Wilson were awarded the Nobel Prize in physics in 1978 for their work. This section consists of a dual profile of them. I have split the profile up in this way because Penzias is now the vice-president of Bell Laboratories in charge of research. He thus continues a tradition, which began with the beginnings of the Labs, of having someone who has an exceedingly strong background in research administer research. I wanted to give Penzias a separate chapter in which he could describe his version of the future of Bell Laboratories. Clearly with the divestiture Bell Laboratories is at a watershed. If all goes well it can continue its great tradition of basic and applied research, and if things do not go well it runs the risk of becoming just another large, conventional, industrial laboratory. As the reader will learn, Penzias is devoting all of his very considerable energies to making sure that things will go well. The reader will learn what he has in mind.

It is important for me to make clear that this book was not sponsored in any way—financially or otherwise—by AT&T. No one was looking over my shoulder when I wrote it. I was given the privilege of wandering essentially freely around Bell Labs and talking to those people with whom I wanted to talk. I think that I was granted this opportunity because the people in charge had some confidence in my ability to absorb—at least eventually—the relevant technological and scientific information, and they had confidence that anything that I was told in confidence to help me with this task would remain in confidence. One person I interviewed said, "I regard you as a friend, and I am talking to you as I would talk to a friend." That made an enormous impression on me, and I hope that all of the people whom I talked to still regard me as a friend and will continue to do so. With a subject this complicated, the way I work is to show what I have written to the people involved. For me this is an invaluable part of the learning process. That so many experts have read this book, in one form or another, gives me some confidence in the accuracy of its contents. I am grateful to William Brinkman and Robert Ford at Bell Labs and to my colleagues Elihu Abrahams, Gerald Feinberg, and John Bell, not only for their counsel but also for the time they spent correcting my mistakes. I am also grateful to Marshall De Bruhl and Joel Honig of Scribners for their immense help in turning a very complex manuscript into a book.

This is, in many ways, an Aspen book, and I would like to acknowledge my debt to the Aspen Center for Physics and to Sally Mencimer's crew of typists and xeroxers, especially Karen Kashinski, Nancy Gargel, and Candi Coe. I am also grateful to Eleanor Gehler of the Physics Department at the Stevens Institute of Technology for her help in typing some of the pieces. In many ways, it has been the most difficult writing project that I have ever undertaken—difficult in terms of the material that I have had to learn, digest, and then recreate. I hope that most of this effort, like the preparation of good cuisine, will be invisible and that the reader will find the result fun to read as well as enlightening.

JEREMY BERNSTEIN

*Aspen, Colorado*
*August 1983*

# Contents

# Introduction

THEODORE N. VAIL returned to AT&T at age sixty-two as president in 1907, twenty years after he had left it. He had served as the first president from 1885 to 1887, having been general manager of AT&T's predecessor, the American Bell Telephone Company. Alexander Graham Bell had invented the telephone in his laboratory at 109 Court Street, in Boston, in 1875 and had taken out the basic patents on it in 1876 and 1877. In 1880 he resigned from the telephone company and thereafter had no further connection with it. Both he and Vail had a common vision, which Vail described in 1910 as "One policy, one system, and universal service" and of which Bell had written in 1877, "I believe, in the future, wires will unite the head offices of the Telephone Company in different cities, and a man in one part of the country may communicate by word of mouth with another in a distant place." Vail had left the company in frustration when he decided that he and it did not agree that "universal service" was a credible goal. The situation that he inherited when he returned is described in "The Emergence of Basic Research in the Bell Telephone System, 1875–1915," an article written by the physicist and historian of science Lillian Hoddeson, who has studied various aspects of the history of Bell Labs.

The Bell System's financial position became increasingly fragile in the decade and a half after Alexander Bell's original patents expired in 1893 and 1894. Many independent telephone companies sprang up, for example the Home Company and the Farmer's Lines. By 1900 there were over 6,000 companies, and by 1907 almost half of the telephones in the United States were non-Bell. Subscribers were becoming increasingly dissatisfied with the service. For example, they would often accidentally reach one of the other companies, and in most cities they had to pay two or more telephone bills each month. The Bell System, having developed out of many different companies, was inefficiently and uneconomically organized. In April 1907, AT&T finding itself in severe financial straits, underwent a management reorganization which brought a New York banking syndicate under J.P. Morgan into control of the company . . . and company headquarters were moved [from Boston] to New York City.

In 1880, before Bell's patents expired, there were 54,000 telephones in the United States, which were rented to customers by American Bell. By 1910 there were 7,635,400 telephones, most of them rented by AT&T. Indeed, Vail meant "universal service" by AT&T and its subsidiary companies. One of these was the Western Electric Company, which American Bell had taken control of in 1881. Prior to that year, there was no formal department at Bell that dealt with technical matters, although Thomas Watson, the instrument maker who had been Bell's assistant when the telephone was invented, was put in charge of technical services and held the post until his retirement from the company in 1881. Hoddeson notes that in the early days of the telephone, customers were "encouraged to make their own electrical connections and string their own wires, but for an additional fee, the proprietors [the telephone companies] would carry out these jobs for them." By modern standards the early telephone service was woefully primitive with all sorts of static, cross-conversations, and fadeouts on the line. It did not go for very long distances either. The first service, over a private telegraph wire between Boston and Cambridge in 1876, went for two miles; but it had been extended to span the 900 miles between New York and Chicago by 1892. The attempt to lengthen the telephone routes eventually led the Bell System into basic science.

Prior to the invention of the telephone, the transmission of electromagnetic signals over wires had been confined to the telegraph. But the dot-dash signals of the Morse code represent an entirely different problem—and a much simpler one—than the transmission of the high-frequency electromagnetic analogues of sound waves. What Bell's telephone did, in essence, was to convert sound waves into analogue, oscillating electromagnetic waves. These waves in voice transmission can oscillate at frequencies of thousands of cycles a second, and the problems of transmitting such rapidly oscillating electric currents are very complex. For example, among the things that were not known in the early days was the so-called "skin effect." A varying current tends to concentrate on the outer layer—or skin—of a conductor, and this dramatically decreases the conductor's effectiveness. As a result, the telephone companies were forced to use thick—and very expensive—copper wires: thick to counter the skin effect, and copper (as opposed to iron) because it is a much better conductor. To cope with matters like this, the American Bell Company established its Electrical Department in 1881 and added a Mechanical Department, or Engineers Department, in 1884. When the two were merged in 1902, they had about 200 employees. A similar department was also associated with the Western Electric Company.

None of these departments was engaged in anything like what we would now consider to be the sort of unstructured basic research found in a university, although there were a few Ph.D.'s employed in them. The first Ph.D. to join the company was William Jacques, who had one of the first Ph.D.'s in physics granted in the United States. He took his degree from The Johns Hopkins University in 1879, a year before joining the telephone company. Hoddeson notes that he formed an "Experimental Shop" in 1883 to supplement the Electrical Department. Among other things, they tested copper wires and helped to decide what patents were worth buying. Hammond Vinton Hayes came in 1885; his doctorate in physics was only the second to be awarded by Harvard. Hayes, who became director of the Mechanical Department, seems to have had a real vision of the potential worth of basic research for the telephone company. As Hoddeson points out, in 1887 he wrote to John Hudson, who was the president of AT&T, that his Mechanical Department should address not only the daily practical problems of the company—what in modern Bell Labs language is called "fire fighting"—but should also deal with the "many problems daily arising in the broad subject of telephony which require solution but are not studied as they will not lead to any direct advantage to ourselves. . . . All these questions should be answered and I write to ask you to allow me to broaden the field of our work to embrace such problems." Hoddeson does not record Hudson's answer. However, in 1897 Hayes hired the first of what became a long tradition of truly first-rate theoretical physicists at Bell, a young man named George Campbell.

As Hoddeson notes, Campbell came to Bell with a superb education in physics and mathematics. Having taken a bachelor's degree in engineering from the Massachusetts Institute of Technology in 1891, he was awarded a master's degree from Harvard in 1893. There then followed three extraordinary years in Europe: one in Göttingen, where he studied with Felix Klein, one of the most celebrated mathematicians and teachers of that day; one in Vienna, with Ludwig Boltzmann, a founder of statistical mechanics; and one in Paris, with Henri Poincaré, generally regarded as the greatest mathematician of his age. Campbell's acceptance as a student by these three men is, in itself, testimony to his ability.

When he arrived at the Mechanical Department, Campbell set to work on the problem of increasing the distance over which telephone signals could be propagated along copper wires. Building on some prior work, especially by the British scientist Oliver Heaviside, he developed the theory of "inductive loading." It turns out that if a magnetic coil is wrapped at regular intervals along a telephone wire, it increases dramatically the distance that an oscillating electromagnetic current will propagate along that wire. The key to the practical use of this technique was to determine the distance between the coils that would optimize transmission. This was done by Campbell and, independently, by Michael Pupin of Columbia University. The ensuing patent fight was won by Pupin in 1904, and the company then bought the patent, an activity that it engaged in fairly often over the years. It was with the aid of cables loaded every eight miles with low-resistance magnetic coils that the Bell system succeeded in extending telephone service the 2,100 miles from New York to Denver in 1911.

However, three years before, Vail had made a decision that would effectively render this method of transmission obsolete and that would take the Bell System into modern science. Following the suggestion of some California businessmen, Vail had decided that AT&T would build a transcontinental telephone line between New York and San Francisco and that it would be opened in time for the San Francisco Panama-Pacific Exposition scheduled for 1914. The problem was that New York to Denver represented the practical limit of transmission along loaded lines. The cost of these lines was prohibitive, so to send voice signals accurately and economically some 3,000 miles something better would have to be found. The clue to how to go about it came from telegraphy. Transcontinental telegraph lines functioned by the use of "repeaters," relay stations that can receive the weakened signal, reamplify it, and send it on its way. In telegraphy this is relatively simple, since only dots and dashes are retransmitted. Telephone conversations are another matter.

The first attempt, using a so-called mechanical repeater, was made in 1903 by Herbert Shreeve of the Mechanical Department. As Hoddeson reports,

[It] proved to be effective on relatively short lines (e.g., between Amesbury, Massachusetts, and Boston [a distance of about forty miles]) but was not adequate for long lines, since it favored certain pitches over others and was highly distorting when used two or more in series. It was also disproportionately insensitive when the incoming signal was weak, and it failed entirely when connected into loaded lines. Shreeve's device consisted of a telephone receiver, through which speech current entered; a mechanical diaphragm, which the current activated; and a carbon transmitter, which transformed the current into amplified speech at the output. The mechanical repeater's difficulty on long-distance lines lay in its diaphragm being too sluggish to vibrate over the band of speech frequencies while driving the electrode of the carbon-button transmitter at each frequency.

A few years later Campbell suggested that making a really good repeater might have something to do with using electrons, that is, atomic physics. This proved correct, and it led Bell into the next step toward creating a modern scientific research laboratory.

In 1904, acting on a suggestion from Campbell, Hayes hired Frank B. Jewett, who had taken his doctorate from Albert A. Michelson at the University of Chicago in 1902 before going on to M.I.T. as an instructor. At Chicago, Jewett had developed a friendship with Robert

Millikan, then an instructor in physics and later noted for his work on the properties of the electron, one of the things for which he won the Nobel Prize in 1923. In 1910 Jewett paid a visit to Millikan and explained to him the Bell System's problems in developing something better than the mechanical repeater. He asked Millikan to send to Bell a few of his best students, especially those who were working in electron physics. The first of several students Millikan sent over the years was Harold D. Arnold, who arrived at Western Electric in 1911. But, unknown to all concerned, the key to the first successful repeater had already been created in 1906 by the American inventor Lee de Forest.

I will give a more detailed discussion of de Forest's invention, which he called the "audion," in the section on the solid state. Here, suffice it to say, it was what eventually evolved into the three-element vacuum-tube amplifier, which is usually known as the "triode tube" and is probably familiar to anyone old enough to have examined the interior of a pretransistor radio or television set. Word of the audion came to AT&T in 1912, when a former employee of the Mechanical Department, John Stone, sent a copy of a paper he had written about it to John Carty, the self-educated electrical engineer whom Vail had placed in charge of a newly organized engineering department at Western Electric in New York in 1907. (This department, eighteen years later, would become the Bell Telephone Laboratories.) Carty had the final responsibility for developing whatever technology would be needed for the transcontinental telephone line. After reading the paper, Carty arranged for Stone and de Forest to come to AT&T in late October 1912 to demonstrate the audion. It was not an entirely auspicious occasion. When they ran it at high enough voltages for it to amplify the kind of currents needed to transmit telephone calls, it filled with what was described as a "blue haze" and then refused to transmit "further speech." At this point—literally the day after the first demonstrations—Harold Arnold took over the problem and began transforming the audion into the vacuum tube, which de Forest ultimately sold to AT&T for $340,000, into a usable device.

Arnold realized that the blue haze was caused by radiation produced by the collision of air molecules in the tube—the tube that housed the electronic components of the audion. The solution was to evacuate the tube—to remove most of the air. (Independently, Irving

Langmuir of the General Electric Company, reached the same conclusion. Many years later he lost his patent fight about the development of the audion in the Supreme Court.) Arnold's work got the research department at Western Electric into the business of producing high vacuua and also into the business of how to make the other components of the vacuum-tube amplifier. Carty, it appears, drove his minions night and day to complete work on the audion and the rest of the technology by the time the now postponed San Francisco exposition opened to the general public in the winter of 1915. The revamped audion repeater first went into service on the New York–Baltimore telephone line in 1913. With seven repeater stations, including one in Winnemucca, Nevada, the telephone line had crossed the country by July 1914. It consisted of four copper wires strung on 130,000 telephone poles across thirteen states. On 25 January 1915, with Alexander Graham Bell himself stationed in New York, the line was used to transmit again the first words ever uttered over a telephone—"Mr. Watson, come here. I want you!"—spoken by Bell to his assistant, Thomas A. Watson, on 10 March 1876. Watson, then in San Francisco, rather than a few feet away as in Boston, replied, "It will take me five days to get there now!" Housed in the Palace of Liberal Arts at the Exposition, the first transcontinental telephone attracted throngs of visitors who could, at prescribed hours, listen over the telephone to the breaking of the Atlantic surf on Rockaway Beach, in New York City.

By 1914, the year before all this took place, some 550 engineers and scientists were working in the building at 463 West Street, in New York City, that had been built on property bought by Western Electric in 1896. In a 1914 stockholders report, President Vail noted that among the scientists were "former professors and instructors of our universities, postgraduate students and other graduates holding various engineering and scientific degrees from 70 different scientific schools and universities, 60 American and 10 foreign institutions of learning being represented. . . . No other telephone company," he boasted, "no government telephone administration in the world has a staff and scientific equipment such as this." By 1924 the staff had grown to some 3,000, and that September a notice was posted that an organization was about to be formed that would be known "by some such name as Bell Telephone Laboratories."

On New Year's Day 1925 the new organization, indeed called Bell Telephone Laboratories, was ready to begin work. It was to be responsible to AT&T for fundamental research and development and was to develop and feed directly to Western Electric potential products for manufacture and sale. AT&T and Western Electric were each to own 50 percent of the common stock in the new corporation. Frank Jewett, who, as assistant chief engineer at Western Electric since 1912 had the actual technological responsibility for the first transcontinental telephone line, became the first president. Jewett, as I have mentioned, had a strong background in research and technology. He began the tradition of Bell Labs administrators with strong technological backgrounds, which extends to the present, and sixth, president of Bell Labs, Ian M. Ross, who made major contributions to the development of the transistor. In the same tradition, the vice-president in charge of research has always been a distinguished research scientist. The first such director of research was Harold Arnold—of the vacuum tube—and the present one is Arno A. Penzias—who with Robert W. Wilson discovered the three-degree cosmic photons.

The first patent ever awarded to a Bell Lab employee went to C. Bordmann in 1926 for a clamping and supporting device. In the week of 13 August 1983 three staff members, Daniel L. Flamm and Dale E. Ibbotson, chemists, and Vincent M. Donnelly, a laser-development engineer, were issued the twenty thousandth Bell Labs patent, for a method of etching semiconductors. Indeed, in 1981, the year before the divestiture was ordered, members of the technical staff at Bell Labs were issued 311 patents. They also, that year, produced 5,725 technical talks and papers and received eighty-nine scientific and engineering awards. Between 1925 and 1981 the number of employees of Bell Labs had grown from a little over 3,000 to 24,078, of whom 3,328 had Ph.D.'s, 5,753 had master's degrees, and 4,007 had bachelor's degrees. Most of them were under forty. They worked in twenty-one different laboratories in eight states, ranging in size from the one in Holmdel, New Jersey, which had 4,810 employees in 1981, to the lab in Lincroft, New Jersey, which had seven. From the beginning, Bell Labs had field stations outside New York City, and in 1926 Bell bought property in Whippany, New Jersey, for radio work. This is now the fourth largest of the Bell Labs, with 2,800 employees. Murray Hill, New Jersey, which was opencd in 1941 and now has about 4,000 employees, is the site of most of the basic research.

The interconnection of basic and applied research at Bell Labs has been very complex. Until the mid-1930's there seems to have been no entity that was simply turned loose to pursue completely unstructured research. (In the mid-1930's a new solid-state physics department was created simply to do whatever research it felt motivated to do, and the activities of this group would ultimately lead to the invention of the transistor.) However, apparently specific technological and economic needs led the Labs, often almost by chance, to discoveries of a fundamental nature.

A case in point was the all-but-accidental discovery in 1927 by Clinton Davisson and his assistant, Lester Germer, of the wave nature of the electron. Davisson was awarded the Nobel Prize in physics in 1937 for this work—the first Bell Labs scientist to win a Nobel Prize. He had come to the Engineering Department of Western Electric— the institutional predecessor of Bell Labs—in 1917 from the Carnegie Institute of Technology. He intended to remain at Bell, where he had come to work on vacuum tubes for military communication, only for the duration of World War I. After the war he decided to remain there in the vacuum-tube department, which had been created to deal with the matter of the repeaters. In the course of trying to understand the behavior of electrons in a vacuum tube he and Germer did a series of experiments in which they bombarded a crystal of nickel with a stream of electrons. Although they did not realize it initially, the results of their experiments could be interpreted only by attributing to the electron a wavelike character. This had already been suggested by Louis de Broglie and Erwin Schrödinger, and so, in effect, Davisson and Germer's experiments provided one of the first confirmations of the new wave mechanics. While this did not have any direct applications to telephony, the publicity that it engendered had great advantages for the telephone company. To give one example, in 1936 William Shockley came to Bell Labs from M.I.T., where he had been a student in theoretical physics—specifically with the idea of working on vacuum tubes with Davisson. A short time later he joined the new solid-state research group.

In the fall of 1982, I encountered a man I knew who has been chief

administrator of a large engineering school. I told him that I was
writing a book about Bell Labs, and he remarked that—contrary to
what most people might think—Bell Labs represented the Ivory Tower
and that the universities, including his own, represented the real world.
He was, of course, referring to Bell Labs as it was constituted prior to
the divestiture. At Bell Labs, he explained, scientists do not by and
large have to compete in the continual rat race for money that university scientists do, usually by writing innumerable contract proposals to
government agencies that fund research. At Bell Labs scientists and
engineers do not have their productive lives dissipated by endless hours
of teaching or by the kind of committee work so characteristic of
academic life at all but the very best universities. At Bell Labs, unlike
the universities, salaries have kept pace with inflation. At Bell Labs
there is a politically protected environment; for example, during the
McCarthy period Bell Labs was a haven for some university people,
such as those teaching in the University of California system, who were
harassed because of their political views. Although no one really has
tenure at Bell Labs, almost no one is fired. Somehow, people are shifted
around in order to maximize the vitality of the various research and
engineering departments. When someone becomes less productive in
research, he or she may move rather naturally into administration or
into one of the development areas. For that reason the age profiles of
the research departments remain relatively youthful; while in many
universities, with their tenure system and their inability, for financial
reasons, to hire young people, the departments get older and older.

The reason that the "ivory tower" atmosphere of Bell Labs has been
maintained is, clearly, that its parent company, AT&T, as a regulated
monopoly and one of the richest in the world, has had the wherewithal
to supply the $1.63 billion that it took in 1981 to operate the Labs. As
of 1 January 1984, the face of the telephone company was transformed.
The first effect of this on Bell Labs was that to service the entities
created by the divestiture 7,000 employees of the Labs were transferred
into newly created laboratories that will support AT&T Information
Systems and the seven newly formed regional operating companies. As
of 1 May 1983 AT&T announced that it would become organized
along seven "lines of business." These include network systems (which
will sell switching and central office products to the operating compa-

nies); components and electronic systems (which will sell products to original equipment manufacturers); processors (which will sell computers and other business machines); international (which will deal with the international side of the business); consumer products (which will sell to consumers and small businesses); government (which will deal with defense and other government systems); information systems (which will sell business communications and information-processing systems).

As to how this affects the Labs, at the time this reorganization was announced, Ian Ross remarked, "We are now structured so that we can capitalize on the markets we serve but we have organized in a way that best suits the talents of the units within the sector. As for development support, Bell Labs is essentially organized in parallel with the new lines of business. We have some fine-tuning to do to ensure the interfaces and accountabilities are clean, but our primary task is to deliver what the lines of business need in a timely, cost-effective manner."

One of the consequences of the "fine-tuning," it would appear, was the divestiture in 1982 by Bell Laboratories of its Economics Research Department, set up in 1968 under the direction of the mathematician and engineer Edward E. Zajac. Eventually it grew to comprise thirty professionals who were divided into three groups: Economic Analysis, Economic Modeling, and Economics and Econometrics. It had an annual budget of more than a million dollars, was responsible for an AT&T-sponsored journal called the *Bell Journal of Economics,* and was widely regarded as one of the top half-dozen economics departments in the United States. Because its salaries were said to be somewhere in the $40,000–$60,000 range, it was able to attract some of the best young Ph.D.'s available. The main emphasis of the group was on the economics of a regulated monopoly, which, of course, was what was relevant to AT&T. Since the department was disbanded, some of its members have gone back to the universities, and others have gone on to the new Bell operating companies. The journal, one of the best in its field, will be taken over by the Rand Corporation. Perhaps a department devoted to the economics of an extinct enterprise—the Bell System—was simply no longer needed. Perhaps this is the first sign of a movement by the management of Bell Laboratories to trim away all of the enterprises it sponsors that are not fairly closely related to telephony or some other line of business. It is too early to tell. In what follows, the reader will find out what the people who have most at stake feel about the future of Bell Labs—namely, those who work there.

In writing this book I have deliberately not expressed my own point of view on the wisdom of the divestiture. It may come to be viewed as a total folly that disrupted the world's best telephone system. Or it may turn out to have been exactly the competitive spur needed to prod a whole segment of American technology into a viable competitive mode. I do not know. What I am certain of is that if the divestiture changes Bell Labs' fundamental character—the special mixture of basic and applied science, of long-term and short-term research, of science and engineering—then the United States will have lost one of its greatest technological assets. That, I believe, *would* be total folly.

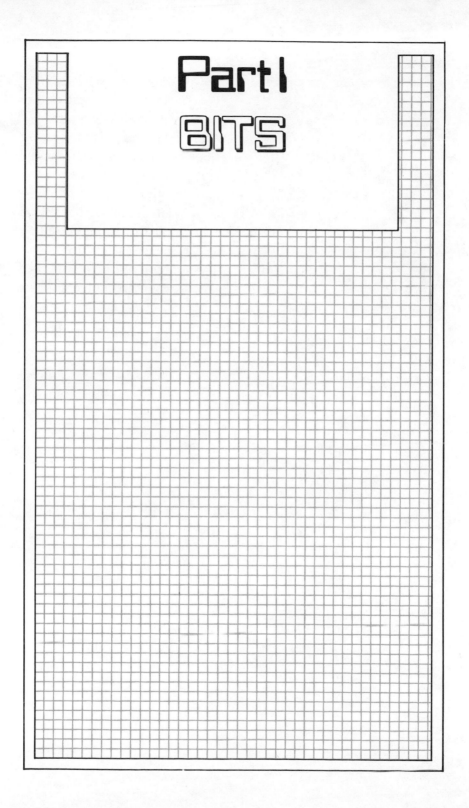

# Part I
# BITS

# CHAPTER 1

# Ronald L. Graham

SOME YEARS AGO the Bell Telephone Company had, in a room in one of its New York offices, a very large map of the United States. This map showed all of the major cities with long-distance service, connected by strings representing telephone lines. When one calls long-distance between New York and Los Angeles, for example, the call may be routed through Atlanta or Detroit—or through many other cities, depending on the availability of circuits. These routes can differ in length by hundreds, if not thousands, of miles, but one is charged the same amount—based on the minimum distance—no matter what path the call actually takes. To determine the shortest route of a telephone call, if it went over existing facilities, the lengths of these strings were measured and compared to other possible routes.

By the mid-1950's, after Bell Labs had taken delivery of the largest computers being manufactured by I.B.M., the question arose as to whether the strings could be replaced by some model calculation done with a computer. Such a calculational procedure is called an "algorithm," and, in 1957, the Bell mathematician Robert C. Prim, building on work done a year earlier at Bell Labs by Joseph B. Kruskal, found a simple algorithm that was well-suited to machine computation. The strings have now disappeared.

Roughly speaking, there are three kinds of computational problems. In 1936 the British mathematician Alan Turing demonstrated the existence of problems for which no algorithmic solutions exist in principle. They are closely related to the Gödel theorems, which demonstrate the undecidability of some propositions in formal mathematics. Then there are problems for which an algorithm exists—the problem is "decidable"—but the computer time needed to use it would grow exponentially with the "size" of the problem. For all practical purposes such an algorithm is useless, since it might take, for example, a time equivalent to the present age of the universe (some 12 billion years) for a computer—or, for that matter, any realistic number of computers—to produce a solution. Such problems are called "intractable." Finally, there is a class of problems—mathematicians working in this field tend to call them the "easy problems"—for which there exists an algorithm of such a character that the computer time does not grow faster than some polynomial in the size of the problem. For example, if the size is $n$, then the computer time might grow only as fast as $n^2$.

Although all of this might seem somewhat academic as far as the telephone company is concerned, it is not. The fixing of tariffs for "Private Line" telephone service is a practical application of such algorithms. Many large corporations have private lines connecting their operations in various locations. The history of how tariffs for these lines were arrived at seems to be rather obscure, but one factor has to do with minimizing the length of the telephone lines connecting the locations. Below is a diagram of four locations, which, for simplicity, I have put on the corners of a square.

☎          ☎


☎          ☎

Let us assume that existing telephone lines connect these points. As the next diagram shows, at least three lines are needed in order to connect all four points. If the edge of the square has length $a$, then the total length needed to connect these points is $3a$.

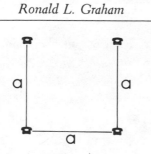

There is nothing very obscure about this, but this is not how the effective length *a* was computed for determining the tariff. To illustrate how this was done, I have put a hypothetical point in the middle of the square. This point need not correspond to an actual point on the telephone network; in fact, it generally won't correspond to such a point. There need not even be a telephone there. It is simply an arbitrarily chosen point that could, in principle, correspond to a telephone exchange.

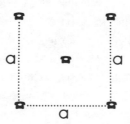

In the next diagram I have connected the imaginary telephone exchange by four imaginary telephone lines to the corners of the square.

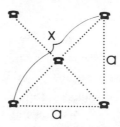

By using Pythagoras' theorem, one can readily show that the length of each of these imaginary lines is $\dfrac{1}{\sqrt{2}}a$, and since there are four of them the length of the imaginary network is $2.8a$, which is less than

*3a* by about 7 percent. It turns out that one can do even better by adding *two* imaginary points, as shown in the next diagram (the central lines meet at 120°):

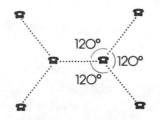

The length of this imaginary network is $(\sqrt{3} + 1)a$, or 2.7*a*. This, it can be shown, is the *best* that one can do, no matter how many imaginary points are added to the square, and according to the tariff structure, this "hypothetical length" is used to figure out the tariff. AT&T was forced to do this because of successful lawsuits that argued that Private Line tariffs should be based on the minimal-possible-length telephone networks and not on some network chosen for the convenience of the telephone company.

Such a network is called a "tree" by mathematicians, and these imaginary extra points are named "Steiner points" after the nineteenth-century Swiss mathematician Jakob Steiner, who studied this problem for the case of three points. The tree that, in the case that we have been considering, produced the smallest net lengths is called the "Steiner minimal tree." The last diagram is the Steiner minimal tree for this case. For certain very simple, symmetrical cases, like the one here, determining the Steiner minimal tree is an "easy problem." But if more cities are added to the Private Line network, and if they are not located symmetrically, determining the minimal Steiner tree exactly is, in a practical sense, hopeless. As Ronald Graham, the Bell mathematician who first introduced me to this problem, put it, "You could have a New Jersey full of Crays [the fastest computer now operating], and you still couldn't solve the general Steiner problem for twenty-five points." Thus, there was no rigorous way in which AT&T could have decided precisely what tariff to charge for Private Line service where a great number of locations was involved.

It has never been clear to me what is meant when someone says so and so *looks* like a mathematician. However, I am quite sure that Ronald Graham does *not* look like a mathematician. He looks, perhaps, like a professional acrobat or juggler, both of which he was. He was once president of the International Jugglers Association, and he is the only mathematician I know of who worked his way through graduate school, Berkeley in this case, by performing in a circus with a trampoline troupe. For some time Graham had a large net suspended from his office ceiling, to catch stray objects dropped while he practiced juggling. (Claude Shannon, the former Bell electrical engineer and computer scientist, who was one of the creators of information theory, was able to ride a unicycle and juggle simultaneously.) Graham, who is blond and about six feet two, and obviously in superb physical condition—a rarity among mathematicians—has recently taken up tennis and immediately became a favorite to win the Bell Labs tennis championship. He is also by all accounts a superb mathematician. He was born on 31 October 1935, in Taft, California, where his father worked in the oil fields. He has been at the Laboratories since 1962 and is now director of the Mathematics and Statistics Center, a group of about sixty mathematicians some of whom work, as does Graham, in discrete mathematics—"discrete" as opposed to "continuous"—which includes the kind of graph-theory problem represented in finding the Steiner minimal tree. The Center publishes something like 250 papers a year, and Graham, alone or with collaborators, publishes about fifteen. In addition, he edits twenty-five journals in computer science, combinatorics, number theory, operations research, graph theory, and general mathematics. He also holds a rather bizarre record, which appears in *The Guinness Book of World Records*, for the largest number ever used in a mathematical proof. As Graham remarked, "It is too large to understand what it actually means." He came across it in 1977. It is inexpressible without special notation and is, appropriately, known as Graham's number.

During Graham's childhood, his peripatetic father moved back and forth between California and Georgia, changing jobs frequently. He finally joined the merchant marine, and he and Graham's mother were divorced. She moved to Florida, where Graham was put into yet another school. But he was a very gifted student and left high school after the eleventh grade with a Ford Foundation fellowship, which he used to enter the University of Chicago at the age of fifteen. In the early 1950's Chicago was involved in one of those educational experiments in which students are taught physics by reading the original works of Isaac Newton—generally a losing move. Although Graham was nominally a science major, he did not take a single course in mathematics. After three years his father offered him the chance to go to a somewhat less adventurous college if he would move back to California. So Graham transferred to the University of California at Berkeley, where he majored in electrical engineering. After a year there, he still had no degree, although he had done the research for his Ph.D. thesis. However, he was eligible for the draft, so he enlisted in the air force and was sent to Alaska. During his off-hours, he attended the University of Alaska in Fairbanks, where he took his degree in physics in 1958— seven years after entering the University of Chicago. After leaving the air force, he now had the means to return to Berkeley and begin his formal graduate work, although he had essentially done the research for his Ph.D. thesis.

Berkeley has a rather traditional mathematics department. As Graham put it, "The department is quite pure. There is a strong emphasis for people who graduate from there to teach and that is what I thought I would be doing; but I wanted to take a look at the other side too." The "other side," in this case, was mathematics as done in an industrial laboratory. In 1962, when Graham got his degree, David Slepian, a Bell Labs mathematician, was traveling around to the major universities to recruit mathematicians for the Laboratories. As Graham explained, "Bell Labs has a whole army of people in different disciplines who are assigned to go to specific schools and talk to potential employees. But I was told by the people at Berkeley that if I went nonacademic I would be mathematically dead in three years. I decided to come anyway, with the idea of trying it out for a few years, making a little money and then deciding what I'd *really* do. I'm still here—twenty-two years later. Slepian was a pretty persuasive guy."

I was curious to know whether Graham was recruited for any particular project at Bell. Mathematicians are so idiosyncratic that it was hard for me to imagine them being recruited to work in a group on some specific project. Graham explained that at the Labs about 10 percent of the work in general is officially designated as "research," the rest being in developmental areas. The Mathematics Center, by and large, does only undirected research. As Graham put it, "Our basic philosophy is to get the best people we can and, in some sense, to stay out of their way. I think in my case Slepian hoped I would get involved in what is called 'encoding theory'—a branch of mathematics of which, along with Shannon and some of the other people here, he had been one of the inventors. It involved techniques that were similar to what I had been using for my thesis. Slepian gave me a book to read and suggested that I might lead a seminar on the book. I looked through it and noted very quickly that many of the people who had created the field were right here, so I thought that my giving a seminar on the subject was, to put it mildly, a little redundant. I learned the material, which was very useful to me later for other work, but we ended up doing a seminar on something else."

Graham, who has had the responsibility for bringing people into his group, told me, "Typically, it takes someone one or two years to learn the ropes well enough here, to get a feel for what goes on and how to function in this environment. It takes time for people to get plugged into the various networks around here. One might mention to a new person a few of the problems that are floating around. One difference between Bell Labs and a university is that here, more or less, everyone comes in every day and the office doors are open. There is a lot more interaction here than in most universities, and a lot less feeling that the problem I am working on is '*my*' problem and that I'll tell you about it when I've dotted all the *i*'s and crossed all the *t*'s. We have much more of a community effort here, and it crosses disciplines. For example, some of the chemists are now looking at the structure of graphs —the kind of thing I do—and they like to get hold of mathematicians to try out their ideas.

"But the atmosphere you work in here is very much a local phenomenon. It depends in a fairly strong way on your local supervision. For example, there are certain regulations about how much vacation you get each year, and there are even regulations about your daily starting time. There are some division managers who apply these regulations pretty literally. Three weeks' vacation doesn't mean four. But within the Mathematics Center it has been a tradition to let each person function the way they do best. We don't expect someone to come in each day and prove two theorems and a corollary before lunch. If you're in the mood, and things are rolling, and you think you have the right insight, you can work. If a problem has really gotten to you, you know you are going to work on it night and day. If not, you are probably going to do a certain amount of paper-shuffling to pass time. Of course in universities you have teaching, which, in a sense, can justify why you are getting paid even when your research is not going well."

This discussion raised a basic question about the Laboratories, and I wanted to get Graham's reaction to it. Universities have a built-in mechanism for dealing with people who have passed their peak research years: they can do more teaching and administration. I was also aware that mathematicians, like many scientists working in these more abstract fields, tend to "burn out" after their forties. Indeed, one of the great problems confronting all but the very best universities is that the average age of their department members is steadily increasing, owing to a mixture of tenure and economics. Tenure guarantees a job for life, and there is not enough additional money to hire young people. Hence many departments are more and more filled up with aging, tenured professors who are, at least in these very abstract fields, less and less productive. Graham said that the average age at the Mathematics Center was definitely below forty. This raised the obvious question of how this favorable age distribution was maintained. He responded, "There is one fundamental way in which Bell Labs is different from a university. There is no tenure here. There is what you might call a weak moral tenure. However, there certainly have been people here who have done good work for a number of years early in their careers, but as time went on they did less and less, until finally, so to speak, they just somehow died. Such people need some real new impetus to get them going again, and there is certainly the mechanism here to provide that. Our vice-president, for example, could say, 'Now you are over *there* in, for example, a developmental area,' which means you are either 'over *there*' or you are out. But I think that the strong factor that motivates people here comes from within the people themselves. Good people here aren't held with their noses to the grindstone.

"No one says, 'You will now do this problem, and then you will do that problem.' Because if you want the very best people to do their best work you must give them an environment that allows them to do that. I think what happens here is that after a few years, during which you have been doing work and getting a reasonable salary with no onerous demands placed on you—time and energy—you can feel something that I wouldn't say is quite guilt. It's rather more like an internal motivation. You say to yourself, 'Let me take another look to see if there is something I can do now that would be really useful for the good of Bell Laboratories.' That's actually quite a strong motivating factor. Many people here go through this kind of soul-searching during their first few years here.

"They ask themselves, 'Why am I here? What am I doing here? Why am I being paid?' and so on. The Mathematics Center has traditionally been a breeding ground for upper-management personnel. People often get promoted kind of diagonally—up and out of pure research—or get put into other areas that are more development-oriented, which don't make the same kinds of demands on one's research abilities. This has certainly been responsible for some of the bias we have in our age distribution in the center."

Graham's own research spans both pure and applied mathematics. In 1972 he shared with two other mathematicians the prestigious Polya Prize for his work in "Ramsey theory," an odd branch of pure mathematics that has to do with finding unexpected order in apparently random mathematical situations. For example, if one arranges the numbers 1 through 101 in any random order, the theory guarantees that there will always be at least eleven numbers arranged in increasing order or at least eleven in decreasing order, so, to that extent, no arrangement is entirely random. Until recently no one had found any application for results like this; but Ramsey theory is now being used in the design of data networks. These are, by and large, the sort of intellectual curiosities that mathematicians delight in.

In contrast, much of Graham's more recent work has had to do with the kind of practical problems that arise from situations like setting Private Line tariffs. Indeed, he initiated a branch of mathematics that he calls the "worst-case analysis." He became interested in this in the 1960's, when Bell Laboratories got involved in writing the software for the then-proposed antiballistic-missile system. Graham knew some of the people working on the problem, which basically involved how to optimize the scheduling of a large number of interrelated tasks—in this case, identifying and locating fleets of incoming missiles. They had discovered that the order in which these tasks were performed made a crucial difference to the end result. More surprising, they also had discovered that an order that appeared good could really be very bad, if each task took a certain amount of time, and if this time were reduced. Prior to this discovery, it was assumed that by adding computers, thereby reducing the waiting time for certain jobs to get started, it would be possible to reduce the time it took to do the whole job. It turned out that adding more computers could actually make things worse. There might be no limit to how bad you could make the overall efficiency simply by doing what, at first, seemed reasonable: bringing more computers to bear on the problem. Graham was able to prove that this was not so. There is a limit to how badly one can make the overall efficiency by adding computers in a problem like this. The fact that such a limit exists enabled Graham to make what he calls "performance guarantees." If one follows certain rules, no matter how quickly or in what order various tasks are done, the end result cannot depart from the best way of doing the tasks by a certain percentage, which, in many cases, Graham could calculate explicitly. One of the situations he analyzed was the NASA Apollo Mission, where three astronauts were asked to accomplish various tasks. The question arose how much worse would their overall performance have been if, following a certain set of rules, they had carried out their tasks in the worst possible way. Among the rules was one that said that if an astronaut were free to do something he should be doing it and once started on that task he should finish it. In this case Graham showed that the worst case was only 40 percent less efficient than the best case.

There is another example of this kind of analysis that Graham likes to give because it is simple to state although very nontrivial to study. Suppose that one is given five weights, two of them weighing three pounds and three of them weighing two pounds. Is it possible to find a strategy—an algorithm—that can be used to divide the weights into two piles which have nearly the same weight. This case is so simple that by trial and error—which is hardly an algorithm—one sees that the solution is to have a pile with two weights weighing three pounds and another pile with three weights weighing two pounds. Each pile will then have a total weight of six pounds. But suppose one wishes to give a systematic method for doing this and one insists that this method will give the best answer in the general case involving any collection of weights. As far as anyone knows this is not a "tractable" problem. There is no known algorithm that would enable a computer, or, as Graham put it, even "a New Jersey full of Crays" to solve the general case in any reasonable time. There are algorithms for sorting them into piles, but there is no guarantee that any of these algorithms will produce the best solution. Graham gave me an example of a simple algorithm, which can be applied to the five weights discussed above.

1. First take the weights and arrange them in order of decreasing weight. We would have then the five weights arranged in the order 3,3,2,2,2.

2. Now we begin arranging these weights into two piles by the strategy of putting the heaviest weight in one pile and the second heaviest in the other pile. So in this case we have one 3-pound weight in each of the two piles.

3. Take the next heaviest weight, 2, and put it into the lighter pile which will tend to even things out. We now have the piles arranged 3,2 and 3,2.

4. Keep repeating the last instruction until all the weights have been placed. In our case we end up with the piles 3,2,2 and 3,2. But this has produced an uneven division, and we know that the best solution is an even division 3,3 and 2,2,2. How much of a mistake have we made? The algorithm gives us a heavy pile of 7 while the "correct" answer—the best answer—is 6 so we are 7/6 off. We can see all of this by inspection here, but Graham proved that if one used this algorithm for *any* collection of weights one would never do worse than being off by this same factor of 7/6. The algorithm will not be wrong by more than about 14 percent which is the "performance guarantee" for this algorithm.

Like so many of the people I talked to at Bell Labs, Graham is worried that the divestiture will change the character of the place—and not for the better. The hiring pattern at the Mathematics Center has already changed: there is now an almost exclusive emphasis on experts in computer science, a very broad subject covering everything from artificial intelligence to the kind of scheduling problems on which Graham is such an expert. Indeed, shortly after my visit he was on his way to the California Institute of Technology, where he functioned as a kind of "interface" between computer scientists and pure mathematicians. He also gave some of his informal "seminars" in juggling, which are immensely popular with students.

Graham told me that the universities are now producing something like 200 Ph.D.'s a year in computer science, well below what companies like AT&T and IBM—let alone, all the universities—can absorb. He worries that industry will gobble up the entire crop of computer science Ph.D.'s, leaving no one to teach. Few universities can compete with the salaries and working conditions that a place like Bell Labs can offer. At Graham's suggestion, some members of his own group have been split off into a computer science group within the Mathematics and Statistics Center—in the hope of strengthening ties between mathematics and theoretical computer science—and Bell Labs has just created a house organ in which they can publish. The *Bell System Technical Journal* may be unique among industrial publications, in that it is produced by a company but contains results of such fundamental importance that workers in certain fields must read it regularly if they are to keep up. At Stanford University, where Graham taught in 1982, the mathematics department had only five or six new graduate students in mathematics; computer science, a very strong specialty at Stanford, had hundreds of applicants. "People know where the exciting problems are," he remarked, "and they have to eat too."

Graham gave me an example of the kind of thing that worries him about the future at Bell Labs. A member of his group is one of the world's greatest experts in the theory of probability. Some years ago his son was stricken with a brain tumor. Graham's colleague became intensely interested in how such tumors can be detected with CAT scanners. This is basically a mathematics problem—the reconstruction of a three-dimensional volume from two-dimensional projections of it. The scanner produces various projections of a mathematical function and the problem is to find an algorithm by which the function itself can be reconstructed from these projections. This is the practical problem of using such a scanner to locate a diseased area in a three dimensional volume. Bell Laboratories is not in the tomography business, although it does do research on machines used for medical diagnostics. (For example, the standard machine used for the bilirubin test on blood plasma—to test liver function—was invented at Bell.) At first, some of the upper management was not very pleased with the proposed switch-over, but Graham's colleague persisted, and on his own initiative he spent six months at a Boston hospital studying tomography. Ultimately he became one of the world's leading experts in computer tomography and recently won an important prize for this work. Graham said this was then "not an atypical sort of switchover of fields for someone who, as in this case, was extremely talented and whom you really trusted. Our feeling was that what he was going to do might take a few years, but that was O.K. We would still be here. Now there is a certain concern, hard to put your finger on exactly, that this long-view atmosphere may get shortened. When I came here there was the attitude that although you were not supposed to do things that were completely irrelevant to the basic mission of the Labs—communication—it was all right if you did something that might have a feedback in ten, fifteen, or even twenty years. We have many examples of things that someone did, and it was only twenty years later that we found that we really needed it, that it was a good thing we had it. The window may now shrink to five years, three years . . . next month.

"There is a term that is used around Bell Laboratories—'fire fighting'—which is what a lot of the people at Murray Hill and other places such as Holmdel do a fair amount of. They have specific problems with deadlines. For example, just down the hall there are some people working on an electron-beam method that will be used to etch circuits on chips. They have a very precise deadline. But that kind of research has limitations. The major developments are unexpected. If you really knew what you were trying to do, that would often be the biggest part of the battle. There does not seem to be any obvious way of knowing how some development here will impact on something over there. You just hope you have good people who are excited and that they can communicate."

# CHAPTER 2
# BELLE

AROUND THE BELL LABS, BELLE is sometimes called "it" and sometimes called "she." "It" or "she" is housed in a metal cage a little over two feet tall and about eighteen inches wide. The ensemble weighs about 133 pounds. In a recent article about BELLE, its—I will, with some reluctance, refer to BELLE as "it"—two creators, Joseph H. Condon, a forty-eight-year-old physicist, and Ken Thompson, a forty-year-old electrical engineer, noted, "It is portable, but one has to be dedicated to take it anywhere." BELLE was, until the fall of 1983, the world's most powerful chess machine. It is often taken to tournaments, involving both humans and computers, to compete and in the fall of 1983 it lost in a tournament to a new "Super" Cray. A rematch is scheduled. To get some idea of its strength it is useful to know that chess players the world over who compete regularly in tournaments are given a numerical rating depending on whom they have competed against and how they did. On this scale the average player—human— in the United States scores 1400. The highest rating, 2780, belongs to Bobby Fischer; while the present world champion, Anatoly Karpov, is rated at 2720. Grand-master rating begins at 2450, and the best commercially available machine is rated at about 1700. BELLE ranks at 2200, which means that it can beat ninety-nine out of a hundred chess players in the world. In the fall of 1983 the International Chess Federation gave Belle an official master rating.

BELLE is not simply a computer program. In the early stages of computer chess, what was done was to devise a chess-playing computer program that was then run on a general, all-purpose computer. These computers are designed to crunch numbers at incredible rates. Since they have nothing special in their hardware that is adapted to chess, when they are used to play the game they are too slow to be really good. To give some idea of how special design matters, it is instructive to examine the evolution of BELLE itself. BELLE began as a program to be run on standard computers. The first program was written in 1973 by Condon and Thompson, who, by their own admission, are not outstanding chess players; Condon told me that he was not even especially interested in the game. Run on a standard machine, this program could evaluate about 200 positions a second. Over the next four years Condon and Thompson constructed their first specialized machine, which had only twenty-five chips. It was not a great improvement over their original program. But having built it, they became hooked on the problem and built a machine with 325 chips that could evaluate about 5,000 positions a second. The present version has some 1,700 chips and can evaluate 160,000 positions a second. As Thompson remarked, "BELLE is the world champion at 100-millisecond chess;" that is, if its opponents were required to make moves at the rate of ten a second they would all lose. Indeed, in the 1982 United States National Open, BELLE tied for second place in speed chess, in which players are required to play a complete game in five minutes.

I asked Thompson, whose responses to most questions tend to be on the laconic side, a question that I had been wondering about ever since I had heard of BELLE. At the age of thirteen Bobby Fischer had played a game with the American grand master Donald Byrne that many people regard as one of the most remarkable ever played. On the seventeenth move—very early on—Fischer suddenly sacrificed his queen. The surprised Byrne struggled on for fourteen moves before succumbing to what had been an inevitable checkmate. This game, if nothing else, convinced the skeptics that Fischer would be a dominant force in world chess. What would BELLE have done if it were put exactly in Fischer's position when he made his sacrifice? Could the machine have found this move? Thompson answered that he had done the experiment. In nineteen seconds the machine sacrificed its queen and then went on to win the game.

Joe Condon is the son of a celebrated American theoretical physicist, the late Edward U. Condon. Condon's older brother, Paul, was my lab partner at Harvard in a particularly onerous course in modern experimental physics. Had it not been for his skill I doubt that I would have survived the course. Joe seemed very amused by this unexpected bit of family history and, in a gesture of bonhomie, invited me to play BELLE. I accepted with considerable misgivings, considering my erratic abilities as a chess player. While I have played for many years, I have never competed in a tournament and therefore have no point-rating at all. I used to play for fifty cents a game in Washington Square Park against a Haitian chess hustler who called himself the "master." I could hold my own against him, but this feat was put into perspective by Stanley Kubrick, who also used to hustle chess in the park and referred to the "master" as a *patzer*. This observation led me to an epic twenty-five-game encounter with Kubrick which continued on and off for almost a year during the filming of *2001*. He beat me, overall, but every fifth game, for some unknown reason, I would do something astonishing and either win or draw—much to Kubrick's surprise and annoyance. Recently I bought a Fidelity Chess Challenger, which I can beat in every one of its six settings except possibly "postal chess," where, it seems, one has to wait days for it to make a move. By the time it moves I have lost interest.

In any event, that afternoon Joe Condon made contact with BELLE to try to interest it in playing a game with me, which he did by typing something into one of the many computer consoles in his laboratory. He discovered that *it* was playing "postal chess" with someone in Germany and had, as it were, no time for another game. Besides, Condon wanted my first encounter with BELLE to be witnessed by his partner, Ken Thompson, who was not around. They had worked until 5:00 A.M. that morning, and Thompson was not expected to arrive before nightfall. Many computer people work at night, at least partly because they have easier access to the large machines at the Laboratories, which are time-shared and extremely busy during the day. So, *faute de mieux*, Condon told me something about Thompson, whom he admires enormously.

Thompson, who was born in New Orleans in 1943, did his undergraduate work at Berkeley, where he majored in electrical engineering.

He joined Bell Labs in 1966 and has been there ever since. He and another Bell engineer, D. M. Ritchie, designed what is known as the UNIX operating system, a system that keeps order among the users of a computer. The UNIX system, unlike most operating systems, consists of small programs that can be assembled like building blocks to do complete tasks. Because of this flexibility, and because the UNIX system can run on the range of computers from tiny microprocessors to mainframes, the UNIX system is one of the most successful systems ever designed and has become adopted at computer centers all over the world. To run it Thompson and Ritchie designed a special computer language called C. For an arcane reason involving some acronym, the first version of the language was called B, and there is some speculation at the Laboratories as to whether the next version will be called D or P. For this work Thompson was elected to the National Academy of Engineering. In October 1983, he and Ritchie received the A. M. Turing Award for the development of generic operating-system theory and, specifically, for implementation of the UNIX system. While Condon and I were discussing this, we were occasionally interrupted by a somewhat eerie voice announcing over a loudspeaker that various people were wanted on the phone. Condon explained that he had helped to create this system, which automatically answers office phones and then pages people by a voice simulator. Bell Labs has been in the business of artificial voice production almost since the creation of the Labs in 1925 and in 1929 developed a reed-type artificial larynx that was widely used. In 1960 a transistorized device was developed by the Laboratories and sold by the Bell System at cost. Condon also showed me a computer screen capable of reading out and simultaneously displaying the output of several different computers. The relative size of each display can be adjusted, so that each output appears in a small square on the screen. It is like being able to read several pages of a newspaper at once. This system, which was then called BLIT and is manufactured for the Labs by the Teletype Corporation, is now available commercially. In one corner of the laboratory is an area where circuit boards can be wired up. The circuit diagrams are stored in a computer and read out sequentially. The wires themselves are attached by means of a special electric tool that wraps them around metal contact posts. No soldering is involved. The device makes a pleasant whirring sound, and Condon finds it very relaxing to sit at the console and put together circuits.

Condon gave me a book entitled *Advances in Computer Chess 3*, which contains the proceedings of a conference held in London in April 1981. In reading through it, I found three comprehensible and fascinating articles. The first, by Condon and Thompson, is about BELLE's specialized computer hardware. As Condon said, "The hardware does not push the state of the art in silicon"; none of it is at the limits of solid-state microchip technology. This, in turn, must mean that if Condon and Thompson keep improving BELLE there is no clear limit to what it can do. To give some idea of what is involved, here is what is done to evaluate the king position. The literal position of the king on the board is tracked by a series of "accumulators." When a new position is written into the machine, the old position is erased and the operative position of the king is recorded. In addition four special registers indicate the existence of "friendly pawns" near the king. There are also four ROM's—read only memories—which evaluate the pawns' positions if they are changed. A fifth ROM evaluates the general pawn structure as it relates to the king's location. A frequent complaint about store-bought chess machines is that they play end games very badly. This special hardware ensures that BELLE can deal reasonably with situations where only kings and pawns are left on the board. BELLE's end-game play is relatively weak compared to its middle game. Equally elaborate special memories deal with the specific properties of the other pieces. Indeed, most of BELLE seems to consist of these specialized memories. The actual "computer"—the processor that keeps all of this information straight—is on one small module, a card, which Condon pulled out of the machine to show me. If there was a flaw with Kubrick's HAL it was that its interior workings seemed to require a huge amount of space. Most of today's supercomputers are about the size of a small steamer trunk.

Incidentally it may have been Condon and Thompson's ability to put special strategic features into BELLE that was responsible for BELLE's downfall when it played the Cray. Condon told me that not long before the tournament they had designed into the machine what they called a "contempt factor"—a rating that they gave to a perspective opponent. The larger the rating the more "contempt" they, and hence the machine, had for the opponent's game. The effect of this is that if BELLE was told not to respect someone's game it would not play for a draw even if the situation warranted it. This is what happened with the Cray, Condon said. "We should have put the 'contempt factor' equal to zero and played for a draw, then we would have tied for the world championship." Condon did not seem particularly upset about BELLE's comeuppance and they plan to play in more tournaments, probably against the Cray.

The second article that caught my eye was by Thompson and deals with his experiment to determine how strong chess machines will become. What Thompson did was to play BELLE against itself—but with a twist. In the parlance of chess, a ply is a half-move. In other words, when a machine searches out its next move at a "depth" of, say, three plies, it is scrutinizing the move in the look-ahead context of its next three moves. What Thompson did was to have BELLE at, say, three ply play against BELLE at four ply—clearly the four-ply BELLE is stronger—and so on, up to eight ply versus seven ply. Each ply added about 250 rating points, he discovered, but it required about a fivefold increase in computing time. In other words, the computing time had to be approximately doubled for each 100 points gained. BELLE was thirty times quicker in evaluating positions than its predecessor, so Thompson would have predicted about a 500 rating-point improvement in its play. Instead, only a 400 rating-point improvement was observed, and Thompson conjectures that it might have something to do with the difference between the way humans and machines play chess; that is, his numerical criterion might apply to only one element in a multidimensional set of factors that determine performance among really good players.

Indeed, this matter is the subject of the third article that struck me, written by D. Kopec and I. Bratko, who were, at the time of the conference, researchers at the University of Edinburgh in the Machine Intelligence Unit. They begin with the premise that further dramatic improvements in machine play may require a deeper understanding of how the great human chess masters play. These masters store about thirty look-ahead positions in their memories, on the average, with a maximum of about one hundred, as compared with BELLE's millions of positions. "This leads to the conclusion," they write, "that a chess master's unique talent does not lie in the ability to perform computer-like feats of memory, but in the ability to conceptualize a position." They then try to clarify and quantify what is meant by the "conceptualization" of a position. To this end they distinguish between "tactical moves," or "tactical positions," and "lever positions." Tactical moves involve either an immediate material advantage, such as the taking of a piece, or some obvious improvement in the mobility of pieces, or the defense against some immediate threat. These are just the sorts of moves that a machine's look-ahead program is designed to evaluate. Lever positions are more difficult to define. They have to do, I think, with what the literary critic and chess player George Steiner has referred to as "fields of force" in chess. They involve, for example, subtle pawn moves that, if successful, eventually bring to bear some field of force on a certain element of the board. Chess masters instinctively sense what these moves are and sometimes make them without even being able to explain why.

Kopec and Bratko searched the literature and came up with twenty-four positions, divided equally between tactical and lever. They then proposed a test that readers of their article are encouraged to take. They present these positions in twenty-four chess diagrams. The reader is meant to study each diagram for at most two minutes and then to make the "best" move. Because these positions have been carefully analyzed in the literature, there is a consensus as to what the best move is. If one finds the best move, one is given one point. If one finds the second-best move one is given half a point—down to the fourth-best move, for which one is given only a quarter of a point. The best possible score is obviously 24 points.

They gave this test to thirty-five human players and twelve machines, including BELLE. The two best human players, both grand masters, scored about 20.5; BELLE scored 18.25. Even more interesting is how humans and machines divided between tactical and lever positions. In both cases the scores were higher in general for the tactical positions. Out of a possible 12, the grand masters scored 10.5 for the tactical positions and 9.95 for the lever positions. BELLE scored 11 for the tactical positions but only 7.25 for the lever positions. Among the other very good chess machines the disparity was even greater. The authors discuss the limitations of this test and of its implications. In international tournament play a chess player is usually required to make fifty moves in 150 minutes, and so the "average move" should take about three minutes. But, of course, this is not what actually happens. To give an extreme example: during the summer of 1972 the Fischer-Spassky world championship matches were held in Reykjavik, Iceland. In one of the games, Spassky contemplated his next move for sixty-three minutes. Having decided on it, subsequent moves were made almost instantaneously. (Spassky, by the way, lost.) So it is quite likely that when first confronted with many of the positions in the Bratko-Kopec test, the original players might have studied them for much more than two minutes. This gives the machine an advantage in the test, since it studies any new position *de novo*. For the machine, each move is, in some sense, a new chess puzzle that must be solved in two minutes. It does not seem to have a sense of the overall ebb and flow of the game. On the other hand, some of the positions in the test would have been known by serious players who had studied the literature. Therefore, for these positions the human subjects knew the right answer from memory. But that is fair enough. One of the elements contributing to the strength of a human master is his exhaustive study of the literature. Despite this, BELLE did slightly better than the two grand masters who took the test on the tactical positions. The clear implication seems to be that a machine like BELLE is at least as powerful as human masters at making purely tactical moves, but it is substantially weaker with the lever positions. But what would happen if BELLE's computing power were increased still further? Would all moves then become purely tactical in some deep sense? No one knows.

Knowing of Condon and Thompson's somewhat "Spanish hours," I made a late-afternoon appointment. Thompson turned out to be a tall, solid-looking young man with a long, mandarinlike beard. He studied me silently while I explained that I had come to play BELLE. He then proceeded to set up the pieces on a chessboard that he has on his desk, giving me, out of courtesy, white, which plays first. I told him that I preferred to play black. "That's odd," he said, "white is about 27 points stronger." I said that I realized that, but I was more comfortable with black. The one opening sequence that I remembered from my study of chess books was the French defense, and I secretly hoped to play it. I asked Thompson if there was anything to be gained while playing BELLE if one deliberately did something absurd. My Chess Challenger often has trouble with irrational moves. Thompson replied that BELLE simply looks for the best move in any position that it is confronted with, absurd or not. He then logged into the machine and moved the white king's pawn up two squares—the standard king's pawn opening. Had *he* chosen that move, I asked, or BELLE? He said that BELLE chooses its openings in a semirandom fashion among the book openings programmed into it. This opening enabled me to play my beloved French defense.

Although the machine had been set to play at tournament speed, we did not try to use clocks. I was nervous enough as it was. Thompson told me that people who play BELLE react to it in one of three ways. Those rare individuals who are better than BELLE have no problem confronting the machine, and those who are substantially worse seem to accept it with good grace. People who think they are about as good as BELLE—and lose—seem to get angry at the machine. This sounded familiar. It is the reason why chess hustlers play the same people again and again, inspiring their opponents to feel that they are just on the edge of beating them.

As I was playing, Condon and Thompson would sometimes sneak a look at the computer terminal into which Thompson was typing my moves. (I would make a move and Thompson would type it in and, after what seemed like a microsecond, would make BELLE's move on the board.) Later, they told me that BELLE had been evaluating my moves, so that as we played they could see what BELLE thought of what I was doing. In the early stages of the game, BELLE had given me fairly decent marks.

I began to try to put pressure on BELLE's king side. On the twentieth move it decided to castle its king right into the pressure. "That's strange," Thompson remarked. This observation sort of unhinged me. Wondering if BELLE had made a mistake and if I would be one of the few people who had beaten it, I began to feel that pleasantly savory feeling that one has before putting an opponent away. On the twenty-second move we exchanged queens. All was going according to the grand canonical scheme. Then the roof fell in. I dropped a pawn and then a rook, and then on the twenty-seventh move I threw in the towel. There was no comment from BELLE—nor, happily, from Condon and Thompson. They had seen this too many times for it to hold much novelty.

That was the only time I have played BELLE, but I have a fantasy. Some night, after Condon and Thompson have gone home, I am going to sneak into their office, and when BELLE and I are face-to-face, alone, I am going to beat the socks off it.

# CHAPTER 3
# Bela Julesz

AMONG THE 160,000 people who left Hungary after the abortive revolution of 1956 was a young engineer named Bela Julesz (pronounced You-less), who was shortly to join the Bell Labs. He was then twenty-eight and had worked as a radar and television engineer in Budapest since 1951. He had just finished his Ph.D. thesis, "Study of TV Signals With Correlation Methods," dealing with the general problem of reducing television bandwidths. The human eye, with its billions of neurons, is so sensitive, compared, say, to the ear, that to make an acceptable television picture something like 100,000 visual elements must be transmitted within a few hundredths of a second. Moreover, the actual rate of transmitting these signals varies with the kind of picture. To deal with this complexity a television station transmits its signals over a frequency band that is at least 600 times wider than a radio station's bandwidth. (It is like a tire track as compared to a pencil line.) Television signals hog the frequency bands and limit the number of channels that can be broadcast in a given geographic region. When Julesz arrived at Bell Laboratories on 31 December 1956, a department was working on the problem of reducing bandwidths while preserving the image quality—something Julesz refers to as "fooling the human eye with a few hundred transistors." He joined it.

Julesz brought with him what he now refers to, with some irony, as two "great ideas" for reducing bandwidths. Had he stayed in Hungary, he figures, it would have taken him some forty years to see if his ideas worked, bringing him well past retirement age. As it happened, Bell Labs had just taken delivery of the first large IBM computer, a 704, which made the organization, then as well as now, one of the world's most powerful computer centers. There is an average of 1.7 computer terminals per employee. Julesz had considerable facility with languages and had earned part of his living in Hungary by translating English books into Hungarian (his spoken English is richly flavored with a Hungarian accent). He decided to apply this skill to learning computer programming and to use a computer to model his bandwidth-reduction schemes. He thought that having just arrived at the Laboratories he might have difficulty convincing technicians to help him construct a real electronic model and decided to produce a computer simulation instead. It took him three months to convince himself that his first idea was wrong. It took him three additional weeks to see that his second idea was also wrong. At the same time he simulated his boss's system, which also turned out to be wrong. That ended Julesz' work on bandwidths. Soon afterward their group was disbanded. "We were one of the first victims of the computer," Julesz recalled, "which was wonderful since if at that time I had been at a university which didn't have computer facilities like that I could have played around with these wrong ideas for the rest of my career."

Julesz soon realized that the basic trouble with his "great ideas" was that he did not really understand how the human eye—the visual system—separates objects. What he did know, as an experienced radar engineer interested in camouflage, was the role that binocular vision seems to play. In the study of vision there is an old and fundamental question: Why do we have *two* eyes? Do we really need both? After all, there is a great overlap between the visual fields of each eye. Indeed, both of them together afford only slightly more panoramic vision than does one eye. Nonetheless, most people feel instinctively that the answer to these questions must have something to do with depth perception, and this, in a general way, is correct. However, the issue is subtle because, as is well known, people with one eye have depth perception. As Julesz remarked, there were aces in World War I who were *famous* for having only one eye, and, indeed, if one closes an eye and looks around, one still has a sense of depth perception. When Julesz began thinking about these matters in the late 1950's, it was almost an axiom in physiological psychology that monocular clues were both necessary and sufficient for stereopsis—the appearance of depth when both eyes are used. In other words, if one could find some method of showing to *each* eye separately something that is total visual gibberish there would be no way that *both* eyes together could make a coherent image out of it.

Julesz was equally sure that this idea was wrong. He based his conviction on his experience as a radar engineer with camouflaged images and camouflage in general. If a camouflaged object is, for example, photographed with *two* cameras from slightly different angles —stereoscopically—it will, in Julesz' words, "jump out" even though it appears essentially hidden when viewed through each camera separately. Julesz was ready to concede that, in those cases, there were always subtle monocular clues—for example, the trees are slightly closer to the viewer than the guns they conceal. So he set about to create pictures in which there could be no monocular clues whatsoever. These random-dot stereograms were, as far as Julesz knows, the first use of a computer to create a nontrivial, novel, visual environment.

Before trying to understand how a random-dot stereogram works, it is worthwhile to recall how an ordinary stereogram is made. In 1838, the British physicist Charles Wheatstone invented the stereoscope; in 1847, the Scotch optician David Brewster developed another version that became extremely popular in Victorian times and will serve as a fine model of how such devices function in general. Two pictures of a scene are taken from slightly different angles. These pictures simulate what the left and right eyes, alone, would see if studying the scene. (One can easily be persuaded that the eyes see something slightly different by looking at an object first with one eye and then the other, and noticing that the object appears to move slightly when one changes eyes.) The photos are then mounted on one end of an instrument that is rigged up with a viewing device at the other end. When one looks through the viewing device, which enables one to look at only one photograph per eye, the scene appears stunningly three-dimensional. Crudely speaking, that is because the left and right images correspond to what they would be if one were *really* looking at the three-dimensional scene and not just photographs of it: the brain has been fooled into reconstructing a three-dimensional image.

Prior to Julesz' arrival on the scene it was assumed that this reconstruction worked as follows. Each eye examined the object and each separately recognized what it was. *After* this took place, the two ocular inputs were combined in that portion of the brain that combines each input into binocular vision. Once that fusion had occurred, then stereopsis—three-dimensional vision—took place. It was precisely this picture that Julesz showed to be essentially incomplete. The key to this was his invention of the random-dot stereogram.

To make such a stereogram, one selects some convenient shape, such as a dot or a tiny square, and programs the computer to generate random positions for it on a piece of paper. Typically there are millions of these black-and-white "mosaic tiles," and the result resembles sandpaper. One next selects some figure—a large square, circle, spiral, or whatever—and draws it on the sandpaper. (I am speaking metaphorically here, since in practice one does not want to leave any telltale lines where the disparate piece has been "drawn.") Let's say one has drawn a large square. One may imagine taking this square, with all the speckled dots attached to it, and displacing it, say, to the right. This leaves blank some space where the square has been pulled, so one covers this space up with more random dots. The result is something that once again looks like sandpaper. Now one does the same thing on another, but identical, collection of random dots, but this time one displaces the square slightly to the left. Now one has two pieces of "sandpaper," neither of which offers any clue, when looked at normally, that it is anything but a collection of random dots. However, these mats may now be used as the two halves of a stereogram. When one does this something quite uncanny happens. After some number of seconds—unless one is what Julesz has called "stereo-blind"—the square emerges out of the maze and is seen to hover over the background. In practice the two images are printed in inks of different colors, red and green, for example, and one looks at them through a pair of glasses with one red and one green lens. Some of the pictures show very complex geometric shapes and are extremely beautiful. As Julesz commented, "It took Seurat ten or twenty years to make a picture of less complexity than that, and I can now generate them with a computer—twenty in a second. Of course, I am not making any comparisons to Seurat's sublime art but only to the process of placing thousands of dots on a piece of paper according to some rule."

Julesz' first conclusion from his random-dot stereograms was that conventional understanding of stereopsis was incomplete. In recognizing the hidden objects in a random-dot stereogram—that is, the objects that seem to exhibit three-dimensional visual behavior—the brain must first combine the two sets of information it receives from each eye separately. As Julesz pointed out, we know where in the brain these two pathways meet, so that, anatomically, it is known from his work that this kind of stereopsis cannot take place in the brain prior to this junction. "I was able to do psychoanatomy without a knife," Julesz commented. It is only after the stereopsis that the brain is able to reconstruct the hidden meaning in the stereogram. The brain has used the stereopsis—the three-dimensionality—to find the hidden clues in the stereogram, rather than using these clues to produce the illusion of three-dimensionality.

Having discovered that the information that is hidden to each eye is first processed much further back in the visual pathway than had been realized, Julesz went on to see if this was true for other aspects of visual perception. For example, there are certain classical optical illusions in which two figures of identical length are drawn so that they appear to have quite different lengths. Julesz reconstructed these figures using his random-dot method. Seen binocularly, the arrows, for example, appear to hover over the background. In most cases the optical illusion—the apparent difference in size—is still there. This demonstrates that the first six or seven processing stages in the central nervous system are not involved in creating these illusions; it is done farther back along the visual pathway. In 1971 Julesz collected all of this work in his classic study *Foundations of Cyclopean Perception.* It is now clear, from this work, that depth perception is produced by at least two different mechanisms. If an object is moving with respect to a background, it will appear to move faster the closer it is to the viewer. This clue, which can be picked out with a single eye, is called "monocular movement parallax" and is, in general, the dominant clue when we reconstruct three-dimensionality. This is why someone with only monocular vision can still have reasonably good depth perception. However, if none of the objects is moving, this clue no longer works. One can test this by closing one eye and trying to sort out the relative depths of, say, the flowers in a bouquet. For this kind of depth perception, binocular stereopsis—that is, two eyes—is needed. As Julesz puts it, "It was very important in our monkey ancestry to be able to see which branch of a tree was nearest, otherwise a monkey might make the wrong jump and fall out of the tree and die. Even more important, the evolution of stereopsis enabled our lemur ancestry to penetrate the camouflage of an insect prey hiding in the foliage." That there were *two* mechanisms at work in depth perception was unknown until Julesz made his random-dot stereograms.

Among the first to understand the implications of Julesz' discoveries were the neurophysiologists. Prior to 1960, when Julesz first published his work, the generally accepted view was that of the early twentieth-century British neurophysiologist Charles Sherrington, who held that explanations of binocular phenomena would have to await an understanding of how a single eye can recognize forms—something that still eludes us. But Julesz' stereograms exhibited the phenomenon of binocular form-recognition in the absence of monocular form-recognition. This discovery led a number of neurophysiologists to turn their attention to binocular vision. For example, David Hubel and Torsten Wiesel shared the 1981 Nobel Prize in physiology or medicine primarily for their pioneering work on the cortical development of binocular vision that they had begun in the 1960's.

When Julesz began this work he was still nominally a television engineer. But because of his stereograms he began to read papers in physiological psychology and, after several years, had "metamorphosed into a physiological psychologist," in which field he has already published 120 papers. In asking Julesz whether this kind of switching created problems for him at Bell, I was aware that switching fields in a university, with its carefully delineated tenure track lines, is very difficult and often impossible. At Bell, he said, "no one ever asked whether I was an engineer or a physiological psychologist. The world started to regard me as a physiological psychologist. The top management at the time encouraged me. John Pierce, who was my boss's boss, took an instant liking to my work and to me, which helped a great deal. He would even distribute the red- and green-colored glasses at my lectures. We had a slogan here at the Bell Laboratories, 'Either you do something very useful or you do something very beautiful.' "

By 1964, the sort of work that Julesz was doing had grown to such an extent that he was made head of the Sensory and Perceptual Processes Department. There were essentially no limits imposed by management. "We might not work on the sex life of the octopus because that is, one gathers, very irrelevant to human beings, but we could, and did, work on, say, frog vision and hearing." A few of the applications of Julesz' work serve to illustrate the odd and often quite unexpected connections between pure research—such as the invention of the random-dot stereogram—and its application. These applications in Julesz' case came about because of his discovery, using random-dot stereograms, that about two people in a hundred are stereo-blind. Indeed, because their depth perception is still reasonably functional, they are not handicapped unless they find themselves in, for example, professional situations where binocular stereovision is crucial. The first use of Julesz' techniques was to screen prospective radiologists at the Temple University Medical School. One of the most difficult things a radiologist is called upon to do is stereo catheterization of the heart. Two X-ray pictures, one red and one green, are shown simultaneously, and using red-green spectacles, the radiologist—if he has binocular stereoscopic vision—can see a three-dimensional image of the heart and use it to guide the catheter. Random-dot stereograms are used to weed out those people who cannot make this three-dimensional fusion.

A few years ago at the Western Electric division in Allentown, Pennsylvania, where microchips are assembled into very large integrated circuits, it was noted that too many of these circuits were defective. The problem was traced to wrong or defective chips encapsulated in the circuit boards. These chips are subject to quality-control inspection by inspectors who use stereomicroscopes. Julesz devised a random-dot stereogram so small that it could be seen only with a microscope and arranged it so that if the inspector had normal binocular vision a telephone number jumped out of the background. What Julesz discovered did not especially surprise him—2 percent of the inspectors were stereo-blind. What did surprise him, and everyone else, was that almost half the stereomicroscopes themselves turned out to be misaligned. This became evident when people with normal vision could not see the telephone number either.

While it is not difficult to realign a stereomicroscope, stereo-blindness is uncorrectable in adults, and this led Julesz to the work of which he is proudest. In 1976, after twenty years of research, including a year in Zurich, where he joined a neurological laboratory, he and his collaborators created a device for testing the stereo-vision of babies. Moving random-dot stereograms are projected in red and green on a six-foot television screen. The baby sits on its mother's lap, ten inches away from the screen; two electrodes are glued to its scalp, on which electric potentials are measured. If the infant has proper binocular vision, an electric potential is produced on the scalp within a minute. The capacity for binocular stereopsis manifests itself between the tenth and fourteenth week. If this capacity is not developed by then, it will never develop; and if the deficiency is not corrected, the child will have a form of "lazy eye." Such lazy-eyed children can be operated on provided that the condition is due to a misaligned eye. (Some "lazy-eye" conditions are due to differential near-sightedness.) This will often correct the condition provided it is done in time; precisely when this critical time window occurs is still under study. Julesz, in his colorful way of putting things, refers to uncorrected infants as "wolf children." They suggest to him, by analogy, children who have not learned to speak by the age of five and can never learn how to speak properly.

In recent years Julesz has been studying texture perception, partly with the idea of creating visual textures that simplify reading. In the course of this work, he has discovered what he calls "textons," which he believes are the fundamental elements—the "quarks"—of texture vision. Since 1972 Julesz has had eight postdoctoral fellows, all of whom have gone on to have active research careers in the general field of vision. Julesz himself was elected in 1980 a fellow of the American Academy of Arts and Sciences and, perhaps ironically, an honorary member of the Hungarian Academy of Sciences. In January 1983 he became the first experimental psychologist to receive a five-year MacArthur Foundation fellowship.

When Julesz joined Bell Labs, he was told of various benefits that he could reap if he remained for at least twenty-five years. Having just witnessed the Hungarian revolution, he was rather skeptical that any institution, including a large company, could remain intact that long. He was, as it happened, only slightly wrong. The Bell System remained at least theoretically intact until eight days after Julesz had been given his twenty-fifth-anniversary luncheon. Like almost everyone I talked to at Bell, he is profoundly concerned about the future of the Laboratories, which he describes as an "absolutely unique treasure not only for America but for the whole world. If someone were to ask me if Bell Labs is the Max Planck Institute of America or something like that, I would answer, 'No, it's much more.' In size and in expertise it's a parallel organization to almost all the academic institutions put together." When I asked him to be more specific, he remarked, "You see the tradition at Bell has been, at least up until now, to help each other. We are employed here not to teach but rather to consult. There is an artificial emphasis here on cramped space. When I was a visiting professor in Zurich, my office was bigger than this whole corridor."

While Julesz may have been exaggerating a bit, one of the things that strikes a visitor to the Bell Labs is the compactness of the offices. He went on, "Here the idea is that distances are so constricted that you can, if you have an idea, rush over to someone who is an expert on, say, stochastic processes or invented I don't know what electronic device, and consult him. It's so nearby that it takes you less time to go over and see him than to suppress the idea. In a university you would say to yourself, 'Shall I take my raincoat?' and by the time you make up your mind it's just as easy to suppress the idea. Also here, when you come over to the guy's office, he is pleased to see you. He regards helping you as part of his job and will even wipe off the blackboard for you. You don't feel embarrassed about taking up his time, because you know that later on he will be happy to say, 'So-and-so was over to see me and to ask for my advice.' It's not a favor the guy is doing for you, but it is something that he is paid to do. I read something once which I still think is the best one-sentence description of Bell Laboratories. It is like a big baroque organ. If you are interested in playing one-finger accompaniments on a baroque organ, then you shouldn't be at Bell. But if you have something to do where you have to pull out every register, then this is the place to do it."

One effect of the divestiture on Bell Labs is that each of the pure-research efforts is being reevaluated to see if it justifies continuing financial support. Some departments, such as the Economics Department, have been discontinued as specific entities. After several months of review, the management decided to continue to support Julesz' fundamental studies in vision by appointing him, in April 1983, to head the new Department of Visual Perception Research, which replaced

his previous one. Some months earlier, another independent department, which will specialize in machine vision—a branch of robotics—
was established. The general feeling at the Labs is that the establish-
ment of these departments, even in the atmosphere of the divestiture,
could be taken as an indication of continuing support for pure, disinterested research.

As Julesz put it, "This new development is a most encouraging sign
for things to come. According to one of my favorite philosopher scientists, Michael Polyani, fundamental research is like a jigsaw puzzle.
When the puzzle becomes dense the best brains in the field are attracted to it because they can outguess anyone else before another piece
is put down. Applied research goes where the monetary and technological need is densest. Very good research will sooner or later become
exploitable, and the real issue has nothing to do with whether it is called
'applied' or 'not applied.' The question for us is whether the new
management of AT&T, and Bell Labs, will be able to afford to have
us continue to look at things in a fundamental way, or whether we will
have to look where the immediate needs of society, technology, and the
economic return are the greatest. If we can continue to do both, then
the tradition of Bell Labs will be preserved, and I wish the best for
that."

# CHAPTER 4

# Mitchell Marcus

ONE OF THE BUZZWORDS in the commercial computer business these days is *user-friendly*. In essence, it means the ability to communicate with a machine with the same ease that one converses with a friend. We are, by and large, most comfortable with direct verbal communication, and so the "user-friendliest" machine would be one that we could talk to and in a language that is essentially our own. How long before such machines will exist no one knows. Mitchell Marcus, a thirty-three-year-old linguist and computer scientist at the Linguistics and Speech Analysis Research Department of the Acoustical and Behavioral Research Center in Murray Hill, conjectured that it might be within ten or fifteen years. He noted, "We are going to have fairly soon enormously powerful machines with the hardware almost for free. They will be in our TV sets, in our Waring Blenders, and in our microwave ovens, and the right way to communicate with many of them will be to talk to them. To talk to a machine, it has to be able to understand the language, and there are lots and lots and lots of problems that have to be solved before it can do that. We can build machines now that people can talk to in very limited ways. You can only use a very limited number of words, because the speech-recognition technology is still limited. You can only use very limited grammatical constructions, because of limitations in the work that has been done in things like parsing. And you can only talk about a limited number of things, because we don't know how to represent the world widely. That may not be much of a problem for a lot of the applications. For example, there isn't much you would want to talk about with your toaster. But, ultimately one wants to be able to allow someone, either when typing at a data base or talking to the machine, to use a wide range of fluent English and not have to think about it. One wants to be able to talk to a machine like an adult and not to have to talk to it the way you would talk to a three-year-old."

The center that Marcus works in consists of about a hundred people, about half of whom are directly engaged in research. The director, Max Mathews, is a noted pioneer in the composition of computer music. There are social scientists who are working in psychology and artificial intelligence, and physicists and electronics engineers who are working on robotics and industrial automation. Several people are working on "speech coding." This has to do with making use of both the structure of speech and the speech-production mechanism to reduce the amount of information needed to code ordinary speech in a digital yes-no, on-off code. Since much of our telephone conversations is transmitted digitally, this work has direct applications to modern telephony. The less information that is needed to characterize speech, the more telephone calls that can be sent digitally over a single wire. Bela Julesz' newly formed department is also part of the center.

Marcus' immediate boss, Osamu Fujimura, a physicist who came to Bell in 1972 from the University of Tokyo, is, according to Marcus, "one of the few people who knows what your mouth is doing when you talk." Fujimura invented a machine called an X-ray microbeam for observing what happens. A set of pellets is put on a subject's tongue and jaw, and the X-ray beam, which is thinner than a pencil line, tracks the pellets as one talks. As a corollary to this study, Fujimura is working on the design of machines that synthesize speech. Marcus' departmental colleague, Janet Pierrehumbert, works on speech intonation. As Marcus explained, "It used to look to people as if the intonational system of language was quite complicated and used a large number of individual tones. In English, for example, it was postulated that there were four or five tones. In her thesis, which she did a few years ago, Janet showed that all you need is two tones and a small machine that combines these tones. That is enough to realize all the tones you use. She actually built a computer program that does this, and it works beautifully. One should be able to use intonational clues to pull other kinds of information out of the wave form. If, for example, you know you are at the end of a pitch phrase, you can make some good guesses about its syntactical structure, and that can be useful for speech recognition."

Others in the department are working on "reading metrics," a measure of the complexity of a text, with the aim of characterizing why certain texts are too complicated and giving rules to simplify them. Some cognitive psychologists are working on improving the way people interact with machines. Much of this work would, in most places, be called "artificial intelligence"—AI. Artificial intelligence as a recognized discipline arrived at Bell Labs very recently. Marcus described the situation when he came to Bell from M.I.T. in September of 1979. "A year before I arrived no one in my field had come to Bell Labs. So there was no one here and no one at the AI Lab at M.I.T. who knew anything about the place. Most people who left the AI Lab took prestigious jobs at well-known places. I had offers from places like that, but people at them kept asking me whether I was really a linguist or whether I was really a computer scientist. I was deeply offended by the question. If people didn't understand why work on the interface between linguistics and computer science was important, I wasn't really interested in talking to them. I needed to be in an environment where there was real interdisciplinary work going on in psychology, linguistics, and computer science. I came here for a look and was just amazed by the attitude of the people and the spirit of the place. There was a community here where people actually talked to each other based on what they were interested in and not on their fields. People who are engineers, and linguists, and computer scientists, and statisticians, and behavioral psychologists all talk intensively. You discover that a guy you thought was a psychologist is really a physicist by training. People here are sort of widely interested—interested in lots of things and they collaborate with each other. In many places, especially in the academic world, people don't collaborate. But here there is real collaboration. People enjoy getting along with each other."

Marcus was born on 28 June 1950 in Philadelphia. His father is an orthodontist who practices in nearby Easton, where Marcus grew up. The senior Marcus had been an amateur radio operator, and one of Marcus' early memories is of discovering several large boxes of radio parts in the basement of the house. By the age of eleven he was building radio transmitters and receivers and had already gotten his amateur radio operator's license. "I hear from my parents," Marcus told me, "that I spent most of my time in grade school ignoring everything that was going on around me and just sort of thinking and doing things." When he was in the ninth grade he read about an electromechanical "mouse," built by Claude Shannon at the Bell Labs, that could run mazes. As Marcus told me, "I decided that Shannon's mouse was grossly inelegant because it needed all those switches in the maze. I felt I could do better. I ended up designing this contraption, out of pinball machine relays, which went through the maze and didn't need any switches. It needed to know when it was coming to a turn and when it was in the middle of a turn. I found that I could leave little strips of metal in the maze that would tell it, for example, that it was in the middle of a turn. The 'mouse' was a little plastic box about six or eight inches square with four lights on it to tell you which way to push it depending on the situation. There were four marbles that it slid on and four buttons that pushed against the walls when it hit a dead end. The maze that it moved through was about four by four feet. What really interested me was designing the computer that ran it. I spent a year scratching together bits of relay circuits and things. I tried to come up with an extension of Boolean logic that was multivalued to make sense of the fact that this thing was going in many directions. [George Boole, a nineteenth-century British mathematician and logician, invented a kind of logic algebra useful in the design of electric circuits.]

"I came up with a notation to write it down, but it didn't make a lot of sense, and I couldn't really explain it. I got the parts from a used pinball machine. I remember going into the place where they sold them and the guy looked at me and said 'How much do you have to spend?' I said, 'Forty-five dollars and thirty-five cents.' He said, 'That's exactly what I want for it,' and he sold me the machine. I submitted it to a regional high school fair, and they grilled me for what felt like forty-five minutes trying to learn who really designed it. I kept saying that I designed it myself. They were utterly convinced that I was lying. When I told them my father had been a ham radio operator they said, 'Aha! That explains it,' and then they essentially disqualified me. After that I said the hell with science fairs.

"In fact something like that had already happened in the fifth grade with another science fair. I had made a model of an electron tube. It had a plexiglass rod down the middle of it that represented the filament. My father had shown me how to make a line down the middle of the rod, and again they said, 'Aha! Your father designed it for you.' It became a big deal. They called my parents in to complain that I had lied to them. After the last fair I always made sure I collaborated with someone. I had discovered that if you did that, they wouldn't let you enter any of those contests—which I didn't want to do. My parents, apparently, decided early on that I was a very smart kid and that if I were going to turn out normal they had better do everything they could to keep me from knowing this fact. So it wasn't until the eleventh grade, when I got back the scores of an aptitude test, and saw that mine simply were better than everyone else's around me, that I realized that I might be smarter. Before then I thought that it was just that I was interested in these things and other people weren't."

When he was thirteen Marcus took a course in computer programming at the Franklin Institute in Philadelphia. In 1963, powerful, general-purpose computers were not widely available, and the machine used at the Franklin Institute was so small that it could not use a programming language like FORTRAN. Marcus had to translate all his programs directly into machine language, including a program he wrote to search for prime numbers. His high school, Easton High, gave him one morning a week off so that he could use the computer at Lafayette College, where he taught himself to write game-playing programs. With this background one might have expected Marcus to plan to major in one of the sciences in college. Whether because of the science fairs, or simply because of an overdose of science in high school, when he graduated he decided he had had enough. He recalls spending his last year in high school writing plays, poetry, and song lyrics. He entered Harvard in 1968 with sophomore standing earned on the basis of placement tests, determined to major in philosophy. As Marcus recalls, "I took a course in Greek ethics my first semester. I thought I was interested in ethics and I was, but the kind of thing taught in the course wasn't actually what I wanted. The course had three prerequisites, of which I had had none, but I took it anyway. In general,

I just skipped all the elementary courses. It was more fun to be in over my head. I got an A⁻ on the final paper and a B⁺⁺ on the final exam, which gave me a B⁺ for the semester. I was really outraged. I walked into the professor's office and asked why I got a B⁺⁺ on the exam. He said I had written a wonderful exam but that I didn't have enough experience in philosophy, all of which meant that he was damned if he was going to give an A⁻ to a first-semester freshman who didn't have any of the prerequisites for his course. At that point I stopped caring about grades, and I got A's and C's all the way through Harvard; A's in the things I liked and C's in the things I had to take but didn't want to take. I liked enough courses so that I managed to graduate magna cum laude."

Among the courses that Marcus liked was a logic course taught by the noted mathematical logician and philosopher W.O. Quine. He read all of Quine and became interested in his philosophy of language, which hinges on Quine's view that people's minds are a *tabula rasa*— there are no innate structures. Marcus spent a lot of time trying to understand that and became very excited by it. In his second year, he took a course in transformational grammar—Noam Chomsky's specialty. As he said, "It instantly became clear to me that if that stuff was right at all, there had to be all of this innate stuff in the mind that was hard-wired in, which meant that everything that Quine had done was this incredibly elaborate and beautiful castle built on quicksand. What I learned in that transformational grammar course is that there are grammatical constraints that are very technical, very deep, and true of all human languages. For example, in no language are sentences like 'Who did John go to the movies with Bill and?' grammatical. But sentences like 'Whom did John go to the movies with?' are grammatical."

These universal constraints had been worked out in a doctoral thesis by John "Haj" Ross, who is now a professor at M.I.T. He came to Harvard and gave two lectures. To Marcus, these constraints meant that there was a huge amount of hardware, hard-wired into the human head. There was a rich structure in the mind that was basically algorithmic—computerlike. Computer models were relevant to transformational grammar and so to the human mind, which Marcus had decided was his primary interest.

"I felt that transformational grammar was the most beautiful thing that I had ever seen," said Marcus. "At the same time I took a course in historical linguistics in which I discovered that sound change in languages is generally rule-based. You could take a set of roots in, say, proto-European and pump them through three different simple sets of rules and end up with Albanian, Greek, and Slavic. I got to know all about the pronoun and case-marking systems in Eskimo, although I have no idea what the pronouns in Eskimo are. I am not very good at speaking foreign languages.

"I was also taking a course in the use of computers to model linguistic phenomena, a field known as computational linguistics. It was taught jointly by Susuno Kuno, a linguist who had done much of the original research on language translation using computers in the 1960's, and a computer scientist named Bill Woods. After taking that course I decided that that was the area I wanted to work in, and I ended up taking about a third of my undergraduate courses from them. I took just about every course that either of them taught. I really learned how to do science from them."

Since Marcus had sophomore standing when he entered Harvard, he decided to do two junior years. He did the first one as a philosophy major and then switched into linguistics for the second one. He ended up majoring in linguistics and applied mathematics and doing a senior honors thesis with Woods who by then was with a computer firm in Cambridge. When Marcus graduated in 1972, he had taken only one formal course in computer science. He had, fairly characteristically, not bothered to hand in the problem sets until he was informed, two days before the end of the term, that they constituted 80 percent of the final grade. Since he could get only half of them done by the final, he got a C. However, he had had a series of remarkable computer-related summer jobs with a firm called Dissly Research in Easton. Marcus recalls that the first day he walked in, he asked what he should do. He was told by the vice-president, an Englishman named Ron Blanchard, that he should learn the assembly language for the company computer by the following day. Not realizing that this was meant as a joke, he learned it.

"I had never met an Englishman before," Marcus explained, "so I didn't realize that he was being droll. Anyway, after I learned the

assembly language they decided that they might have something interesting for me to do after all." Marcus ended up designing a driver for
an electron-beam recorder. He was told by his bosses that this was an
"easy" problem, and so he did it in three weeks, thus beating out, by
four months, a team of three people who were doing the same thing
for International Harvester. Marcus then became both a regular summer employee and a paid consultant for the company during his entire
stay in college.

"They had a lot of faith in me. I would walk in and they would say,
'Hi, we are thinking of doing $X$. Would you do it?' I would say, 'I don't
know how to do $X$, and they would say, 'O.K., what do you need to
learn?' and I would learn what I needed to know to do the job. I did
this all the way through college. I got $100 a month in the winter for
consulting, which for a student was wonderful. I built a lot of computer
hardware for them. So when I applied to the Artificial Intelligence
Laboratory at M.I.T., I wrote them a long letter with my application
and told them what I had been doing in the summers. I sometimes
think I must have gotten into the AI Lab with the lowest grades anyone
there had ever seen. Before I got in I was interviewed by Terry Winograd, who was a professor there. After that he took me to Marvin
Minsky's office. Minsky was the director. Minsky looked past me at
Winograd and said, 'Well?' and Winograd said, 'He knows his stuff.'
Minsky then talked to me for a couple of hours, and after forty-five
minutes he asked me, 'What are you *really* interested in?' I said that
what I was really interested in was in doing computational linguistics.
He said, 'No you're not. What you are really interested in is how the
mind works.' He was absolutely right. That was exactly what I was
interested in, and, given that, it was clear to me that the AI Lab at
M.I.T. was just the right place for me."

The AI Lab at M.I.T. in the fall of 1972 was legendary. Both the
students and the faculty were extraordinary. Marcus commented, "It
was very good for people who were very smart, very motivated, and very
sure of themselves. If you lacked any of those three things you were in
trouble. But it was a wonderful place for people who had them. The
idea when I applied was that there was going to be a special graduate
program that would be independent of all the standard academic departments and would be interdisciplinary. It would free people up to

do, primarily, research. That is what I basically signed up for. A special committee was supposed to have been created to supervise all of that. But, because of the laissez-faire attitude of the people involved, the paper work to create the committee was never quite done. Nonetheless Minsky always made magic happen in terms of graduate school for people. The place was incredibly exciting. It was just the most intense intellectual atmosphere I think that I have ever run into. For the first couple of years everyone used to sit around at lunch in the "playroom," a big common room that had just been built. People would argue for about an hour-and-a-half at lunch each day. When I first got there I jumped in, but then I discovered that I didn't know anything. So I kept my mouth shut for a semester and read every thesis on AI that I could get my hands on. Winograd had already completed his program SHRDLU—the one that carries out commands and answers questions about geometrical figures such as boxes and blocks—and people were playing with all those new AI computer languages . . . very strange languages that were really different from any that had been put together before. David Marr had just come from Oxford and was beginning his marvelous work on vision. [Marr's *Vision*—published in 1982 two years after his death, gives an enthusiastic discussion of work that Marcus was about to do.] He eventually changed the AI Lab into being more intellectually responsible than it had been. He came first for a three-week visit, and then six weeks, and then three months, and then a year and, when he died, he was on the faculty of the psychology department. With him around, the standards for argumentation went way up. He insisted that his students know the relevant mathematics and the relevant neurophysiology cold. He also believed that the kind of work that I ended up doing was more central to AI than Minsky did. Minsky thought that my work sapped off energy that might be spent on the central problem of cognition and thought."

Minsky, whose own grade record at Harvard and Princeton was at least as erratic as Marcus', had little use for formal requirements and grades. Marcus recalled that many people graduated having failed every major graduate exam they took. In fact one person failed the same exam three times, but Minsky insisted that the person was very creative and would do good work, so he got through.

"Minsky was right," said Marcus. "Afterward that person did very creative work. My own graduate program was a little strange. There were some exams that one was supposed to take at the end of the first semester that were meant to test one's background in computer science, which, in my case, wasn't very broad. Two days before the exams my advisor called me into his office and said, 'You haven't signed up for those exams. Do you realize that if you don't take them you can't get a Ph.D.?' I said that Minsky had told me that I didn't have to take the exams. Well, it turned out that Minsky had not done the paper work to get me out of the exams so I had to take them anyway with almost no preparation. Fortunately I passed. It turned out that I had learned more on my own than I had realized.

"It was well known that the AI Lab was a scary place and that you got into the place at the threat of your ego. That chased a lot of people away and the people who went through were, by and large, good people. At the time, Minsky had the idea that all that was needed to understand intelligence were five big ideas and if you had them you could solve the problem of intelligence. What he wanted to do was to set up an environment where people could come and absorb the vital ideas. Nothing else mattered. I thought that was dead wrong and I think, partly due to the influence of David Marr, the place changed. For me, however, the nonstructured environment was perfect, since I got this research idea—the problem I am still working on—in the middle of my first year of graduate school.

"Once I discovered transformational grammar I was struck by how algorithmic the process was; how you got this very rich structure out of the interaction of a lot of simple rules. But it was clear to me that this was, in Chomsky's term, a *competence model*—a model of what someone knows and not how they use it. I am primarily interested in what happens in the mind when we analyze the grammatical structure of a sentence. It is an explicit assumption of current linguistic theory —for which, I think, the evidence is overwhelming—that every time we hear a sentence the first step towards understanding it is to do a grammatical analysis. It's like the diagramming of sentences that we all learned in the fifth grade, except it's a much more complicated form of that kind of diagramming. Once the grammatical structure of the sentence is made explicit, the meaning can be extracted much more easily. This sort of grammatical analysis kind of happens automatically and unconsciously and I am interested in finding out how that happens. The Chomskian model was intended to be a model of what we knew —of what knowledge we used, in some sense or other, when we did this grammatical analysis."

There were intellectual and personal disagreements between Minsky and Chomsky, and therefore during Marcus' time at M.I.T. there was no contact between the AI Lab and the Linguistics Department. Each side was actively hostile. Minsky viewed the mind as being relatively simple while Chomsky believed there was a whole complex cerebral system devoted just to grammar, a view that Marcus shares.

"Chomsky thought—at least until Marr's work—that what was done at the AI Lab was intellectually vacuous," said Marcus. "He felt that Marr's work was invaluable. Much later, when I had finished my thesis, I got up my courage and went to see Chomsky. I started to talk and he said, very politely, very pleasantly, 'Oh, but . . . oh, but then what you are saying is vacuous because of so and so. . . .' And I said, 'No you misunderstand' and then got another sentence in. And he'd say, 'Oh, but then what you are doing is simply wrong because. . . .' And I'd say, 'No, you misunderstand.' This went on for twenty minutes. It was the best thing that could have happened to me since I was incredibly nervous. It was a chess game which I understood and I just lost my nervousness and played it. At the end of the twenty minutes he found that he couldn't dispose of me, and he cancelled his next appointment. So, for the next half hour, I told him about my thesis. At the end of it he asked me if I would like to take a postdoctoral fellowship with him. I didn't need a fellowship, but I thanked him and we began to talk regularly. Since then there has been a rapprochement between the AI Lab and the Linguistics Department and a fellow who was my student, before I left, had Chomsky for his thesis advisor.

"When I learned about Chomsky's model as an undergraduate, what shocked me was that it didn't give any kind of natural process account. To see what I mean, imagine trying to explain what happens when you throw a ball. You can give an explanation in terms of torques and forces and Newton's laws and all of that, but that would really not help very much in explaining how in the world you tell your muscles what to do. Chomsky's model was a little like that. It wasn't going to tell what happened when one actually made one of those grammatical analyses. So I became interested in processing models—models of how one actually did it. The first one that I learned about that got me excited was constructed by my undergraduate teacher William Woods. It allowed you to specify a network of abstract relationships, and then it had a processor that searched the network to find some path through it that amounted to a grammatical sentence. It did it by making guesses, and, when it got stuck, it would back up and try something else, and if it got stuck again, it would back up again, and on and on. Sometimes it would have to make forty guesses in a row until it found a path through. It was an example of what we call simulating a non-deterministic machine. The sort of sentence that would hang it up would be, 'Have the students who missed the exam take the exam.' When it encountered the first *have* it couldn't tell whether this would be followed by *take* or *taken* as in, 'Have the students who missed the exam taken the exam?' so it would have to guess and then keep track of all of its guesses. All of this was implemented in a computer program which I still have the code for in a drawer.

"The network looked like a cabalistic chart. Woods used it as the front end for a system he did around 1970 which he called Lunar. You could ask it questions about the Apollo moon rocks. Incidentally, because of Woods's program there are all sorts of people in computational linguistics who know all sorts of geological terms without knowing what they mean. It could answer about 80 percent of the questions one asked it provided one used the technical language of the lunar geologists. I used to sit and watch Woods's program analyze sentences like, 'Is the block sitting in the box red?' and it would stupidly try all sorts of possibilities. I kept saying to myself, 'What if it merely sat there and *thought* about it? It would have been clear what the right thing to do was.' Of course this machine doesn't have a mind anywhere. There isn't a homunculus there to go and think about it. I became very frustrated with all of this. It struck me as exceedingly unlikely that *people's* minds could be going through this huge bookkeeping and guessing process, or that we had unlimited processors to try each path in parallel—which is the other option. I found it difficult to believe that language is the only cognitive system we have that is a pure artifact, which has not been forced upon us by the environment. Our visual system has evolved to see the world. Tools can be very nearly matched to the shape of our hands. There would, I felt, be some kind of a match between the grammar of language and our cognitive abilities. I didn't believe that language was *that* complicated. So I decided to look into the possibility that, despite all appearances to the contrary, and the conventional wisdom in the field, that the match was, after all, simple. I decided that, if you did it right, it had to be the case that you could go right through a sentence and make the right decisions. I also decided that the simplest model to try would be to go straight through using only syntactical information—no semantic information about the world—and this is what I began to do in my first year in graduate school."

Marcus married Sue Manning, a philosophy and mathematics major at Wellesley, in the summer of 1972, just after he graduated. Their first child, Joshua, was born on 6 January 1976. They now have a daughter, Rachel, born in 1979 and another son, Benjamin, born in 1982. Joshua's birth date sticks out in Marcus' mind for another reason. On the day after, he had the first meeting with his Ph.D. thesis committee. By this time he had been working for three years on his thesis with no supervision whatsoever. He had actually built a machine —a computer program—that parsed sentences along the lines that he had decided to try during his first year in graduate school. He talked to Terry Winograd in the spring of 1973 before Winograd left M.I.T. to go to Stanford and showed him his proposal. Winograd said, "Yes this looks like exactly the right thing. Do it." And for Marcus, "That was more or less that. There was a group of language students at M.I.T. and we met once a week for lunch and read a paper and discussed it. We did just fine by ourselves."

Marcus explained to me something of the evolution of his machine. "Take the sentence, 'Is the block sitting in the box red?' as opposed to 'Is the block sitting in the box?' In Winograd's program SHRDLU, the machine always guesses that 'sitting in the box' is a relative clause. In the first case it is right and it can parse that sentence in fifteen seconds. In the second case it is wrong and it takes it forty-five seconds to unravel the grammar even though the sentence is shorter. It seemed to me that once you had this piece 'sitting in the box' you should be able to store it somewhere and look around to see what else was in the sentence before you had to make any guesses. To deal with this I introduced something I called the buffer.

"I tend to view a machine like this in an almost physical way, so I view the buffer as a set of three pegs on the wall on which I can hang parts of a sentence until I have decided what to do with them. The fact that I need *three* pegs is empirical. I found that two were too few and four resolved grammatical ambiguities that people can't resolve. I will give you some examples later. I see this process as building a parse tree —the grammatical structure—out of tinker toys. I am sort of sticking things together. I have a set of rules for putting them together but the instructions, by themselves, aren't good enough always to determine what to do. So I have these three pegs on the wall and I build three pieces of the sentence and then put them on the pegs. From what I can see on the pegs, and from what I have built so far, and from what I know about the language, I can then decide what to do next. I may want to take something off a peg or build something else and put it on a peg and so on. You need to know a little bit of what is coming up next in the sentence in order to know what to do next. For example, in the sentence, 'Is the block sitting in the box red?' my program puts 'sitting in the box' in the buffer until it looks ahead and encounters 'red.' It does not proceed by trial and error. It simply keeps moving from left to right.

"Before I actually built my first machine I spent six months trying to find a counter-example on which it wouldn't work. I thought that my idea for making such a machine might be crazy. The other programs that people were using for this kind of grammatical analysis all used a great deal of semantics—word knowledge—and I didn't want to use any, or, at least, as little as possible. By the way, one thing should be made clear, as yet no one, myself included, knows how to build a parser that can parse a sentence taken at random, say, from a magazine. We don't have a complete enough characterization of English syntax. What I am talking about is the ability to parse a somewhat simplified, but still useful, form of English: the kind one might use to communicate with a foreigner. I was looking for a counter-example that was, or might be, a kind of prototype of something my machine couldn't handle."

Marcus discovered that children's magazines are ideal for such sentences. He found the following in a *Humpty-Dumpty* story about an Indian boy named Red Moon: "When Red Moon saw the pony he was to choose from his face flowed many tears." He said, "I realized that because of the way that sentence works if you get only three pieces of look ahead you can't decide what to do. I wrote the sentence down on a big piece of paper and was staring at it on my desk when a fellow walked in and looked over my shoulder and said, 'Those words are nonsense.' " Marcus had left out a comma. The sentence should read, "When Red Moon saw the pony he was to choose, from his face flowed many tears." There are whole classes of such sentences—Marcus calls them "garden-path" sentences because they lead you down a grammatical garden path. One of his favorites is, "The cotton clothing is made of grows in Mississippi." These sentences have the interesting property that the reader takes the wrong turn and gets dead-ended or takes the right turn and never realizes there is a problem. Marcus did informal experiments at M.I.T. by putting garden-path sentences on three-by-five cards and wandering around the halls testing them on people. When spoken, most of these sentences are not garden paths because of intonation. "That is what you would expect," said Marcus. "Language was really developed for speech. But when you use only the written language you degrade the system a little and this tells us how the system breaks. In a certain sense these garden-path sentences are an artifact of the written system. By the way the sentence that usually garden-paths anybody is, 'Have the soldiers given their medals by their sweethearts.' You think, at first, it is going to be a yes–no question. Recently there have been experiments which involve tracking people's eyes when they read one of those garden-path sentences. The data indicates that people recover much more rapidly if the semantic clues are strong. I found that if the resolution point in the sentence is five off, most people get sandbagged. For example, in the sentence, 'Have the soldiers given their medals by their sweethearts,' the *by* is the resolution point and to see it you have to look at four additional phrases, including *have*. Everybody I have tried that on got zapped except for two people, and I think that one of them was lying. It turns out that this is also a property of my model parser. It couldn't handle the sentences that people couldn't handle and it seemed to predict which ones these would be. At that point, I sat down and actually wrote a program. A little later I will run a version of it for you. It became a marvelous contraption, but the first one was a mess. I built it incrementally just adding stuff to it as I discovered I needed things. It ended up being about 8,000 lines of code. Most of it deals with things like plurals. If I feed it the word *knives* it says, 'Oh, this is the plural of knife.' That is one piece of code, and requires about 600 lines. It was much less complicated than Winograd's program SHRDLU which even he couldn't keep track of."

After working on his program for some three years with no supervision, it dawned on Marcus that he had better have a thesis committee if he was actually going to get a Ph.D. His nominal advisor was John Allen, who was in the Research Laboratory of Electronics at M.I.T., which he now heads. In addition, the committee consisted of Ira Goldstein, of the AI Lab, and Seymour Papert, a noted polymathic computer scientist. Marcus recalls that Papert who was, to put it mildly, not an enthusiastic admirer of Chomsky's views on language "sat there at that first meeting of my committee and proceeded, with a scalpel, to slice away all the parts of my program that were fluff. He separated the parts that I really hadn't thought through from the parts that it was clear to him that I understood. It was really Papert who ended up focusing what I was trying to do. Later he read the first two chapters of my thesis and said, 'This is really very interesting,' and then didn't show up for the thesis defense. After that meeting I went off for a year-and-a-half and wrote the thesis. As I started to write it, various things became clear to me that hadn't been clear before, including the fact that the machine behaves in such a way that makes it unable to produce sentences that are forbidden by various language universals. I discovered that one day when I was looking at the machine and thought, 'Oh, my God! the machine automatically has that behavior.' I had decided that I would write up the thesis as a publishable document, so, much of it was tutorial. I intended it to be read by computer scientists, by psychologists, and by linguists so I had to explain a lot of everything in it. I had an offer almost immediately from the M.I.T. press to publish it as a book, but I couldn't bring myself to revise it until it was clear to me that there was no additional small change that would make it absolutely correct. I had this gut feeling that this might be the only time that I could sit and do a bang-up job getting everything right. I was very compulsive about my thesis. I wanted it to be as perfect as I could make it so I wasn't going to finish by a deadline. I was going to finish it when it was done."

Marcus' thesis was published as *A Theory of Syntactic Recognition for Natural Languages* by the M.I.T. Press in 1980. By then he had come to Bell Labs. After Marcus got his degree in February 1978 he took a postdoctoral position at M.I.T. He was being considered for a faculty job when, as he recalls, "I woke up one morning and decided I didn't want to be on the faculty at M.I.T. despite the fact that, for years and years, I had assumed that was exactly what I wanted. I then walked into the office and withdrew my name as a candidate.

"What happened was that in the fall of 1978 Mark Liberman from Bell Labs—he is in my department—came to M.I.T. for a semester to replace Chomsky who was going on leave. Mark had gotten his Ph.D. from M.I.T. two years earlier after having written a thesis on phonology that utterly revolutionized phonology and linguistics. I had already met him at a conference and had been tremendously impressed by him. He is a linguist who has this incredibly deep understanding of computation. He had read my thesis and had become very excited by it and when he came to M.I.T. he decided to teach a seminar that began by studying my thesis. That just blew me away. About half-way through the seminar, Mark found a new way of looking at the problem of speech recognition that got me very excited. He asked if I wanted to come down to Murray Hill to look the Labs over. I was surprised when Mark suggested that, because no one at Bell was then working on the higher level aspects of language such as syntax. No one I knew had ever come here.

"When I came for my visit I was just amazed by the people and the attitude. Here, on these two corridors where I now have my office, were people like Saul Sternberg in psychology and Bela Julesz in visual perception, both of whom talk to people like Mark Liberman, Osama Fujimura, and each other. There was, and is, a community of people who talk to each other depending only upon what their interests are and not on their fields. At a place like M.I.T., for example, psychologists work with psychologists, linguists work with linguists, and computer people work with computer people. They don't get close to each other unless they are writing an interdisciplinary grant proposal. When I came here for my interview, I asked people what they did, and how the place worked, and, basically, everyone said you sort of do what you are interested in, and if it's good work you are fine. I thought, until I got here, that those people had some sort of conspiracy worked out so that they all told me the same story. I just didn't believe I would have *carte blanche.* It took me awhile after I got here to realize that it really is true. The other thing that impressed me about people in this place, and continues to impress me, was, that unlike many people in academic life, people here don't sell themselves constantly. In a very soft-spoken way someone will show you something they had built, but only after telling you what the limitations of it were. They would go out of their way to tell you what was wrong with what they were doing, and then they would show you this astounding thing. They let their work speak for itself. It seems to me that to do good science you have to keep your ego down as much as possible. This place seemed to be good at that. So, much to the astonishment of the people at M.I.T., I came here. They thought that I was just about to step off of the edge of the world."

Since Marcus' arrival at the Bell Laboratories in 1979, the computer-science and artificial intelligence activities have been expanding. Marcus himself has been continuing his work on parsing machines. The program he now has running is a variant of his thesis program, which he called PARSIFAL. Like most Bell Labs scientists, Marcus has a computer terminal in his office. In his case he is hooked into the network that enables computer scientists to send messages to each other all over the country. For some reason, Marcus was not able to rouse his program from the main computer by using his terminal, so we went upstairs to a room filled with people working at computer terminals. Marcus began typing away at a free console. His program is written in a special version of LISP (List Processing) code, which, he says, looks like English but isn't. After a few passes, the machine was ready to go. He asked me to pick a sentence. For some reason, I chose, "My birthday is the 31st of December"—which is true, but not, I would imagine, of any special interest to the machine. Before we proceeded, Marcus reminded me of exactly what was going on.

"The model," he said, "consists of two parts. It consists of a grammar and what I call a grammar interpreter. The grammar is actually a program, and the grammar interpreter is a special-purpose machine that interprets the program. The properties of the grammar interpreter embody the things that are universal—in Chomsky's sense—to all languages, and the way languages vary is built into what I call the grammar. There are then two components in the model, one language-specific and one language-universal. It also has a lexicon for the language. For example, it knows in general that *can* can be a verb, or a noun, or a modal. It has a set of properties for each word that can tell it what sort of a word it might be. Its job is then to say, for example, that such and such is a sentence with a noun phrase 'so and so,' which consists of a determiner, and a noun, and so on—just like you were taught to do in the fifth grade. If you give it something that is a nonsentence, this parser will parse the first fraction of it that looks like it might be a sentence and then it will stop. The parser that we are about to build will take the fragments and tell you possible sentences that might be built out of them.

"Getting philosophical for a second, what I am really interested in, as I have told you, is the structure of the mind as viewed as a computational process. Since most of the mind seems to be quite inaccessible to scientific study as opposed to philosophical speculation, I have focused on grammar as one area where there seem to be some reasonable data. We have these strong and clear intuitions about which sentences are or are not acceptable to us. What I am really interested in is trying to understand what the computational process in our minds looks like that is doing grammatical analysis. The assumption is that every time we hear a sentence we analyze its grammar subconsciously and automatically before, and as a step toward, extracting the meaning."

Marcus' machine, as opposed to some of the other parsers that have been built, uses what he calls the determinism hypothesis. This is the assumption that the syntax of natural language can be parsed by a deterministic machine that functions continuously from left to right without backup or parallelism. He has a deep belief that the way the mind does this syntax must be simple and elegant. He eliminates anything in the model that is not. A researcher at M.I.T. has written a version of Marcus' parser that works for Japanese, and two summers ago Juliet Sutherland, who was a summer student at the Labs, built a version that can parse sentences that consist of exactly the words *he, she, it,* and *can*—sentences like "Cans can can cans." and "Can cans can cans?" "We did not try to handle *cancan* as a noun, but I don't think it would be hard," said Marcus.

The machine's first reaction to the sentence "My birthday is the 31st of December" was to reject it out of hand. The machine appeared to take special umbrage over the usage "31st." This puzzled Marcus, until he remembered that a summer student had recently been using the program and, for some reason, had arranged it so that numbers had to be written out. Marcus then rewrote the sentence to read, "My birthday is the thirty-first of December." This appeared to placate the machine. The next thing that happened I found rather poignant. The machine sent Marcus a message that read, "Sorry, I don't know the word *birthday*. Tell me a word like *birthday*." Marcus informed the machine that a *birthday* was a kind of *meeting*—a word in its lexicon. The machine then went into a sort of brief trance during which Marcus commented that it was "garbage collecting." The machine then emitted a printout written in computerese, but it is not too difficult to decipher. It considers each of the eight words in "My birthday is the thirty-first of December." It starts with *my*, which it identifies as a possessive pronoun; *birthday* it identifies as a noun. The verb *is* it reinterprets as "is during" and identifies *is* as a third-person-singular, present-tense auxiliary verb and *during* as a preposition. I cannot make out what it has decided that *the* is, but in the context of the sentence it has decided that *thirty-first* is a date. It identifies both *thirty* and *first* as numbers, *of* as a preposition, and *December* as a noun referring to a month. Its last entry is to note that "." is the final punctuation. It does not know that "the 32nd of December" is not a date, so it will also happily parse the sentence "My birthday is the thirty-second of December." If it mattered, this calendrical information could be programmed into the computer.

Marcus can envision when a more sophisticated and easier-to-use version of this parser could be part of a future electronic office. It might analyze the grammar of a letter and say, "This is ungrammatical," and rephrase it. If an office computer is ever to talk, it must be able to do syntax—that is, parse—or it will not get intonations right. Some of Marcus' colleagues at Bell are trying to produce what they call a writer's workbench, which attempts to tell a writer if the grammatical structure of his text is too complex for the intended audience. Marcus can imagine this task being done by some future version of his parser, and is working on such a parser with Bell Labs consultant Donald Hindle. As Marcus explained, all of the present generation of parsers, including his, have difficulty with conjunctions. For example, sentences like "Birds eat small worms and frogs" or "Our baby-sitter loves to take care of small boys and girls" have the possible meaning that both the frogs and the girls are small. Marcus' parser would at best get the meaning that only the worms and boys are small—the frogs and girls are just frogs and girls. The parser that Marcus and Hindle are building constructs descriptions of parse trees, rather than parse trees themselves, and it is flexible enough so that one description simultaneously conveys both interpretations of such conjunctions. They hope to have it running within a year.

Any kind of commercial payoff of these ideas is years away—maybe even decades. In view of this, I was interested in finding out how Marcus thought the divestiture would affect the kind of nonapplied research that he is doing. "There are incredible transient responses at the moment," he said, "which are affecting people's behavior. My own perception is that it's wrong to think that we have to work on things that will pay off immediately. But I don't think that there will be support for things that aren't *ever* very likely to pay off in some financial way, even if they are good work. But I think that has always been true. I have the feeling that we are returning to an older spirit at the Laboratories that has been very productive. At the moment there is a paranoia here that we are going to have to do things on a short-term basis. The kind of work that I am doing, if it succeeds, would lead to things that might be useful ten years from now. But the payoff for research is a continuing process. The work that we do this year will, by and large, not be the products that AT&T is going to manufacture this year. That work was done ten years ago. At times I have been worried, but at the moment I am almost excited by what is happening. We have even gotten signals that while some of our people have been doing an incredible job of aiding people in development, they were not spending *enough* of their time in basic research. I think that my own tastes and interests will fit in nicely with our long-term needs."

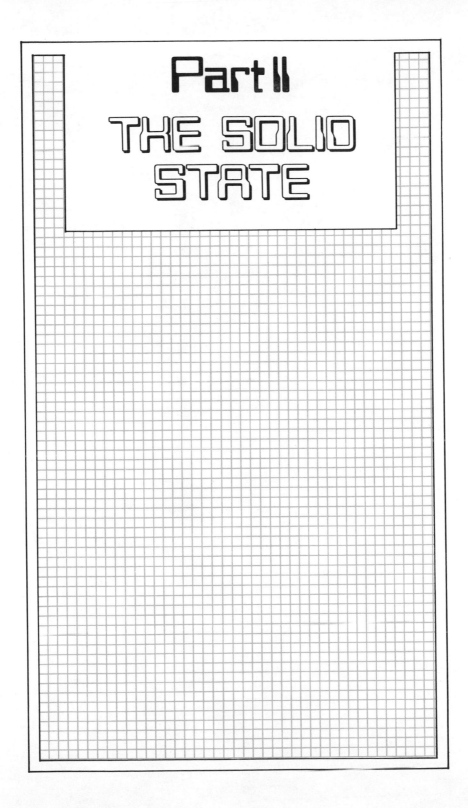

# Part II
# THE SOLID STATE

# CHAPTER 5

# Russel Ohl

BY THE EARLY 1930's engineers at Bell Labs realized that the practical limit to vacuum-tube technology had been reached. Used in the telephone system since 1915, these tubes soon came into general use and, by the mid-1930's, had been improved to the point where they lasted about ten years and required a tenth of the power of the original tubes. Nonetheless, they were still unreliable, expensive, and bulky; and some sort of solid-state device would have to replace them. In the mid-1930's a program in solid-state physics was inaugurated, and in barely a decade it produced, among other things, the transistor. One of its remarkable side effects was an accidental discovery made in 1940 by Russel Ohl.

Ohl was a chemist who had become a radio engineer during World War I. In 1939 he was a member of a radio group working in the Holmdel, New Jersey, division, about thirty miles away from the main laboratory in Murray Hill. He was interested in the problem of detecting very-short-wave radio signals. These were harder to detect with vacuum-tube circuits, as Ohl knew, than with a cat's whisker rectifier, a fine metal wire that is brought into point contact with a crystal. According to Lillian Hartmann Hoddeson, by 1939 Ohl had tested over a hundred crystalline materials to find the one that worked best as a detector. He finally decided on silicon, but the art of refining it was still in its infancy and available samples were far from uniform. Ohl asked two metallurgists on the staff, Jack Scaff and Henry Theurer, if they could produce some uniform samples. In an interview with

Hoddeson in 1975, Scaff described what happened. "We sent some beautiful ingots [of silicon] down to Ohl . . . Ohl would send these ingots out to be cut into pieces for physical measurements and other experiments. We didn't have a diamond saw in Bell Laboratories at that time. He would send them out to a jewelry outfit down in Perth Amboy, to grind them and cut them and make the samples, and had produced some beautiful little samples, oh about an eighth of an inch in diameter, and an inch long. Nice cylinders."

For some reason, Ohl did not feel like measuring the electrical resistance of these "nice cylinders," and he could not get anyone else to do it so the samples lay on a shelf for months. Finally, in disgust, he decided to measure the voltages himself with an oscilloscope. The electric fan that he used to cool the laboratory was placed in front of a bench light, interrupting the light at regular intervals as it spun. As the choppy light shone on Ohl's silicon, something very queer began to show up on the oscilloscope. The voltage seemed to follow the chop of the light. Ohl had no idea why this should be, and he called a couple of colleagues into his laboratory. This took place on a Friday. On Monday he showed the effect to his boss, Harold Friis. Ohl recalls, "Friis couldn't make anything of it and said you had better take this up to Bown (the director of research) and show it to him. . . . Bown was astute enough to know that here was something that had some importance but he didn't know what it was. So he said you better show this to Kelly (Bown's boss). I went up to Kelly's office and he thought this was very interesting saying that 'I think so and so ought to see this thing.' So he called Dr. Williams and Rob Burns who is Dr. Williams' assistant. And then he said, 'Well, I think Herbert Ives ought to hear about this.' [Ives had directed, at Bell Labs, the development of the first American television transmission, on 7 April 1927.] So he called these fellows and said to drop their work and come on up here and take a look at something. Then all of these men gathered in Kelly's office."

What Ohl had accidently discovered was the photovoltaic effect in silicon. Scaff and Theurer had unknowingly prepared their silicon sample in such a way that when light fell on it an electrical current was produced. Ohl had hit upon the essential ingredient for producing photovoltaic solar electricity.

A number of people at the Laboratory came to know of Ohl's

discovery—including Walter Brattain, one of the inventors of the transistor, who witnessed a demonstration in 1940 and was "flabbergasted." Nothing came of it, however, for nearly fifteen years, one reason being that during the war essentially the entire resources of Bell Labs were mobilized. Indeed, it was not until 1954 that three Bell Labs scientists, G.L. Pearson, C.S. Fuller, and D.M. Chapin made the first solar battery—using strips of silicon, each about the size of a razor blade.

# CHAPTER 6

# Transistor I

ON THURSDAY, 1 July 1948, several notes of potential interest to radio listeners and television watchers appeared in "The News of Radio" column of the *New York Times:*

> "On Your Mark," a new audience-participation item, will be added to WOR's schedule next Monday. It will be heard at 2:30 P.M. each weekday afternoon thereafter and will include prizes for questions which are correctly answered. Paul Luther will produce and announce the program.

This was followed by:

> George Shackley's original composition, "Anthem for Brotherhood," will have its first television performance at 5 P.M. Sunday over WPIX. The rendition will be a part of the station's "Television Chapel" program.

The last item read:

> A device called a transistor, which has several applications in radio where a vacuum tube ordinarily is employed, was demonstrated for the first time yesterday at Bell Telephone Laboratories, 463 West Street, where it was invented. [The transistor had in fact been invented at Bell's Murray Hill laboratories.]
>     The device was demonstrated in a radio receiver, which contained

none of the conventional tubes. It also was shown in a telephone system and in a television unit controlled by a receiver on a lower floor. In each case the transistor was employed as an amplifier, although it is claimed that it also can be used as an oscillator in that it will create and send radio waves.

In the shape of a small metal cylinder about a half-inch long, the transistor contains no vacuum, grid, plate or glass envelope to keep the air away. Its action is instantaneous, there being no warm-up delay since no heat is developed as in a vacuum tube. . . .

Along with these electronic demonstrations, Bell's public relations department had provided an eight-foot model transistor on wheels, intended to explain just how simple the whole thing really was. The press conference preceded by two weeks publication of the first scientific paper on the transistor, which was written by its two inventors, John Bardeen and Walter Brattain, and appeared in the *Physical Review* of 15 July 1948. This paper acknowledged the help of William Shockley, who would later invent the version of the transistor—the "junction transistor"—that came to dominate the field. The three shared the Nobel Prize in physics for 1956. Bardeen then went on to win a second Nobel Prize in physics in 1972, which he shared with Leon Cooper and J. Robert Schrieffer, for the theory of superconductivity. Bardeen, who is now at the Unviersity of Illinois, is the only person to have won two Nobel Prizes in the same science.

Bardeen and Brattain had discovered the "point-contact" transistor in December 1947 and had demonstrated its ability to amplify audio signals on the afternoon of 23 December. This unexpected Christmas present, which culminated two years of research at the Laboratories— and many more if all of the efforts that contributed indirectly are included—was kept secret for almost seven months. Even the editor of the *Physical Review* was asked not to divulge the contents of the paper.

There were several reasons for this secrecy. In some sense the transistor was "in the air" in physics; indeed, a group at Purdue University was exceedingly close. Brattain later recalled that in January 1948 a member of the group had described to him a potential experiment that surely would have led to the discovery of transistor action. "Yes,"

Brattain commented before walking away, "I think maybe that would be a very good experiment." He knew that it would be a good experiment. He and Bardeen had already done it. Had someone else discovered the transistor while Bell was preparing the patent applications, things could have become very sticky. Another reason for the secrecy, oddly enough, was to keep the discovery out of the hands of the military before it became public knowledge. Bell did not want any unnecessary or shortsighted security restrictions placed on its development. (The transistor was shown to military authorities on 22 June, eight days before the public announcement). A third reason was to give the company time to figure out how to develop and exploit the device. Given the transistor's subsequent history, it was remarkable just how little impact Bell's press conference announcement had.

This curious fact is commented upon and analyzed by Ernest Braun and Stuart Macdonald in *Revolution in Miniature*, an outstanding study of the history and development of the field.

"The announcement of the transistor," they write, "excited so little reaction that it was a decided anti-climax to the months of secrecy at Bell. . . . Even the technical journals mostly managed to control their enthusiasm, many waiting until late 1948 to report the event, some until 1949, and some not bothering at all. This seems strange considering the excitement of the transistor's inventors. . . . However, at the time of the announcement, the transistor was little more than a laboratory curiosity. It was to be some years before the device was made to do something useful."

Indeed, things moved at a glacial pace. It took nearly four years before Western Electric, in October 1951, began manufacturing extremely primitive transistors. Transistors did not appear in the telephone system until 1952, and not until 1953 were they used commercially outside communications, in Sonotone hearing aids. Because of Alexander Graham Bell's interest in the deaf, AT&T granted the license to use transistors in hearing aids cost-free, and Raytheon became the first commercial firm to supply them to hearing-aid manufacturers. By March 1953, Raytheon was producing some 10,000 transistors a month for use in hearing aids. Whatever their merits, these hearing aids were initially three to four times more expensive than the conventional variety, which used vacuum tubes. This could be traced directly to the cost of the transistors, which, at about $9 each, cost more than eight times as much as the vacuum tubes. The first commercially mass-produced transistor radio—the Regency—was jointly produced in October 1954 by Texas Instruments and the IDEA Corporation. It was a commercial failure. At $49.95—or about $210 in today's money— it was too expensive for what it was. But, whatever it was, it had taken six years to produce it.

To understand this extremely slow pace, why transistors and other semiconductor devices were so fiendishly difficult to produce, one must know something about the discovery of the transistor itself. From the point of view of their capacity to conduct electricity, materials can be divided into three classes: conductors, insulators, and semiconductors. Conductivity, or ability to conduct electricity, is conventionally measured in terms of how much resistance they offer—or, shall we say, do *not* offer—an electric current. The unit of conductivity is expressed in terms of the inverse of the resistance per unit length. The higher the number, the greater the conductivity.

Conductivity also depends on the temperature of a material. At room temperature, metals that are good conductors have (in units of inverse resistance) conductivities of from between about $10^4$ to $10^6$; insulators, like amber or glass, range from $10^{-22}$ to $10^{-10}$. So the entire range of conductivity from the best insulators to the best conductors comprises some twenty-eight orders of magnitude. Semiconductors such as silicon and germanium have conductivities somewhere in between—in the range from $10^{-9}$ to $10^3$. In addition there are also superconductors—materials that in the neighborhood of absolute zero temperature have essentially infinite conductivity.

However, a semiconductor is not just a poor insulator or weak conductor. It is physically something quite different. The first difference was noted as early as 1833 by the British physicist Michael Faraday. If we raise the temperature of a conventional metal conductor, its conductivity decreases. The reason for this is simple: as the temperature is raised, the electrons in the metal move more rapidly and collide more frequently with the metal atoms. Thus the flow of electrons—which *is* the conduction of electricity in a metal—is impeded, and the conductivity drops.

With a semiconductor, on the other hand, as Faraday discovered, the conduction *increases* with rising temperature, until it reaches a maximum, from which it then drops as the temperature is increased still further. From the point of view of classical, prequantum physics this result was totally incomprehensible. In 1840 the French physicist Alexandre-Edmond Becquerel noticed that an electrical current could be made to flow in some semiconductors if light was made to shine on them, and in 1873 the British physicist Willoughby Smith observed that light altered their conductivity. Both effects were also incomprehensible on the basis of classical physics. Finally, in 1874, the German physicist Ferdinand Braun discovered the phenomenon of "rectification" in semiconductors, that under certain circumstances they conduct electric currents in only one direction. This ability turned out to be the key to their utility in electronics, although it was not appreciated for many years. But Braun's general work on radio transmission was appreciated, and he shared the Nobel Prize in physics with Guglielmo Marconi in 1909.

By the late nineteenth century, it was well understood that certain electromagnetic circuits oscillate; that is, they can vary periodically in time in both magnitude and direction. The simplest example is a circuit consisting of a device that can store magnetic energy—an inductor—connected to a device that can store electrical energy—a capacitor. In a circuit these two devices are connected by a current-carrying wire. As the capacitor loses energy, this energy is gained by the inductor; when the inductor acquires *its* maximum energy, it begins to lose it to the capacitor. The result is that the energy in the circuit will oscillate rhythmically back and forth between these two devices, at the "natural frequency" of the circuit. The whole thing resembles a pair of springs that have been hooked together. When one spring is compressed it will expand and thus compress the other spring, and so on, back and forth indefinitely—or at least until both springs lose all their energy by giving off heat.

Now, such a circuit can be connected to an external source of electric power. If this source is itself oscillating, the circuit will try to follow these oscillations. If the frequency of the external oscillation and the "natural" frequency of the circuit just match, the two are said to be in "resonance." The "natural frequency" is the frequency at which the circuit oscillates when there is no external oscillating source of power. At resonance, the current flowing through the circuit will be maximized. But it is possible, by varying the characteristics of the capacitor, to make the circuit resonate at various frequencies. In my youth I used to take apart radios. Behind the dial that one turned to select different stations I discovered an odd-looking device. It consisted of two sets of parallel metal plates, each of which looked like a circular metal surface cut in two. I thought of them as round cookies that had been half-eaten. When I turned the dial one set of plates rotated together, while the other was set rigidly. Although I did not have the foggiest idea of what this gadget did, it was clear to me that by turning it I was somehow able to tune to different stations. In the language of what I have been describing, what I was doing was changing the geometry of the capacitor, thereby changing the natural frequency at which the radio circuit would oscillate.

A radio station broadcasts at a definite wavelength, or frequency. When this "carrier" wave is picked up by an antenna, it produces just the kind of externally oscillating voltage source discussed above. By adjusting the dial of the radio, one changes the natural frequency at which the circuit oscillates, until it exactly matches the frequency of the carrier wave. This circuit acts as a detector of the radio signal. But the carrier wave is a very poor source of information. It serves only to tune the receiver to the transmitter. To transmit information, such as audible sound, the carrier wave must be "modulated"—varied in some characteristic way. Information is imposed on the carrier wave by changing either its frequency (FM broadcasting) or amplitude (AM). It is this change that carries information. The shape of the carrier wave then becomes distorted, and to "read" the information contained in this distortion, the radio circuit must have a device that can separate the *modulations* inflicted on the carrier wave from the wave itself. This device must somehow be able to "read" the information contained in the carrier wave. Enter the rectifier.

A rectifier is a device that conducts more current in one direction than in another. An ideal rectifier would conduct current in, say, the "forward" direction but not in, say, the "reverse" direction. In practice, rectifiers can produce preferentially forward currents that are several thousand times greater than the reverse currents. The great utility of a rectifier is that it changes alternating current (a.c.) into direct current (d.c.). Alternating current, by definition, changes its direction periodically, sixty times a second in American households, fifty in many European countries. This rate of change is called its frequency. If a source of alternating current is attached to a rectifier, then the rectifier will pass only that part of the cycle in which the current is flowing in the preferred direction. The alternating current has been transformed into direct current. How well a rectifier works depends on the frequency of the current. Typical AM radio carrier waves have frequencies of about a million cycles a second. But the modulations that carry the information—the voices and the music—are of relatively low frequency, ranging from about twenty to twenty thousand cycles. The high-frequency oscillations can be rectified, but many rectifiers are inefficient for the low-frequency oscillations. The rectifier acts to separate the carrier wave from the part of the signal that carries information. Hence building a radio receiver boils down, in a certain sense, to making a rectifier.

As mentioned above, in 1874 Braun discovered that the mineral, galena, was a natural rectifier, and by 1900 an Anglo-American electrician, David Edward Hughes, had discovered that the combination of a tungsten needle in light contact with a carbon block acted like a rectifier. In fact, the tungsten needle acted as a kind of radio antenna, and this combination was used as a primitive radio receiver. By 1903 the American engineer Greenleaf W. Pickard began trying out various crystals in place of carbon as rectifiers, and in 1906 he discovered that silicon was especially good. Thus began the era of cat's whiskers crystal sets; the cat's whisker refers to the metal needle in contact with the crystal. Ironically then, the first radio receivers were solid-state devices and, in this sense, have more in common with the present generation of electronic equipment than does what came in between. The era of what came in between began in 1904 with the discovery—or invention—by John Fleming of the "thermionic valve" —the first electron tube.

Fleming, an English electrical engineer, died in 1945 at the age of ninety-five, having been scientifically productive for most of his life. He had visited Edison in the United States in 1884, and was aware of the "Edison effect" in which electrical particles—electrons—can be "boiled" off a metal that is heated in a vacuum, such as the filament of an electric light bulb, and then made to move to a positive electrode. This became the model of the first vacuum tube. In this tube—usually made of glass—a filament is introduced that can be heated by an external current. A metal plate collects the electrons emitted by the heated filament. Both the filament (cathode) and the plate (anode) are housed in a partial vacuum inside the glass tube. The voltage between the cathode and the anode can be arranged so that current flows only in one direction. Hence this two-element tube, or diode, functions as a rectifier and was so used in some early radio sets.

The invention of the diode would, by itself, probably not have been enough to render the cat's whisker obsolete, except that in 1906 the American inventor Lee de Forest had the idea of inserting a third element, a grid, between the cathode and the anode, and thus invented the "triode" vacuum tube. The triode—some claim that de Forest himself did not really understand it—made both radio and long-distance telephony practical. De Forest's feelings about the latter remain elusive, but of the former he once asked a group of radio executives, "What have you gentlemen done with my child? The radio was conceived as a potent instrumentality for culture, fine music, the uplifting of America's mass intelligence. You have debased this child, you have sent him out in the streets in rags of ragtime, tatters of jive and boogie-woogie, to collect money from all and sundry." Be that as it may, de Forest's "audion," especially as developed by Harold D. Arnold, Bell Labs' first director of research, Irving Langmuir of General Electric, and Fritz Lowenstein, an independent inventor, was a creation of real genius. Lowenstein appeared at Bell in January 1912 with his version of the audion in a sealed box so that Bell officials could see it—or hear it—in operation without learning how it worked. Some years later Bell bought the rights to Lowenstein's idea of making the grid electrically negative by attaching it to a battery which he had patented.

In the triode, as in the diode, a stream of electrons flows from the heated filament to the plate. However, this stream is modulated by the voltage on the grid; and the voltage, in turn, depends on the amount of current that flows to the grid. In other words, any change in the grid current will be reflected in changes in the electron stream; the grid current, so to speak, "imprints" its profile on the electron stream. But grid currents are, as a rule, very small—they may arise from relatively weak radio signals—whereas the cathode-to-anode current can be substantial. Thus, in effect, these weak grid currents become amplified. Hence a triode acts not only as a rectifier but also as an amplifier of weak signals. This latter role makes it absolutely essential to such tasks as boosting telephone signals coming down the wire or reamplifying radio signals coming through space. Without the audion, the long-distance telephone service between New York and San Francisco inaugurated in January 1915 would never have been successfully completed. The cost of a three-minute call in 1915, by the way, was $20.70, or about $207 in today's money.

As marvelous as the triode was, by the 1930's some of the more visionary members of Bell Laboratories realized that something would have to be found to replace vacuum tubes. J. R. Pierce, the Bell engineer and general polymath who took Arthur C. Clarke's 1945 suggestions of a communications satellite and made it into a reality, once remarked that "nature abhors a vacuum tube." Hence, in 1936, after a Depression-related hiring freeze of six years, Mervin J. Kelly, who was then the director of research at Bell Labs, began to hire what would now be known as solid-state physicists. He assembled a small group, including Shockley, who came to the Labs in 1936, and Charles Townes, who came in 1939. Their job was to learn about the physics of the solid state, in general, with the vague hope that whatever came out of their effort might be useful for communications and, in particular, for the telephone business. What came out of it, among other things, was the transistor.

In the meantime a separate enterprise was taking place at the Holmdel branch of Bell Labs. In the late 1930's some members of this group became interested in detecting radio waves of very short wavelengths—a few centimeters, as opposed to the several-hundred-meter wavelengths characteristic of AM radio-station carrier waves. This activity was carried out in connection with radar, which, for the Bell System, became a major enterprise during World War II. The Bell System did about half of the research and development that went into the successful United States effort to develop radar. As Lillian Hoddeson notes, "In the late 1930's George Southworth and other members of Bell's radio group at Holmdel, New Jersey, were seeking new methods for the detection of very short (40 cm) radio waves. Vacuum tubes, which had replaced cat's whiskers rectifiers, were insensitive at high frequencies. Southworth decided to reexamine point-contact detectors [cat's whiskers] and constructed one first from parts found while rummaging in the famous secondhand radio market on Cortland Street in lower Manhattan. He found them to be much superior to vacuum tubes in the high-frequency [short wavelength] range. This discovery prompted a large and continuing research effort on point contacts. The attempt to find materials that work best in point contacts led in turn to a program of studies of silicon." This is the program that engaged the interests of Russel Ohl and his two colleagues at Holmdel, Jack Scaff and Henry Theurer.

Scaff and Theurer were, as we have seen, in the business of producing silicon ingots. In September 1939 they accidentally produced the remarkable ingot of silicon that had a bizarre property: two of its parts rectified in opposite directions. It was this sample that Ohl had sent out to the jewelry outfit in Perth Amboy to cut up into the "nice cylinders"—those nice cylinders in which an electric current was produced when the choppy bench light shone on them. These cylinders had the property that one region had one direction of rectification while the other had the opposite. The photo voltage developed across the junction between these two regions. Having decided that they should have a different name for each region, Scaff and Ohl called one region "*p*-type" (positive) and the other "*n*-type" (negative). It is not clear just what crystal ball they were looking into when they selected these names, but they have been with us ever since. Now we understand why these names were exactly right.

By 1940, while this work and its sequels were being done, the theory of semiconductors, which had been evolving almost from the discovery of quantum mechanics in the late 1920's, had begun to assume something like its present form. For purposes of illustration it is useful to begin with the discussion of what would be an ideal insulator. Below is a sketch of a diamond which is a lattice of carbon atoms.

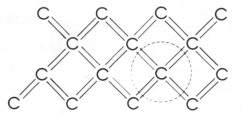

*The four lines emanating from each C represent the
carbon atom's four valence electrons.*

The reader may imagine extending this picture in various directions. Now, each of the four valence electrons can combine with an electron from a neighboring carbon atom to make what is known as a valence bond. There are four nearest neighbors in this tetrahedral structure, which is also characteristic of germanium and silicon. If one applies an electric field to this diamond, no charges will move, since all of the valence electrons are used up in the bonding. Hence such an idealized diamond lattice would be a perfect insulator. If, by some means, an extra electron is inserted in this structure it is free to move in an electric field, and such electrons would be called "conduction electrons." They are the electrons that conduct current in a conductor. But there is another way of producing electronic conduction in such a lattice. Let us imagine that somehow one or more of the valence electrons holding a carbon atom to its neighbor is removed. This will make an altered bond as shown below:

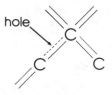

Removing a valence electron leaves a "hole" in the lattice structure. An electron from a neighboring bond can jump into this hole—which, in turn, leaves *another* hole. This hole gets filled, and so the hole propagates throughout the lattice. We could follow the motion of the hopping electrons, but it is much simpler to follow the motion of the holes. Since these holes move, in an electric field, in just the opposite sense to the jumping electrons, they are completely equivalent in their behavior to the propagation of a positive electric current through the lattice. Now one can begin to get an insight into what the *n* and *p* really mean in the two regions of Ohl's semiconductor. The *n* region is a region that has an excess number of electrons, and the *p* region has an excess number of holes. A neutral region would be a region in which all the holes are filled. Before we discuss how, in practice, these regions are created, it will be useful to present these same ideas in a somewhat different, but deeper form, using the notion of energy levels.

An electron that moves around a proton cannot have arbitrary energies. The allowed energy levels are what are called "quantized." Only certain values are possible, and these are determined by quantum mechanics. If many atoms are put together in a solid—say a metal or an insulator—then something remarkable can happen. The allowed energy levels are so many and so close together that they fall into bands. Here are the bands for an insulator:

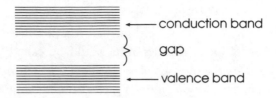

Between the two bands—the conduction band and the valence band—is a gap in which no energy levels exist. In an ideal insulator all of the electrons are in the valence band, which is filled. For an electron to be part of the conduction current, it would have to be promoted from the valence band to the conduction band above the gap. If the gap is wide, this cannot readily happen, so that the material acts like an insulator. In a conductor some of the energy levels in the conduction band are not occupied and this allows the electrons to move and the material to conduct electricity. A semiconductor, on the other hand, is like an insulator in that the two bands are separated by a gap, but the gap is smaller. Therefore, it is relatively easy to promote an electron from the valence band to the conduction band. One way to do this is to shine light on the semiconductor. The light quanta, which carry energy, knock an electron or several electrons out of the valence band and into the conduction band. That is why semiconductors can conduct an electric current when they are exposed to light. It is the essential explanation of how photovoltaic solar electricity is generated. Another way of promoting electrons into the conduction band is by heating the material. This is why semiconductors have increased conductivity when they are heated. Semiconductors can also have their conductivities dramatically altered by adding electrically active impurities, something that is known as "doping." It is clear then that the band theory of solids is an extremely powerful and very successful theory of material properties.

We can now begin to understand the meaning of the *n* and *p* regions and, from that, to understand the transistor itself. It is remarkable, considering the number of potentially possible explanations of these regions, that Scaff and Theurer hit on the correct one almost immediately. Theurer found that if he added minute amounts of boron—less than .01 percent—to the molten silicon then, when it cooled, its *p*-type conductivity was enhanced. He also found that phosphorous added to the melt would increase the *n*-type conductivity. He and Scaff reached the reasonable conclusion that these impurities must somehow be responsible for the regions of opposite conductivity. Hoddeson tells us that when Scaff first reported this idea to Walter Brattain, it seemed so unlikely that Brattain reacted by telling Scaff that he was crazy. Not only was Scaff not crazy—he was right, and this work led to a general observation that was the key to the manufacture of semiconductor devices. It was noticed by Scaff and Theurer that the doping materials that worked—that produced these conducting regions—fell into two classes. There was a group comprising elements such as phosphorous, antimony, and arsenic that, in a certain sense, have one electron too many (these elements have five valence electrons per atom). Hence when they are inserted in a lattice made up of atoms having four valence electrons, such as carbon or silicon, there is one electron too many for each atom that is inserted. These electrons have to go somewhere, and it is very easy for them to pass into the conduction band. Hence, if one dopes silicon with one of these elements, one turns it into an *n*-type semiconductor. Another class comprises elements having one valence electron too *few*—three per atom; members of this class include boron and aluminum. When an atom of this class is substituted for a carbon or silicon atom, it leaves a hole. Thus to make a *p*-type region one must dope the silicon with boronlike atoms. What Scaff and Theurer had done, accidentally, when they produced the sample of silicon on which Ohl had found photoconductivity, was to dope the silicon with just the right impurities so as to produce contiguous *n* and *p* regions. What was not accidental was that this event took place in an environment in which its significance was immediately apparent, although, as Brattain later remarked, the first time he actually saw the huge photoeffect in silicon, "I even thought my leg, maybe, was being pulled." As Pasteur wrote, "In science, chance favors only the prepared mind."

# CHAPTER 7

# Transistor II: Addison White

IN 1941 a large part of Bell Laboratories was moved from 463 West Street in New York City to its present location in Murray Hill, New Jersey. By 1945 the staff had nearly doubled, to some 8,000 people, reflecting the growth that had taken place during World War II. Much of that work had focused on radar, and next to nothing was done in the way of fundamental research on semiconductors.

In 1942, William Shockley and Walter Brattain left the Laboratories for a year to work in separate laboratories involved in submarine-detection research. In 1944, after they returned to Bell, Mervin J. Kelly became executive vice-president of the Laboratories, and in July 1945, with the authorization of Bell Labs' president, Oliver E. Buckley, he made a sweeping change in its organization. It had become clear to Kelly that fundamental research in solid-state physics was the key to further progress in semiconductors. To this end he created, among other things, a small solid-state physics group with Shockley as its head. One of Shockley's first accomplishments was to hire John Bardeen, who had gotten his Ph.D. in 1936 with the distinguished Hungarian-born theoretical physicist Eugene Wigner at Princeton and had spent the war at the Naval Ordnance Laboratory in Washington, D.C. Then, as now, space was at a premium at Murray Hill, so Bardeen found himself sharing an office with two experimental physicists, Brattain and Gerald Pearson, who had been working on semiconductors since the early 1930's. It turned out to be an ideal arrangement, since Bardeen was challenged to explain the experimental results that his office mates were producing.

Shockley and Bardeen represented the two sides of the coin of theoretical physics. Shockley is a phenomenologist, a theoretician whose deep insight into the workings of physical phenomena is expressed almost pictorially and with a minimum of mathematics. Bardeen, as well as being a phenomenologist, is a master at constructing profound mathematical structures that explain and coordinate many experimental phenomena and that become richer the further they are explored and developed. Both sides of the coin are necessary in theoretical physics, and occasionally—as in an Einstein, for example—they come together. Einstein was not only a master of "pictorial physics" —what he called thought experiments. When it came to his general theory of relativity and gravitation he also was able to construct a vast mathematical edifice that revealed and predicted entirely new phenomena—for example, black holes.

One of the first things that Shockley's group did was to review all available knowledge about semiconductors. By 1939 there were the beginnings of a deep theory as to why junctions between the $n$ and $p$ regions of a semiconductor, and the junctions between a metal and a semiconductor—such as tungsten points and silicon—rectify. Much of this work had been done in Germany by Walter Schottky and in England by Sir Nevill Mott. The findings were collected and summarized in a basic text, *Electronic Processes in Ionic Crystals,* written by Mott and Ronald F. Gurney and published at Oxford in 1940. Schottky's work had appeared in Germany in 1939, but at that time Bell Labs was no longer receiving German journals. Hence, to some extent, it was reinvented at the Laboratories by Addison White, a young chemist, who had been lent to the metallurgy group, which was led by Jack Scaff and accidentally discovered the $p–n$ junction and its photoelectric properties. These results seemed totally mysterious at the time, but White was able to make some sense out of them by applying the available literature to the problem at hand.

As early as 1939 Shockley and others at Bell had been trying to construct a solid-state device that would amplify electric currents like the de Forest triode audion. But none of these prewar experimental devices showed any desirable characteristics, and there the problem rested until the group returned to it in 1945. That April, Shockley came up with the first design for a transistor. He imagined applying a strong electric field perpendicular to a thin slab of a semiconductor in order to modulate the flow of current along the slab. He drew up the circuit design in his laboratory notebook, and it was then tried experimentally by Brattain and others. The problem was that it didn't work; no current modulation took place. By March 1946 Bardeen had come up with an explanation of this apparently paradoxical behavior, based on what he called the "theory of surface states"—states on the surface of the semiconductor that trapped electrons so that their flow could not be modulated. In the 1950's it was finally understood how to overcome this problem and make Shockley's original device work. It is now called a field-effect transistor, the kind of transistor that is most commonly used at present.

Early in December 1947, Bardeen and Brattain were working on a version of the field-effect transistor. Having had some success in controlling the electron flow, they were now trying to improve the device's performance. They were using germanium as the semiconductor, since they were able to get samples of very high purity. On 11 December, Robert Gibney, a physical chemist in the group, prepared a germanium sample for Bardeen and Brattain. This sample had been doped so that it was *n*-type, that is, the excess carriers of electric current were negatively charged electrons. Gibney evaporated a circular spot of gold onto the germanium, leaving a small hole in the center so that a tungsten point could be inserted to make electrical contact with the germanium. When Brattain went to use the sample he accidentally set off a spark between the tungsten and the gold. This spoiled the hole. In frustration he put the tungsten point alongside the gold but separated from it by a tiny distance. He attached this device to a power supply, expecting to see something like a field-effect transistor with a flow of electrons. There was a substantial modulation of current, but something was odd. Much to his astonishment, the current was flowing the *wrong way.*

Almost immediately, Bardeen and Brattain understood, in a general way, what was going on. This is made clear in an entry dated 19 December in Brattain's notebook: "It would appear then that the modulation obtained when the grid point [the gold] is bias + is due to the grid furnishing holes to the plate point [the tungsten]." In other words the gold contact was drawing electrons *out* of the semiconductor rather than, as they had expected, injecting them *into* it. In the language that we have used earlier, the gold contact was injecting "holes" *into* the semiconductor. For this reason they coined the term *emitter* to describe what was happening at the gold contact and *collector* — "collector of holes"—for what was happening at the tungsten, and these terms have been used ever since. What was really surprising was that these holes could propagate through the germanium from emitter to collector. Prior to these experiments it had been assumed that if holes were injected into *n*-type germanium, the surplus electrons would simply fill them immediately so that there would be no propagation. Holes in *n*-type semiconductors are called minority carriers since, in an *n*-type material, the majority carriers are electrons. The possibility of propagating minority carriers was the key to the invention of the transistor.

This effect was nearly discovered at the same time by the Purdue group, but by their own admission, they did not understand the physics and were unable to use the phenomenon to design an amplifier. Indeed, after their discovery on 11 December, it took Bardeen and Brattain several days to make an amplifier. Five days after they had first observed the minority-carrier effect, Brattain made a new version of the device. In this one, the distance between the gold emitter and the tungsten collector had been reduced to a few ten-thousandths of a centimeter, in the hope of improving performance. When they plugged this gadget into their circuits they found, on the first try, an amplification factor of fifteen. By 23 December they were confident enough to stage a demonstration in the Laboratories. Brattain wrote in his notebook the next day, "The circuit was actually spoken over and by switching the device in and out a distinct gain in speech level could be heard and seen on the scope presentation with no noticeable change in the quality." The age of the transistor, as yet unnamed, had begun.

In a 1975 interview Brattain described how the transistor got its name. "When the question was asked, 'What should we name it?' Bardeen and I were told, 'You did it, you name it.' We were aware that de Forest had called his three-electrode vacuum tube an audion, and that this name did not survive. We also knew that whatever we named it might not take. We knew a two-syllable name would be better than three or more syllables. J. A. Becker had originated names for other semiconductor devices, namely, *varistor* for the rectifer and *thermistor* for the temperature-sensitive device. We wanted a name that would fit into this family. We had many suggestions, some ending in *-itron*, which we did not like. Bardeen and I were about at the end of our rope when one day J. R. Pierce walked by my office and I said to him, 'Pierce, come and sit down. You are just the man I want to see.'

"I told him about our dilemma, including that we wanted something to fit in with varistor and thermistor. Now Pierce knew that the point-contact device was a dual of the vacuum tube, circuitwise. . . . He mentioned the most important property of the vacuum tube, 'transconductance,' thought a minute about what the dual of this parameter would be and said, 'transresistance,' and then said 'transistor,' and I said, 'Pierce, that is it!'

"Some years later," Brattain continued, "I came across a story by J. J. Coupling, entitled 'The Transistor,' in a science-fiction journal. The last phrase in the story was 'and an obscure individual by the name of J. R. Pierce named it.' Pierce had written many science-fiction stories, and he signed them all J. J. Coupling. I knew this and was somewhat chagrined that maybe we had not given him proper credit, though everybody knew who had named it.

"My late wife, Karen, said when she first heard the name, that it would probably be shortened to *sistor* before too long. When the award of the Nobel Prize to Bardeen, Shockley, and me was announced, my father was out in the Bitterroot Mountains of Idaho. The only way my mother could send him a message was by forest reserve telephone to tell Ross Brattain, etc. . . . She wanted him to get the news before everybody else on the line knew, so her message was, 'Tell Ross Brattain the transistor won a Nobel Prize.' The message my father received was, 'Your sister won a Nobel Prize.' My father did have a sister, but he knew she had not won this prize. When we went to the first International Semiconductor Conference in England (1950), the English scientists were not using our name for the device. We asked them if by chance they did not think the name *transistor* was appropriate. Their answer was that they thought we had copyrighted the name and were therefore being very proper in not using it. We told them this was not so, that they could use the name if they wished."

The type of transistor that Bardeen and Brattain invented is called a point-contact transistor, since the electrical contacts to the semiconductor were originally made with two points—gold and tungsten. Put into production by Western Electric in 1951, it remained an engineer's nightmare because of its general unreliability and difficulty to manufacture: no two transistors seemed to have the same characteristics. Whatever patents Bardeen and Brattain had were assigned—as were all patents on inventions made by Bell staff members—to the company for a dollar apiece. "You sold your soul for a dollar," a Bell engineer once said, jokingly, to me. The dollar no longer changes hands. Patent rights are assigned to Bell Labs as part of the employment agreement. Many people seem to have the impression that Bell, having invented and patented the transistor, collects a royalty on each one. In 1956, under an antitrust consent decree, Bell waived all patent rights to the transistor. Five years earlier, perhaps in an attempt to stave off the decree, the company had begun to share its knowledge with others entering the field. In *Revolution in Miniature,* Ernest Braun and Stuart Macdonald report that in April 1952 the company invited—at a cost of $25,000 per "invitee"—all comers to attend an open symposium on transistors. There were thirty-five takers. Since Bell had invested, according to one estimate, about a million dollars in research on the transistor up to 1948, the company just about recovered its costs until 1956, by selling manufacturing licenses to newcomers such as Raytheon and Texas Instruments. The public-relations benefits to Bell were enormous.

It was clear to Shockley as early as 1948 that something better than the point-contact transistor was needed if the device were ever to play a role in electronics. By then the theory of the $p$–$n$ junction rectifier —what Russel Ohl had stumbled on in 1939—was reasonably well understood, at least by Shockley. In essence it is the following. On the $p$-side of the junction, holes dominate in number over free electrons; while on the $n$-side, electrons dominate over holes. Hence, if a suitable potential is applied across the junction, holes flow easily into the $n$-region while, at the same time, electrons flow into the $p$-region. On the other hand, if the potential is reversed, then both the holes and the electrons encounter a barrier at the boundary of the $p$–$n$ region, and the flow of current is greatly reduced—in silicon, for example, by a factor of up to a million. Shockley apparently had arrived at the theory of the $p$–$n$ junction by January 1948, but the *Physical Review* rejected his paper for what they considered its lack of rigor. It was published in the *Bell System Technical Journal* in July 1949. In this fifty-four-page memoir Shockley also produced a design for what is known as a *p–n* junction transistor. It took two years before Shockley, in collaboration with Morgan Sparks and Gordon Teal, actually made the device.

In essence Shockley's idea was to put two *p–n* junctions back to back. Below is a schematic drawing of a so-called *p–n–p* junction transistor circuit. The *n–p–n* transistor can be made by reversing the roles of *n* and *p* in the diagram.

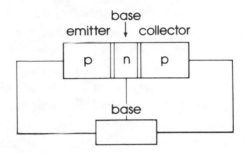

In this device two *p*-type regions make a sandwich that envelops a thin *n*-type region—a thousandth of an inch thick, or less, in an actual transistor. If a suitable voltage is applied to the emitter, a current of holes can be made to flow to the base—the thin *n*-type region. If this region is thin enough, these holes can diffuse across the base and into the collector region. This current can be modulated and the power amplified. Thus the device is a rather precise analog of de Forest's vacuum-tube amplifier. Although it may look simple on paper, it took another year before Western Electric began to manufacture these junction transistors—and then at a rate of only a hundred a month.

But by the spring of 1950 the problems of making a workable transistor had become so complex and multidisciplinary that some special arrangement within the Laboratories was necessary to deal with them. A triumvirate of leaders was established to coordinate activities in what was effectively a development, rather than a research, effort. Shockley was put in charge of the physics part; J. A. Morton, the development side; and Addison White, the young chemist "lent" to the metallurgists before the war, was placed in charge of the materials side—assigned the terribly difficult problem of producing physical semiconductors that bore some resemblance to the idealized theoretical models that Shockley and his colleagues were using in their designs.

Addison White is a very distinguished looking grey-haired man of seventy-four. He does not visit the Laboratories too often now, but he agreed to come by on a few of my visits to talk to me not only about the evolution of the transistor but about the evolution of the Laboratories which he joined in 1930 at the age of twenty-one.

White was born near Fresno, California, in 1909. His father was a farmer with a wide-ranging curiosity that he instilled in his son. As White put it, "I soon found that I was curious about the world in general, but I was not drawn to any one aspect of it. I enjoyed my high school courses, but I got no indication in high school of what my future calling would be." In 1926, White entered Occidental College in Los Angeles, a small, liberal arts school. He had taken only one general-science course in high school and had no intention of becoming a scientist. Money was short, so he took part-time jobs. The steadiest, and most financially rewarding, was as a chemistry laboratory assistant, and he ended up by majoring in chemistry with a minor in mathematics. "I would just as soon have majored in Latin, or history," he remarked, "except that they didn't have any assistantships. When I graduated in 1930, the only recruiter who talked with me was from Bell Labs so, *faute de mieux,* I accepted his offer and came. I went to work with the avowed purpose of treating my job as a means to an end . . . that is, eating."

The timing of White's entry into Bell Labs was extremely fortuitous, not only for him but also—considering what he would accomplish —for the Laboratories as a whole. Soon afterward the Great Depression struck, and hiring was suspended until 1936. By then it had become company policy to recruit essentially only Ph.D.'s for scientific research. As White noted, "If I had come in after 1936, with the qualifications I had, I probably would have been a technical assistant at best." In 1939 he had a chance to work, for two years, with Lester Germer and Clinton Davisson, whose classic experiment in 1927 demonstrated the wave nature of the electron. In 1937 Davisson won a Nobel Prize in physics for this work, which played a vital role in the development of the quantum theory. Davisson was the first of the seven staff members at Bell Labs to win a Nobel Prize in physics.

By the early 1930's it was generally recognized that a knowledge of quantum mechanics was essential to understanding not only chemical processes but also solids. As early as 1931 Brattain attended a lecture course given by the great German physicist Arnold Sommerfeld in the Michigan Summer Symposium in Theoretical Physics at the University of Michigan. After he returned, various members of the Labs decided it was vital that they too learn quantum mechanics. So in 1935, at the suggestion of his supervisor, Stanley Morgan, White took a course in quantum mechanics from Isidor Rabi at Columbia University. This course was held during working hours and involved commuting to the city from Summit, New Jersey. Two years later Shockley started a quantum mechanics seminar at the Laboratories, which White joined. "Even though I didn't have a degree in physics," White commented, "I was able to carry my load in the seminars partly by virtue of having studied with Rabi. We did all the work among ourselves and took turns chairing the seminars." After 1936 they included people like Shockley and Charles Townes. The seminars must have been a great success since, by 1941, White was able to use his knowledge of quantum mechanics to provide some sort of explanation for why doping certain crystals with certain materials makes them $n$ or $p$ and how a point-contact semiconductor rectifier works.

White continued to work on semiconductors and related matters. "During the war," he told me, "Bell Laboratories had gotten—entirely by accident, since it had nothing to do with our communications mission—a little part of a project at Columbia University. They were designing a membrane to be used in separating different isotopes of uranium, something that was essential in the construction of the atomic bomb. The man in charge of the project left the Bell Laboratories and left the company holding the bag, in some sense, because there were contracts to be fulfilled. By that time I had moved to Murray Hill, but I was sent to New York to liquidate this project. There was a group of about six or eight staff members and technical assistants, and, entirely through their ingenuity, we solved the problem of making a membrane that would work and stand up to corrosion within the year that I had been given. It was later used in the $600-million plant that was then going up at Oak Ridge, Tennessee."

This effort must have made a considerable impression on White's superiors at the Laboratories. Soon afterward he was put in charge of what might be called the chemical electronics, and then, of the physical electronics group. By 1948, when White had his first contact with the transistor group, a project had been started by Gordon Teal and J. B. Little that would completely change the materials aspect of making transistors. Prior to the war silicon samples, like those used by Ohl when he discovered the photovoltaic effect, had been made by melting silicon and then freezing it. The resulting ingots consisted of many crystals—polycrystalline silicon. The great disadvantage was that, at the boundaries between crystals, a hole or electron injected into the sample would in effect disappear as a minority-charge carrier. Because the boundaries acted as traps for these carriers, any current injected into the semiconductor would "evaporate" in less than a millionth of a second. In an imperfect material like this, it would have been impossible to make the kind of transistor that Shockley was trying to design. Thus, Gordon Teal decided to try to grow a large, single crystal of germanium. He chose germanium because it melts at 937.4°C., whereas silicon melts at 1410°C. The silicon melt is so brilliant that one cannot look at it with the naked eye. From all accounts, Teal's efforts were at first regarded with considerable skepticism by his colleagues, particularly the metallurgists, at the Laboratories. But he persisted, and in 1948 he and Little managed to produce single crystals of germanium. The technique that they used was invented in 1917 by J. Czochralski and is known as "crystal pulling." It consists of melting the germanium in a carbon crucible, since carbon and germanium do not react at this temperature (it is crucial not to contaminate the sample). A tiny crystal of germanium—the seed—is put into the melt so that the melt wets it. The seed is on a sort of spindle that can be rotated and slowly withdrawn from the melt. If the temperature is properly controlled, the melt freezes on the continuously withdrawing seed in such a way that the atoms of the solid are arranged in the same nearly perfect order as in the original seed. The crystal is thus slowly pulled out of the melt like a piece of taffy. The result, a sort of torpedo-shaped object 8 centimeters long and 2.5 centimeters wide, took a few hours to grow. It was so structurally perfect that it could maintain hole, or electron, currents long enough to make transistor action possible. Without this advance in crystal-growing, it is hard to imagine how the transistor could have been developed at all. Teal and Little published their paper on the single germanium crystal in June 1950 in the *Physical Review,* and by 1951 Shockley, Stanley Morgan, Morgan Sparks, and Teal, using crystal-pulling techniques, had made the first *p–n* junction transistor. (Teal, incidentally, left Bell Laboratories in 1953 for Texas Instruments, where he headed the newly founded research laboratories that turned the company into a major factor in the semiconductor business.)

White did not learn about the transistor until several months after it had been invented. As he told me, "People in the company who knew about it didn't talk much about it for the first few months. An occasion like the discovery of the transistor opens up all kinds of opportunities for creative invention, since it was something quite new. So they wanted about six months to explore the matter intellectually and legally. The really effective use of transistors in the Bell System came, as you know, many years later. But there was a great deal of local excitement here among the physicists, chemists, and electronic engineers following the announcement. I wasn't personally involved until the project had been growing for awhile. At that time I was head of the physical electronics department. In 1948, the director of research, Ralph Bown, asked me—I suppose on behalf of Shockley—what, in general terms, our department could do to help the transistor project.

"I think what Shockley had in mind was to detach some people from the group I was in charge of. I did not think this was a very good idea. Shockley was a very brilliant physicist but, by his own admission, not a particularly good manager at that time. But we were able to contribute anyway. After a year or so I was really enlisted. That's when I became part of the triumvirate. I think that Shockley saw me as a chemist, but one with quite a bit of training and experience in physics. So he must have thought I could bring the chemists and metallurgists into working more effectively on the project. At that stage—the spring of 1950—I began to know well what was going on and to be confronted with some of the urgent problems of developing this device. I think, by the way, that we didn't enlist anyone against his will into the transistor project. Indeed, once or twice we found a man who had been contributing well, whom we wanted to stay on the project, and who said, 'No, I want to work on something else.' Which he then did.

"This sort of freedom is a very important part of preserving a research laboratory's *élan.* The project had been steadily expanding but in an orderly way, about as rapidly as was humanly possible as problems became defined and new ideas evolved. Incidentally, as a comparison, I think that our country has been conducting its affairs in an absurd way on cancer research, much of which is being done without a guiding idea. We are trying to throw hundreds of millions of dollars at the problem without enough ideas, which is nonsense. It would have been the same sort of thing if we had tried to move more rapidly in the case of the transistor."

Characterizing the problems that he and his group confronted in 1950, White explained, "The theory of the transistor as developed, for example, by Shockley, assumed that one is dealing with an absolutely perfect crystal lattice, to which a carefully controlled set of impurities has been added in such a way that the impurity atoms become a part of the lattice. For example, if the lattice is silicon, the theory assumes that one simply replaces a certain number of silicon atoms—say, one out of a million—in the lattice with a certain number of, for example, arsenic atoms, in a sort of one-to-one swap. The problem that we confronted was that the material we were working with was something quite different. It was fairly pure germanium but in a polycrystalline ingot, something very far removed from the idealized theoretical model."

While Teal and Little's success at growing single germanium crystals appeared to resolve the structural problem—at least for germanium —it did nothing to resolve the matter of the unwanted impurities. This was solved in 1951 by William G. Pfann, a member of the Metallurgy Laboratory who was working on transistor materials. As White put it, "Bill Pfann came along with an idea that was pure genius and just as simple as could be. You start with an ingot, a long rod, of contaminated germanium in a 'boat' of very pure graphite. You melt the germanium along narrow transverse zones by moving induction coils along the rod. [A coil of metal wire encircling the boat and germanium rod, an induction coil "induces" a high-frequency heating current inside the germanium rod.] Nearly all the impurities have a greater affinity for the molten germanium than for the solid. As the coil is moved along, the impurities move with it and finally accumulate at the end of the rod, where they can be cut off. The machine can be set up automatically so that it comes back and does the same thing again—as often as you want—and gradually sweeps the impurities out of the rod. It turned out that this method was capable of refining germanium to less than one part in ten million of unwanted impurities."

This method, called zone refining and previously used—but much more crudely—in refining aluminum, was adapted soon afterward by Pfann for *adding* impurities in a controlled fashion to the germanium. A tiny pellet of doped germanium is placed in contact with a heated zone of purified germanium. This seed crystal is partly melted, and the impurities—the *desired* impurities—get passed along the rod as the heated zone is moved. This technique produces a carefully controlled concentration of impurities—what is called an impurity profile—in the volume of the germanium.

In 1951, shortly after the first junction transistor was actually made, Shockley came by to talk to White. "That first transistor," he recalls, "was made by a very able man named Ernest Buehler, who was working under Morgan Sparks's direction. Well, a little later, Bill Shockley came around to me. He was very worried because Buehler hadn't succeeded in reproducing that first crystal. I was in a position, on the basis of my experience on the development side of things, to reassure Shockley that when you are first starting a development process like this nothing ever works reproducibly. It just doesn't happen that way. So *I* didn't worry very much about Buehler's failure. Sure enough, after a week or so he succeeded in growing another junction transistor."

White also has a distinct, if less happy, memory of an article, written at that time by a university physics professor and published by a national magazine, claiming that the Bell System was monopolizing the transistor, "sitting on it, so to speak so as to protect our investment in plant already in place. Meanwhile a hundred men here were busting a gut trying to make the thing work. In terms of total effort by highly skilled personnel, development is likely to require several hundred times as many man-hours as does invention. There were just an enormous number of things that had to be done in order to make reproducible devices."

One of the most difficult things was learning to work with silicon as opposed to germanium. In *Revolution in Miniature,* Braun and Macdonald make it clear why silicon was crucial. "While a large percentage of the earth's crust is composed of silicon in the form of sand, germanium is a rather rare element. At the time of the invention of the transistor, annual world production of germanium was about six kilograms [somewhat over thirteen pounds], obviously too little to support any sort of transistor industry. Fortunately, germanium was available as a by-product of other extraction processes. In the United States it could be obtained from zinc refining in the form of germanium dioxide. In this form it cost about $300 per kilogram in 1952; by the time it had been purified it was worth more than gold by weight, though the germanium in each transistor weighed only about .002 gram." Therefore, as late as 1953 top-quality transistors were selling for $8.00 each ($30.00 in today's money), more than ten times the price of a vacuum tube designed to perform the same function. Apart from the economics, silicon was a better choice for technical reasons as well. Silicon promised superior transistor performance. What was not known then was that only silicon had the surface chemical properties that make a semiconductor suitable for integrated circuits, which are now the backbone of the electronics industry. But very early on, the people in the transistor business understood that silicon was the material of choice.

At first it appeared, as White put it, that working with silicon "was a perfectly hopeless problem," even though by 1952 Teal and Buehler had succeeded in growing single crystals. Most of the difficulty came from silicon's high melting point, 1410°C. If one tried to melt it in a graphite crucible—like that used for germanium—one would simply end up with silicon carbide, a useless mess. Therefore, fused quartz (silicon dioxide) was used as a crucible, but this created a new problem. "We would take silicon, as pure as it could be," White explained, "and then melt it in one of those crucibles. After we did that, we found the resistivity of the solid silicon changed radically, making the material impossible to use as an electronic component. That was one of the major material problems on which various men worked for years until we finally understood it scientifically. It turned out that oxygen was dissolving from the crucible wall into the silicon and then would form complexes that were electrically active. But as to transistor development, this problem was solved in 1953, when Henry Theurer came up with the "floating zone" method of refining silicon. In that, a rod of silicon is rigidly clamped at both ends in a vertical position. It is encircled by a high-frequency induction coil that melts a small region —what is called a floating zone—of the silicon. Because of the properties of the silicon, this globule of liquid silicon can hold itself together between the solid members of the silicon. So Pfann's zone-refining technique can be carried out without any crucible at all. And this is what solved the contamination problem, along with producing a single crystal. It's what everybody has done ever since.

"Then in 1952 Calvin Fuller had invented a new way of doping silicon and germanium crystals. What had been done until then was to pull the crystals out of the melt just as Teal had done. That was hopelessly impractical when it came to actually manufacturing transistors, because you had to melt a whole chunk of, say, germanium just to get one layer containing two *p–n* junctions that you could slice up into transistors. What Fuller did was to heat up slices of the crystal in the presence of a gas containing the impurity, so that the impurity diffuses into the semiconductor without involving any liquid. The precise amount of the impurity can be controlled by varying the time of exposure of the semiconductor and its temperature. The diffusion process is fundamental to the way all microcircuits are made now."

In 1953 Teal left Bell, and in 1954 the first commercial silicon transistor was produced by Teal for Texas Instruments. That year Shockley left Bell to found his own company, an enterprise that was ultimately a good deal less successful than Teal's. By then, many of the major discoveries involving the transistor had been made, and the field was rapidly developing commercially. In 1953 White became the laboratory director in chemical physics and, when Shockley left, director of semiconductor research as well. He held these positions until 1958, when he became executive director of research for all of the physical sciences, retaining the post until just before his retirement.

I asked White to give me something of a perspective on his career, covering nearly forty years at Bell. "My philosophy," he replied, "was completely different from that of most of the research men in the Bell Laboratories, in that I had no real calling for research or any other technical work. I had drifted into chemistry in the first place. I was therefore willing to do whatever the company wanted me to do. When it came to the transistor I had no real ideas of my own, and that, I think, is a good thing for a technical manager, because it means that he does not compete professionally with the men who are reporting to him. I think Bill Shockley's fundamental problem as a manager was that he was competing. Perhaps because of my personal history, I have always been utterly skeptical that any school of business administration can teach people how to manage. My own concern has always been, how does one motivate these extremely able people? Part of the answer is, of course, to hope that one way or another you can arrange it so that they will be doing work that is just a little beyond their capacity. That's the way people grow. I think that when it came to the responsibility I had for the materials side of the transistor, it worked. A good deal of this early transistor work was really development as opposed to physics research. When it comes to research, about all one can do is to recruit very able people in fields relevant to the Laboratories' mission and turn them loose, as is done in a university.

"The first person I reported to in 1930, Stanley Morgan, was a role model for me, since he exhibited this kind of attitude toward me and the other men. It was always *their* benefit that was uppermost in his mind. That gave me a chance to see how management could be conducted. So the first time I had a group to manage, I made very sure that each man understood that his role would be emphasized by me and that my name would never come up in connection with any technical achievement. I followed that principle all the way through my managerial career, and the word got around. Of course, many other Bell Labs managers followed similar policies. I was able to influence the actions of my transistor group strongly in various ways. For example, I held weekly meetings in which everybody could discuss the problems they were working on and the progress being made. This meant that people understood what was needed better than they would have otherwise, and it created a forum for acknowledging contributions."

By the time of White's retirement in 1967 he had the responsibility for some 500 people, about half of whom were Ph.D.'s. "The fact is," he commented, "the jobs that management people should be doing are fairly dull. So the higher my responsibility became, the duller the work was. I was enjoying my life outside my work greatly, and I was looking forward to retirement. I would have been able to demand retirement at my own option at the age of sixty, which would have been in 1969.

But I was able to gain two years on this by good-natured kidding of the top management. I sent them several memos in which there was a serious point. You see, Bell Laboratories didn't begin to go Ph.D. until it resumed hiring after the Depression hiatus, which lasted from 1930 to 1936. So at that time a good many men here were like me. We had been recruited even though we had no advanced scientific training at all. In due course, for lack of any alternatives, we began to occupy a lot of top-management positions. So, starting in 1965, I kept pointing out that it would be a good thing for all of Bell Laboratories if some of the younger Ph.D.'s who were coming forward could move into management and if the 'old fogies' could be 'induced' to retire early. Everybody knew that when I wrote memos to that effect I was thinking of myself. But it finally had an impact, and, furthermore, what I was saying was right. Shortly before my retirement my division was split in two, and after I left each part was put under the direction of a very capable Ph.D. Everybody was better off—including me."

In 1950 White had visited Paris with his wife and fallen in love with the city. "I decided instantly that I wanted to live there after my retirement. A great motivation was the idea of learning a foreign language and, to the extent possible, a foreign culture, opening the doors to something totally new." Therefore, in 1967, he applied for early retirement and moved to Paris, where he and his wife lived until 1979 when they returned to Summit, New Jersey. "When we moved to Paris we got a tutor to teach us about both modern and classical French literature as well as the language. It was wonderful. I think the twelve years we spent in Paris were the best years of our lives."

# CHAPTER 8

# The Blue Zoo

IN THE INTEGRATED-CIRCUIT BUSINESS a gate provides a sort of natural unit for measuring the complexity of a circuit. As the name might suggest, a gate is a circuit element that allows current to flow if—and only if—certain conditions are met. For example, in an element of a computer memory, a gate, if opened, might allow the passage of a certain number of electrons that are then trapped in some tiny region of a semiconductor. The presence of these electrons constitutes a "bit" of information—a "1"—and when they are released, by reopening the gate, their absence constitutes the lack of this "bit" of information, or a "0." Because gates serve all sorts of functions, the number of gates in a circuit is a convenient measure of the circuit's complexity. There are four standard, approximate, divisions:

| | | |
|---|---|---|
| SSI | small-scale integration | 1–30 gates |
| MSI | medium-scale integration | 30–300 gates |
| LSI | large-scale integration | 300–10,000 gates |
| VLSI | very-large-scale integration | 10,000 gates or more. |

Some people reserve VLSI for at least 100,000 gates.

The digital watch and the pocket calculator are LSI devices. A microprocessor—a single silicon chip the size of a thumbnail—which might contain several hundred thousand circuit elements and which is the central processing unit of a modern computer—is an example of

VLSI. So is the new 256K RAM memory chip that AT&T has begun to produce commercially. RAM is an acronym for random access memory, and 256K means that the memory chip, again the size of a thumbnail, can store about 256,000 bits of information—the amount of data in, say, a page of a newspaper. A 64K memory chip (64,000 bits) costs about $5.00 and is more than likely made in Japan. The Japanese are also expected to get into the 256K memory business, along with several other American semiconductor companies. The chase is on.

As far as I can tell, the integrated-circuit industry was founded on a discovery made in 1954 by Carl J. Frosch and L. Derick of Bell Labs. (The notion of an integrated circuit—an entire electronic unit on a single chip—was conceived in 1958 by Jack S. Kilby of Texas Instruments.) Frosch and Derick were attempting to diffuse impurities into silicon, presumably to make transistors. The impurities were contained in a heated gas to which the silicon surface was exposed. They noticed that when the gas contained oxygen—steam will do—a very thin, uniform layer of silicon dioxide, $SiO_2$, a kind of glass, formed on the surface of the silicon. This layer is both electrically neutral and chemically inert, and thus it blocks any new impurities from diffusing into the silicon. Frosch and Derick also noticed that if they etched windows into the silicon dioxide, which can be done by treating selected spots with hydrofluoric acid, the impurities could be diffused through these "bare" spots and positioned with great precision on the surface of the silicon. This, it turns out, is the basic technique in making an integrated circuit. By the way, if germanium is exposed to steam, the surface layer of germanium dioxide that is formed is chemically active and will not block impurities. For this reason almost all integrated-circuit chips are made of silicon.

Many steps go into making such a chip. The first is to grow a boule, a single crystal of silicon. A typical boule is about a meter long and ten centimeters in diameter and looks somewhat like a large sausage. The boule is then sliced into wafers a fraction of a millimeter thick that resemble oversize and extremely thin poker chips. The surface of the wafer is polished so that it shines like a mirror. The wafer is then heated to a temperature of about 1000°C., while being exposed to steam. This exposure coats the surface with a one-micron-thick layer of silicon-dioxide. In a certain sense, the microcircuits will be "printed" on these wafers. To that end, an organic polymer, called a "photo resist", is deposited on the silicon-dioxide surface. This material is sensitive to visible light.

The circuit itself is designed on a computer, and wall-sized diagrams of these circuits can look like the street plans of some futuristic city. These designs are then tremendously reduced and transferred onto, typically, a glass plate, or "mask," on which the circuit lines are traced out by a metal pattern. Several masks are needed for each circuit element. For example, a gate consists of about ten devices, and each device requires about five masks to make. On each of these there are about twenty metal lines. Since a VLSI circuit contains at least 10,000 gates, it requires at least 10,000,000 lines, on various masks, to define it. That is why such circuits are designed by computers. Actually a mask contains many copies—or clones—of whatever circuit element it represents, because several identical chips will be cut from one wafer. The chips usually resemble tiny postage stamps—a few square millimeters in area.

The wafer is now covered with a mask and exposed to light—optical lithography. An image of the mask is projected onto the wafer. Light cannot penetrate the metal lines on the mask, and so these places on the surface of the wafer are not exposed. When the wafer is then bathed in hydrofluoric acid, the places protected by the metal lines on the mask, become places where the silicon-dioxide coating on the wafer does not get eaten away. Thus the pattern on the mask is transferred to the wafer. These exposed lines on the wafer can now be penetrated by diffusing impurity atoms, such as boron or phosphorus. So, for example, one can create $n$- and $p$-type regions, and thus transistors or gates or whatever. In such a circuit a transistor is not much larger than a typical human blood cell, and the connecting wires are so small that a human hair is like a boa constrictor by comparison.

I had a chance to make this comparison at the Bell Laboratory's "Blue Zoo." Formally known as the Murray Hill Integrated Circuit Design Capability Laboratory, the Blue Zoo very likely gets its name from the azure surgical gowns that are required attire—as are a surgical mask and surgical gloves. The air is specially filtered, and the laboratory's strangely sterile ambience is accentuated by oddly garbed and masked figures peering into microscopes and manipulating silicon objects by remote control. A visitor may observe their activities through a picture window. In a visitors' gallery outside is a full-size replica of the first point-contact transistor. (The real one is in the lobby at Murray Hill.) It is hard to believe that this forlorn and discarded relic started the modern electronics revolution. On a nearby table, a high-power microscope has been set up for visitors to look at a modern chip, with its tens of thousands of transistors. If the microscope is focused on the microchip's lines—its wiring—the human hair placed alongside becomes a blur. If the microscope is focused on the hair—Gulliver in a land of Lilliputians—the lines vanish.

My tour guide was Evelyn Hu, "supervisor"—a position prominent in the development areas and intermediate between member of technical staff and department head—of the VLSI Patterning Processes Group. The principal concern of her seven-member staff is to put more things on a silicon chip than anyone ever thought possible. Using optical lithography, writing with light, she and her group are trying to produce features as small as one-millionth of a meter (a micron). As Hu remarked, "I don't think that anyone yet is manufacturing devices with one-micron lines and spaces and with the severe alignment criteria that we are working with now. In fact, for a long time, people were saying that with optical lithography, which is what we use, it was not possible to go to one-micron features. We are doing that, and at the same time we are still doing a bit of the 'older' two-and-a-half-micron technology. Our main product was the Western Electric thirty-two-bit microprocessor. That's VLSI. Some of what we're doing now has twice the resolution, but it's not quite VLSI. A cutoff some people have suggested is to call 100,000 transistors on a chip minimum VLSI."

Evelyn Hu was born in New York City on 15 May 1947. Her father is a mechanical engineer with a strong interest in science, and her younger sister, Esther, is an astrophysicist with NASA in Greenbelt, Maryland. Until she came to work for Bell Labs in 1975, Hu had never left New York. She attended Hunter College High School and Barnard College, graduating summa cum laude in 1969, and then took her Ph.D. in physics at Columbia in 1975. While at Columbia she did not take one course in solid-state physics, her present activity. "Elementary-particle physics," she explained, "was what was and is emphasized at Columbia. My Ph.D. advisor was C.S. Wu, and we did an accelerator experiment at the Brookhaven National Laboratory."

She and Miss Wu, a very distinguished experimental nuclear physicists, studied so called exotic atoms, which can be produced only by using the large accelerators that manufacture exotic particles such as K mesons, antiprotons, and sigma particles. These particles can be "captured" by heavy target nuclei, and in the course of this process radiation is given off. By studying the energy of this radiation, one can learn about the structure of these atoms in which the usual electrons have been replaced by the strange particles. It is fine physics but far from practical, and this troubled Hu. Furthermore, she did not look forward to the kind of high-energy experimental physics usually done by teams of people with machines run for them by specialized engineers. As she put it, "I really wanted to have more of a kind of tabletop experimental arrangement, where things were more easily controlled by one person or by a few people, in a more localized setting where you have more of a direct handle on both theory and experiment." Miss Wu made some inquiries on Hu's behalf at Bell Labs, and at about the same time—and coincidentally, "a Bell Labs physicist named Solomon Buchsbaum [now executive vice-president of Customers Systems] came to Columbia in 1975, just as I was finishing my thesis, to give a seminar on optical communications. I thought it was just fantastic. It was fascinating. It was beautiful, because there was a natural analogy between optics and electronics. It was useful and wide-ranging in its implications, and I decided on the spot that this was the sort of thing I wanted to do."

Hu went to both Murray Hill and Holmdel for interviews. "I interviewed with several people," she explained, "and while a lot of things were revealed to me that I had not been aware of before—a whole host of solid-state experiments were presented to me—I stuck to my original resolve of wanting to do something in optical communications—that sort of thing." Asked which group she wanted to work with, she chose that of P.K. Tien, whom she describes as the "founder of integrated optics." As it happened, an entirely new method of making integrated circuits, known as "molecular-beam epitaxy," had just been developed at the Labs. "Epitaxy," she explained, "means, in this case, the growth of crystals on a single crystal substrate—a template." In essence, if atoms arrive at the surface of a crystal under just the right conditions, they can fit perfectly into the original lattice and continue the crystal-growing process. It is as if the new atoms were forming a sort of skin on the original crystal. In this way extremely thin layers can be deposited—one layer of atoms at a time, in fact. Hu went on, "One can do homoepitaxy and deposit, say, silicon on silicon or gallium arsenide on gallium arsenide or in many cases, one can do heteroepitaxy and deposit, for example, aluminum gallium arsenide on gallium arsenide. The lattice constant—the basic unit that defines the size of the crystal cell—must be the same or at least close in the two cases, otherwise there's a mismatch and one won't get good crystal growth. In epitaxy one is actually creating more of the same crystal, adding an orderly array rather than, for example, depositing a piece of liquid plastic over a surface. Epitaxy is a growing onto rather than a painting over."

In molecular-beam epitaxy a source of the material to be deposited on the crystal is heated in an oven. Some of the atoms escape from the surface and are allowed to pass through a hole in the oven into a vacuum chamber. These escaping atoms or, more generally, molecules form a "beam"—a molecular beam—and if a silicon wafer, for example, is put in its way, these atoms can be deposited epitaxially on the silicon. By controlling the temperature of the oven, the precise rate of epitaxial growth can also be controlled. In this way a uniform layer of impurities, a few microns thick, can be placed on the wafer.

When Hu arrived at Bell the equipment for molecular-beam epitaxy—she describes it as a "very expensive piece of high-vacuum equipment"—had just become available. She decided to use it to do research in the construction of Josephson junctions. In 1962, when the British physicist Brian Josephson was a beginning research student at Cambridge, he attended a course given by Philip Anderson, who was then on leave from Bell. The latter part of the lectures dealt with superconductivity, the total elimination of electrical resistance in certain materials that occurs when they are cooled to temperatures approaching absolute zero ($-273.15°C.$). Electrical currents set up in superconductors will continue to circulate, literally, for decades. After listening to Anderson's lectures, Josephson got the idea that if two superconductors could be separated by a thin layer of oxide, then pairs of electrons could tunnel through such a layer of what is now known as a Josephson junction. This effect is one of the rare examples of quantum mechanics—which is usually applied to subatomic phenomena—manifesting on a macroscopic scale. The first Josephson junctions were made at Bell in 1962 by Anderson and John Martin Rowell, a young experimental physicist. They may be used in very advanced computers because they can be switched in substantially less than a billionth of a second and use very little current.

The "classical" Josephson junction consists of two superconductors separated by an oxide layer three microns thick. These junction layers were made using optical lithography. What Hu and her collaborators wanted was to use the new molecular-beam epitaxy technique to make a semiconductor junction, thinking that it would have significant new properties. "In a very naïve way, we took the molecular-beam epitaxy apparatus and started depositing semiconductors," she explained. "First we tried to use silicon, but its melting point is so high that it is difficult to work with. Then we began using elemental germanium, but it seemed as insulating as an oxide, so we decided to dope it to increase its conductivity. It turned out that to make a useful Josephson junction we needed to add about 25 percent tin to the germanium. Once we found that, we began exploring different ways of fabricating Josephson junctions. I began by working with only one other physicist, Larry Jackel. We formed a nucleus and then started adding to our group until we had a sort of critical mass. We began to work on ways of getting the areas of the junction down. When we began, they were a hundred thousandth of a meter by a hundred thousandth of a meter; but very soon we were getting them a millionth of a meter by a ten millionth of a meter. Because of that we became interested in the general problem of fabrication at very small dimensions, not only of superconducting devices but eventually of semiconductor devices as well. First we used optical lithography to do our patterning, and then we also experimented with beams of electrons. Under certain circumstances, such as in an electron microscope, electrons have wavelike character with wavelengths even shorter than ultraviolet light. So electron beams can be used for patterning at dimensions even smaller than those that can be realized optically. We became very interested in the kind of structures you can make with dimensions of a few hundred angstroms—a hundred millionth of a meter. How do the characteristics of these circuit elements scale when you make the dimensions smaller and the circuit elements become denser—more complex circuits in a smaller and smaller area? Eventually the physics that adequately describes larger scales may no longer apply. There are going to be some kinds of breakdowns. Some of them are already well understood, but we don't know whether *they* are going to be the limiting factors on what one can put on a chip or whether it is going to be something else."

Hu's early work at Bell Labs was done in Area 11, the area of pure research; but after a few years she switched to Area 52, the development side of the Labs, where the Blue Zoo is located. "It was logical for me to come into this department where, in many ways, we are at the cutting edge of what can be done in a real industrial or production sense. We are by no means a manufacturing line such as Intel has, or Hewlett-Packard, but we're as close to it as you can get. We are at the forefront of this kind of patterning and design. I wanted to see the impact of our research on the development and manufacture of devices, so I came here. Our laboratory—the Blue Zoo—is intended to be a processing line for integrated circuits. It is set up with state-of-the-art equipment: production equipment, pattern-transfer tools, and the whole host of processes needed to fabricate integrated circuits. All of these processes should eventually be transferable to a real production line, like the one that AT&T has in Allentown, Pennsylvania. Because ours is a fairly small, tightly organized facility, we have the ability to give a rapid-turnaround proof of the capabilities of new designs. Even though we are not now directly feeding into the marketplace and hence don't have that kind of demand for high output, we do have our own deadlines to meet. And we are very conscious of the mundane problems —like pieces of dirt on a wafer—that can affect production. These are not things that represent a breakthrough in science, but they are crucial in determining whether or not a process will work in practice. As I said, we're a small facility working with state-of-the-art equipment, trying to find ways of rapidly assessing the feasibility of a given design."

As a souvenir of my visit, Evelyn Hu gave me a tie clip. I don't usually wear a clip, but this one is unusual. In the middle of it is a silicon chip no bigger than a postage stamp. It is in fact a 32-bit microprocessor, with twice the capacity of previous commercial models and nearly the capacity of a modern medium-sized mainframe computer. I would need a powerful microscope to see that the chip contains a hundred thousand transistors.

# CHAPTER 9
# Phil Anderson

PHILIP WARREN ANDERSON, the youthful-looking sixty-year-old Bell theoretical physicist, who won the 1977 Nobel Prize in physics for his seminal work in the quantum mechanics of the solid state, has what he calls a "perennial nightmare that actually happens every once in a while. It's like the sensation that I sometimes have in a dream, of being caught partly dressed on a podium, or something. It happens when someone says to me, 'Now Doctor Anderson, what did you actually *do* to win your Nobel Prize?' and I know that as a rule I can't actually tell them." Anderson is not inarticulate or unwilling to explain. Rather, there is an enormous gulf between people with what one might call "quantum literacy" and people without. Quantum mechanics is not something that most of us need or use in our daily lives, although we are increasingly surrounded by artifacts, such as solid-state electronic devices, whose workings cannot be understood at all without the rudiments of quantum mechanics. In fact, one cannot even understand the difference between a metal and an insulator—to say nothing of a semiconductor—without quantum mechanics. The invention of something like the transistor, for example, would have been almost inconceivable without quantum mechanics. Nevertheless, it took well over a decade after the theory was created in the mid-1920's until it really came into use at Bell Labs, where the transistor was invented.

Lillian Hartman Hoddeson, who has written extensively about the Labs' contributions to physics, has traced the arrival of quantum mechanics at Bell. The theory of quantum mechanics was invented largely by Erwin Schrödinger, Werner Heisenberg, and Paul Dirac around 1925–1926. Almost immediately, physicists like Wolfgang Pauli, Hans Bethe, and their teacher, Arnold Sommerfeld, began applying the theory to give the first correct account of what a metal is. This was followed by an intense effort by Heisenberg, the Dutch physicist Peter Debye, and the American physicist John H. Van Vleck to understand the electromagnetic properties of matter, for instance, to give a real theory of how a substance like iron becomes magnetized—"ferromagnetism." In 1931 the British physicist Alan Wilson first presented the energy-band diagrams, of the kind reproduced in Chapter 6, which show clearly the difference between, say, an insulator and a semiconductor. This work was built on a celebrated 1928 Ph.D. thesis by another of Sommerfeld's students, Felix Bloch. The few Americans who played any role in quantum mechanics did so by traveling to Europe, especially to Germany, where this physics was being unraveled. By the early 1930's quantum mechanics was making inroads in the United States, in part because of the migration of European physicists and in part because Americans like Van Vleck, J. Robert Oppenheimer, and I.I. Rabi deliberately decided to import the new physics from Europe.

From the point of view of the quantum theory of solids, there are two examples of this migration which illustrate each of these cases. The American physicist John Clarke Slater spent parts of nearly a decade visiting various European centers before becoming chairman of the physics department at M.I.T. in 1930. One of his early students was William Shockley, who came to Bell from M.I.T. in 1936. On the other hand there is, for example, Eugene Wigner who was born in Hungary, although he had his advanced education in physics in Berlin in the 1920's. When Wigner came to Princeton in 1930 he already had an international reputation and, indeed, he had planned to spend part of each year teaching in Berlin. But, in 1933 he settled in America permanently. His students in solid-state theory included Frederick Seitz and Conyers Herring, now at Stanford, and John Bardeen, both of whom came to Bell soon after World War II. Prior to the arrival of this post-1935 cadre there were no physicists or chemists at Bell who might be described as professional quantum mechanicians. Nonetheless, some of the people who were there, even before 1936, felt so strongly about the need for learning this new, or relatively new, physics that they set about to teach it to themselves. The crystal chemist Alan Holden reported that, around 1933, he was approached by the Bell metallurgist Foster Nix. "You know," he said, "we've got to learn this new physics. I don't know any of it and you don't know any of it, and one way to do this is for us to get together once a week and go through a book. . . . We worked awfully hard. We met once a week after having covered a chapter [of a quantum mechanics text] each week, and having done all the problems on it, met once a week to correct each other's problems—we worked good and hard."

In 1936, Mervin J. Kelly, who had been involved in vacuum-tube research at Bell, became general director of research at the Labs. He had a clear vision that fundamental research, especially in solid-state physics, was the key to advancing beyond vacuum tubes in telephone transmission. The Depression-related suspension of hiring was lifted in 1936, and one of Kelly's first appointments was of Shockley, who came directly from M.I.T. In 1938 Kelly created a kind of quantum-mechanical solid-state group centered around Shockley, Nix, and Dean Wooldridge, a new appointee from the California Institute of Technology, who later became a founder of the Ramo-Wooldridge Computer Company. Given almost total research freedom, they functioned, at least in some respects, like a university physics department in miniature with, among other things, their own "journal club." By the beginning of World War II, the group had expanded to include Walter Brattain and Charles Townes, and Addison White was able, with official sanction, to take university courses at Bell's expense in purely scientific subjects like quantum mechanics. Research scientists will generally gravitate to a place where they find the scientific environment congenial, even though some loss of salary may be involved. The presence at Bell Laboratories of so many Nobel Prize laureates has undoubtedly had an immense impact on recruiting.

When Anderson first appeared at Bell Labs in the spring of 1948 there was, as he recalls, "an appreciable percentage of all of the solid-state and low-energy physicists in the country here at that time. Bill Shockley, Walter Brattain, and John Bardeen were inventing the transistor. Charlie Townes was working on microwave spectroscopy. That work eventually led to the maser and laser, and several others, like Charles Kittel and Gregory Wannier, were extraordinarily impressive."

Anderson was then beginning work on his Ph.D. thesis at Harvard. For some reason that he cannot figure out, Deming Lewis, the Bell Labs recruiter for Harvard, suggested that he give a talk at Murray Hill on his preliminary thesis work. "I knew about Bell Labs and admired them, and I thought, 'Great, that's just the place I would like to work.' They paid for first-class accommodations on the train down from Boston, as they used to do. I gave my talk, which was essentially a summary of how people had tried to solve the kind of problem I was interested in doing for my thesis. Naturally, they weren't terribly interested. They just patted me on the head and said, 'Of course you are not ready for a job, but let us know when you are, and we'll see.' It was sort of a disaster."

At the time of this "disastrous" talk, Anderson was twenty-four. He was born in Indianapolis, Indiana, on 13 December 1923. His family roots go back several generations in the Middle West. "My mother," he explained, "came from Crawfordsville, Indiana. They weren't Crawfords, but it's Montgomery County and they were Montgomerys and had come to this country well before the Revolutionary War.

"My father's family also came early; there seems to be a record of one of our Andersons who fought in the Revolutionary War—a ploughman who had immigrated from Wales. My father's father was an itinerant, fire-breathing Presbyterian preacher who was so strict in his views that eventually he even lost his job as a preacher and took up farming. He migrated through a number of interesting-sounding places like Beanblossom, Indiana, until he ended up in a little town near Crawfordsville called Ladoga. As a result of all this, my father came to reject any sort of religion and got away from the farm as soon as possible. Both he and his brother went to Wabash college and became plant pathologists. Their sister, who stayed on the farm, had seven children all of whom became professionals of one sort or another—for instance an historian at Brookings Institute. It was one of those upwardly mobile farm families from which the professional and academic class often came in those days. My mother's father was a mathematician who taught at Wabash where my father studied. Her brother had gotten a Rhodes scholarship to study English from Wabash—he did his graduate work at Columbia, but, like his father, went back to Wabash to teach."

Anderson's father spent most of his professional life as a professor at the University of Illinois in Urbana, moving back and forth between the biology department and the agriculture school where he ended his career as the director of a laboratory of plant pathology. He was an expert at growing fungi and yeasts and did some important work on antibiotics. From his earliest childhood, Anderson was fascinated by science, especially biology. He recalls collecting butterflies and collecting and classifying plants and flowers. "I used my father's copy of *Gray's Manual,*" he told me, "when I was so young that I didn't have the faintest idea of what a lot of words in it meant. But I could use the glossary, more or less, without really understanding the principles of classification, and I actually got fairly good at it. I think children often learn in this sort of haphazard way, seizing on what they can use."

Many theoretical physicists have memories of very early, and often rather prodigious, mathematical feats—but not Anderson. "In fact," he said, "my grade school years were hardly a great success. At one point I accidentally got an arithmetic book in which the answers were written, and there was a great uproar when the teacher found I was actually reading them off. I don't remember whether I wasn't good at arithmetic or just didn't care much. It was only in high school that I began to show some mathematical ability. Both my sister and I—she is four years older and eventually got a Ph.D. in biochemistry from the University of Wisconsin—went to the University of Illinois High School: Uni-High. It is a remarkable place, run by the School of Education at the university. We had practice teachers from the Education Department (as it then was) as well as university professors. That was back in the days before being an educator tended to shut off the possibility of being educated.

"Anyway, we had a marvelous math teacher, Miles Hartley, who was also an associate professor. He was a fussy sort of guy who played the organ in one of the local churches. He was both a stickler for accuracy and an innovator. In the middle of teaching us algebra he would, for example, spend two weeks on those word problems that involve a matrix of 'Jones speaks to Brown, and Smith is a carpenter' —things like that—and he would show us how to reason them out. In geometry he would give us a theorem to prove as a classroom exercise, and I would test myself to make sure that I could prove the theorem while he was still giving his opening spiel. I became the court of last resort in the class when it came to proving theorems. That high school has produced, so far, three Nobel Prizewinners. I was the first. The second was Hamilton O. Smith, from Johns Hopkins. He shared the prize in 1978 for the discovery of how to do gene splicing. He is quite a bit younger than I am, so we had no high school overlap. James Tobin, the economist, won it three years later. I know him slightly, and he was actually one of the reasons that I went to Harvard."

Anderson skipped a year and graduated from high school in 1940, at the age of sixteen. Four years earlier Harvard had instituted a program of national scholarships with the idea of attracting students from those parts of the country that generally had not sent large numbers of students to Harvard. "Jim Tobin and a classmate of his named Richard Noyes—now an eminent photochemist—went to Harvard on those scholarships the first year they were offered," Anderson noted. "They must have prepared Harvard for the idea that Uni-High students could be pretty good. Toward the end of my junior year the principal said to me, 'You have a chance to do this, but you haven't had any Latin.' One of Harvard's entrance requirements then was two years of Latin. My mother, who was a pretty formidable lady, managed to persuade the chairman of the Classics Department at the university to teach me the first year of Latin that summer. Bill Oldfather was a classicist of considerable reputation. Years later, when I went to Cambridge University, he was one of the few Americans the Cambridge classicists had ever heard of. He had some theories about high school education, and so he consented to tutor me for the whole summer. I then scraped through the second year in a regular class, and in my senior year took the exam offered by Harvard and won one of those scholarships. Otherwise there was no way, financially, that I could ever have gone to Harvard."

Anderson recalls what Harvard was like when he got there. "There is a book about Harvard in those years," he told me, *"The Last Convertible,* by Anton Myrer. It has nothing to do with any of the realities as I saw them. Those people in the book were the sophisticates, mostly from Eastern prep schools, who were two or three years older than me and more blasé and were up to all sort of tricks. Then, in more or less descending social order, were the athletes, and then there were the scholarship boys like me. I didn't socialize much, partly at least because I had to work very hard. The standard advice at the time was to take a very heavy schedule the first year so one could relax the rest of the time. It almost undid me. I didn't know how to study; even in the best Midwestern high schools, no one ever taught you how. It was all too easy. If you'd been good enough to get a scholarship to Harvard, it meant you probably hadn't had to study at all in high school. I suspect that people like me still drown at Harvard at first. In high school I took physics and hadn't liked it much. It seemed to me nonquantitative and gadgety, and I don't take to gadgets. All I remember was learning to use a hand vacuum pump. I was more interested in quantitative science or in broad descriptive science. I want to know how things really work. So when I got to Harvard I thought that I was going to be either a mathematician or a chemist."

When Anderson entered Harvard there was a noted introductory physics course taught by the theoretical physicist Wendell Furry. Indeed, I took the same course seven years later. Anderson had heard about it in high school from F. Wheeler Loomis, chairman of the Physics Department at the University of Illinois and a friend of the family. "I think Loomis said," Anderson recalls, " 'You can pick up chemistry, but you can't pick up physics. That course looks great and you had better take it.' I went to the first class, and Furry said, 'Only half of you are going to be here by the end of the term.' I was intrigued by that and decided I was damned if I was going to be in the wrong half. Furry was a very good teacher and I was hooked. It was a two-year course, and by the time I was through with it I knew that physics was what I would probably do, although I liked writing and wrote poetry. I had dreams of possibly becoming some sort of writer."

Along with the rest of his class, Anderson was accelerated so that, after three years, he graduated, *summa cum laude,* at the age of nineteen. Because of the war and the imminence of the draft, he had taken a kind of engineering-physics curriculum, with an emphasis on electronics and not much on pure physics. He had originally wanted to get into the Air Corps, or ROTC, but was turned down because of poor eyesight and ended up at the Naval Research Laboratory in Washington as a Navy recruit. He was assigned to a group that measured antennas for the radars that were to be used for "identification—friend or foe" beacons. "My boss at NRL," Anderson noted, "was a very difficult man, an engineer from Purdue. He asked me to build detector circuits for him. The first one I built was a little minicircuit in a plastic box. I melted the box completely around the circuit with my soldering iron. Then I was supposed to build a high-voltage transmitter that, in theory, worked between rooftops. I finished it and picked it up underneath and managed to run a spark through my finger. So he had me attach very large pieces of pipe—I was good enough at that—where nothing much could go wrong. Later on I learned how to do mechanical design, and I installed antimissile gear on ships. One of the consequences of being at NRL was that I learned that ordinary people can be bright. I worked with some of the old petty officers from the Navy, and it was quite clear to me that they were brighter than my boss. The other thing was that even though we worked a six-day week, we had a lot of spare time. There was a bibulous old character there, with a Ph.D. in physics, who gave me his copy of a text on quantum mechanics as security for quite a few loans. Eventually I got to keep the book, and I read it throughout the war and taught myself quantum mechanics from it."

In 1945, the doyen of theoretical physicists at Harvard was John Hasbrouck Van Vleck, a remarkable character whose many interests included railroad trains. Apart from knowing all the schedules of every American railroad, he had various arrangements with local engineers who would let him ride in the cabs and make special stops for him. He and Sir Neville Mott of Cambridge University shared the Nobel Prize with Anderson in 1977. In 1945 Van Vleck was, in Anderson's words, "out collecting students," wandering through government laboratories with an eye out for brilliant students. He recruited Anderson for the Harvard Physics Department just after the war. "I began by taking all the courses in physics that I had missed as an undergraduate when I went into electronics," Anderson recalled. "I took Furry's course in statistical mechanics and his quantum mechanics course, which were very well taught. Julian Schwinger, who had just come from the Radiation Laboratory at M.I.T., gave a three-semester course in which he told us everything he knew—all the nuclear physics and the rest. It was terrific. The course was supposed to start at 11:00, but Schwinger would get up at about 11:00 and arrive about 11:30, without notes, and lecture until one—half an hour after the lunchroom closed."

Schwinger was still maintaining "Spanish hours" when I took a comparable course from him a few years later. In 1965 he shared the Nobel Prize in physics with Richard Feynman and Sin-itiro Tomonaga.

"I fell in with a group of people of mixed ages, background, and specialties," Anderson continued. "Some, like Tom Lehrer, were younger, having been accelerated because of the war. Tom was in math and was only seventeen or eighteen. We sang his songs as he wrote them. We also played bridge and did puzzles, compulsively, and various kinds of games—for instance, making up our own Double-Crostics. Tom's were the hardest, based mostly on slang from *Variety*. Tom and Chandler Davis, who wrote science fiction, had back-to-back classes in freshman calculus and in which they instructed and traded doggerel on the blackboard. Tom also enjoyed setting song lyrics to the wrong music, like the words to 'Clementine' set to the tune of 'The Road to Mandalay.' Some of our group were older, having spent longer in the war—for instance, this English major who played the guitar. He had made a collection of World War II songs: 'I wanted wings 'til I got the Goddamn things . . . now I don't want them any more,' and 'Those 88's are breaking up that old gang of mine (There goes Tom, There goes Jim/Off down Snipers' Lane/Never mind, they'll come back/ They just won't look the same.)

"I was having a marvelous time and doing well in my courses, and then came my oral exam. I had never taken an oral examination. The first question was about classical mechanics. I had had a course in classical mechanics from Samuel Goudsmit of the Brookhaven National Laboratory, who had come to Harvard one summer to teach, and it had not covered the sort of thing they asked me. (In fact, I have never liked classical mechanics.) I was told that the examination had not been good enough for me to become a theorist and would I consider becoming an experimentalist. I said, 'I *know* I am not competent in experiments,' so they reluctantly let me become a theorist—'they' being in this case largely Van Vleck, who was the chairman of the department."

Anderson had decided that he wanted to do his thesis work with Van Vleck. Anderson noted, "One of Van Vleck's specialties had

always been the energy levels of molecules. There was a lot of surplus
radar equipment left over from the war, and people were using it to
study molecular energy levels. Van was their guru. He would tell them
where these levels—at what energies—they were located. These levels
have characteristic shapes, called line shapes, and Van set me the task
of calculating them, essentially from first principles. What he did, in
fact, was to give me a few papers in the subject and say, 'Make some
sense out of them.' In those days one did not necessarily have an office
or even a desk in the department. I just went off to my room with the
papers."

This was the spring of 1947. In the summer of 1947 Anderson
married Joyce Gothwaite, whom he had met in Urbana. "We lived in
simple and not too genteel poverty," he said. "Between a fellowship
from Harvard and the GI Bill we had $165 a month. The rent was $95
and everything else came out of the difference. Joyce went back to the
University of Illinois to teach for a term, at least in part to accumulate
enough money for the birth of our daughter, Susan, in 1948. Susan is
still in Boston where she paints. Quite some time after Van Vleck had
given me those papers to read, he called me in to ask what I'd been
up to. I told him that I had understood the force between molecules,
and he told me to write up what I knew, as an exercise. I did that, but
I didn't see what to do next. I didn't seem to be going much of
anywhere in my work. It was at this point that the Bell Labs recruiter
came around and I made that pointless trip to Murray Hill.

"The trip to Murray Hill wasn't a complete waste, however, because on the way back I had my first original idea in physics. A lot of
theoretical tools that we now take for granted didn't exist then. Today,
if someone were given the problem I did for my thesis, they would
almost automatically know how to proceed—how to write down the
relevant mathematical starting point. I had to invent a whole sequence
of methods involving a correlation function, which takes into account
the forces between molecules and how they affect the shape of the
molecular energy levels. It was one of the first examples of the whole
new way of thinking that came to be called 'many-body theory.' Doing
it was incredibly thrilling for me.

"Looking back, I had almost unconsciously made a good decision
as well as a discovery. The decision had been to avoid what was then

the strong current of fashion, which ran toward nuclear and elementary-particle physics and was typified by Schwinger, in favor of the more old-fashioned style and subject of solid-state and low-energy physics, represented by Van Vleck. Wide-open, exciting, and expensive as the new and fashionable fields were, and bolstered as they were by the prestige of the men who had produced the Bomb, they have ever since been an area—at least as I see it—where more and more brilliant people have chased fewer and more exotic results every year.

"The discovery was that the problems in the physics of ordinary matter—Van's kind of problems—were just as intellectually challenging and exciting as those in particle physics. In fact, my new methods were closely related to things I had learned in Schwinger's course. I did not yet see that the two fields could reinforce each other with methods and insights about the nature of the quantum mechanics of complicated systems. I suppose many of my fellow graduate students thought I was picking an easy option, and it certainly wasn't until much later that I myself lost a certain defensiveness about the intellectual respectability of solid-state theory. I imagine at least in my early years, I would have gone off to the Institute for Advanced Study to do "pure" physics, if someone had asked. Luckily, as it turned out, I was never offered that temptation.

"After theory comes the real work of calculation, and I did most of it in the summer of 1948. Joyce and I would wheel Susan around Belmont in her carriage, and I would calculate away. These calculations go very fast once you know how to do them, and it took me only a few months.

"That fall, when Van Vleck returned from Europe, I showed him what I had written up. He said, 'In the first place you write English as though it were German, and in the second place your notation is too compact. I can't understand it.' He then proceeded to work on my prose style, as his father, who was a mathematician, apparently did for him when he wrote his first book on spectroscopy. To satisfy him on the notation I wrote one version with all the equations doubled—which he could read. Then he said, 'I still don't understand what you are doing. Everything should be do-able without quantum mechanics.' So I wrote an entire chapter—most of which is wrong—trying to satisfy him on that subject. The thesis finally became a 340-page book, and my wife typed four versions of it. Since I needed a job as soon as possible, I finished the thesis in February 1949. I really only learned, twenty-five years later, how pleased Van Vleck had been with my thesis. At the time he certainly didn't say anything to *me*. But years later Victor Weisskopf [a noted theoretical physicist at M.I.T.] told me that the reason that he and Schwinger had been asked to constitute my thesis committee was that Van was pretty proud of it. I hadn't drawn that simple deduction myself."

Anderson then faced the problem of finding a job. In the pre-Sputnik days in physics, while funding was much higher than it had been prior to the war, jobs were not easy to find. Anderson went on a job-hunting trip to Westinghouse. He recalls, "The man who was going to be my boss showed me a room with eight desks in it and a little box of transistors that had been sent to them by Bell Labs. He said, 'Nobody around here can make these things work. Maybe you can explain them to us.' Then I went to Brookhaven and talked with Sam Goudsmit. He didn't offer me a job, and years later he told me why. When he asked what I wanted to do at Brookhaven I said that I didn't know, that I'd finished my dissertation problem and didn't know what to do next. He did not believe that a good physicist could lose interest in a problem just because he had finished it. Then there was a recruiter from Washington State College in Pullman. That was the only college, at that time, that went around looking for a miscellaneous new Ph.D. in physics. They offered me a job and so did Westinghouse—at the same salary, $450 a month. Joyce and I spent a long time deciding. I really didn't like that big room at Westinghouse with the eight desks. My parents had lent us the money for a car, and just as we were about to drive across the country to Washington, Van Vleck suddenly asked me where I would really like to go and I said, instantly, 'Bell Labs.' "

I asked Anderson how he had come to that decision. "During the war," he explained, "I had seen Bell Labs in operation. Among other things, our group at the Naval Research Laboratory tested a lot of equipment. When somebody from Bell Labs came along with a piece of equipment there was this tremendous feeling of competence. Nothing crummy ever came out of Bell Labs. When they did something they really 'Cadillaced' it. They produced a clean piece of equipment that was GI-proof and also proof against *us*, which was something. Anyway,

Van Vleck said, 'I will see what I can do.' I think that, literally, he rode the cab of the Phoebe Snow to Summit, New Jersey. That was a fancy train on the Lackawanna Railroad that stopped in Summit only to *pick up* passengers, except for Van Vleck, who got off at Summit when he wanted to. Riding the cab of the Phoebe Snow was how he normally came to Bell Labs. He came and talked to Bill Shockley and other people, telling them that they should hire me. Shockley said that he would think it over. Eventually he called me to tell me I could have a job at the same salary that Pullman and Westinghouse had offered."

When Anderson arrived at Bell Labs in February 1949 he joined three other newly hired physicists who went on to have very distinguished careers. John Kirtland Galt, an American who had been working in England, eventually organized the Device Research Laboratory at Bell—the research counterpart to the Blue Zoo. He is now with Sandia Laboratories in New Mexico. Gregory Wannier, a Swiss-born theoretical physicist, remained at Bell for eleven years before joining the Physics Department at the University of Oregon. Bernd Matthias, a German-born experimental physicist from M.I.T. and a genius at discovering new materials, had come to Bell from M.I.T. "We were not a bad crop for Bell," Anderson observed. "We were over nose count [Bell Labs' term for the number of authorized personnel]. I was hired over nose count and so was Matthias. Wannier and I were put in a big room together, since there was not room enough for an office for each of us. We talked a lot. One of the things Wannier said was, 'If it's a physics department it must have an afternoon tea.' They didn't, so we set up a tea that still functions in the theory group. Matthias had come to Bell with crystals of barium titanate in his pocket—in a manner of speaking. (They are slightly yellowish-looking transparent crystals.) The ones that he knew how to grow were quite flat and about a square centimeter in area. When you cooled them to a critical temperature just above that of boiling water, a positive electric charge would suddenly appear on the top face and a negative charge on the bottom— or vice versa, depending on the voltage you applied. This is called a spontaneous polarization of charge, and materials that do that are called ferroelectrics. When Matthias came to Bell, three classes of ferroelectrics were known. When he left, he had discovered twenty different classes and literally hundreds of compounds. We didn't know

it at the time, but eventually they became important in optical communications. I was hired by Shockley specifically to work on his ideas
on ferroelectrics. They were valid ideas but, as far as I was concerned,
not very exciting.

"I would say Matthias and I were the most important of the
'younger Turks' (if one classes Shockley a 'young Turk') who finished
the job of changing Bell Labs from a typically conservative, industrial
laboratory to the particular institution it is today. For instance,
Matthias in 1951 went on his own initiative on a kind of sabbatical to
Chicago, much deplored by the Old Guard, to learn liquid-helium
techniques. When he returned he started his fantastically successful
search for new superconducting materials, one of our first ventures into
really open-ended research. The resistance of management was less, but
still noticeable, in 1952, when I was invited to spend a Fulbright year
in Japan. But the management here gradually began to realize that the
extra exposure and contacts had been worthwhile. There was a tend-
ency at that time to feel that travel was part boondoggle, a reward for
faithful service but not an essential part of a scientific career. It is hard
to believe now, but my boss, Stan Morgan, didn't let me go to the most
famous and prestigious of all invitational scientific meetings, the Solvay
Conference, in 1955 . . . because I'd been to Japan in 1953! Matthias,
who was a freer spirit, went anyway.

"I always felt that Shockley was the quickest physicist I ever knew
in the first two stages of a problem. He was very good at breaking
problems down to their bare essentials and doing things with what one
might call Gallic simplicity or clarity. His ideas were always very clear
but never deep. I learned a lot from him. In addition I spent some time
writing up my thesis for publication. I was generally encouraged to be
a physicist with some prejudice toward justifying Shockley's ideas about
ferroelectrics.

"When we came to Bell, Shockley was kind to us. The Shockleys
had us stay in their house for a few days while we got settled. When
we moved into our apartment, Bill came over to help us paint it. But
he had another side as well. He liked to test people to see how they
would respond in situations he created. For instance, he took my wife
for a ride in his tiny open Triumph, at seventy-five miles an hour, or
as close to it as he could get, along our narrow New Jersey back roads,
with the bushes rushing past their elbows. It was our first and most

personal example of this side of his character, but in time there were others. For the young people under him at Bell it was particularly disturbing. It was considerably later, some years after he had left Bell to form his own company, that he became notorious for his role in the controversy over I.Q. testing and race.

"Actually, my first bosses were Stan Morgan and Bill Shockley jointly. Stan was a chemist, an easy, friendly person, rather typical of good Bell Labs management at the time. He kept his own counsel and was very relaxed with people. It was felt that his presence was necessary in order to take the rough edges off Shockley."

For about a year Anderson filled a big notebook with calculations about ferroelectrics. He also learned something about the tradition of Bell Labs collaboration. He recalls, "Gregory Wannier, my officemate, had been appointed 'house theorist' for a gaseous electronics group. He is very mathematical, and the poor experimentalists would come in and try to make sense out of what Gregory was trying to tell them. Gregory wasn't terribly good at explaining things to them. I would sit still as long as I could, then finally butt in, saying, 'Look, here's what he's trying to tell you!' That was good training for me. People here are eager for interaction, and management is eager for you to collaborate with the largest possible number of people; to know this is to understand how the Laboratories function. After the war—and I don't know who had the idea, Shockley may have had a hand in it—an idealized picture of a collaboration here as containing one or more experimentalists and one theorist, who was available to consult, was developed. From time to time the theorist would actually be a coauthor of any paper that was produced from this collaboration, although in my first exercise along these lines my idea just appeared as an appendix to the paper of my experimental collaborator on ferroelectrics. The paradigm of this concept of collaboration was a paper written around 1946, just before the transistor, by Gerald Pearson and John Bardeen. That was the first time samples of germanium and silicon were available for which one had a real idea of what the actual concentration of electrically active impurities was. Pearson just ran through the temperature and concentration range that was available, and Bardeen interpreted what was going on. That paper is full of fundamental ideas, supported by experimental results, and became a model from the Laboratories' point of view. After my first learning experience, I got into the collaborative mode fairly quickly. We refined this model of experimental–theoretical collaboration—Bardeen, Shockley, Kittel, and then myself and Conyers Herring—and in the end it propagated through the whole field, which is now enormous. Somewhere around a third of all physics papers worldwide are in the field of condensed matter, and most of them now follow the Bell Labs model.

"It is hard to realize that in most other fields of science this close collaboration is not accepted. The machines are too big, the specialties too sharply defined, and the whole sociology is hostile to inviting a theorist to think about raw data and experimental arrangements or an experimentalist to propose a theoretical model himself. The idea is, 'A gentleman doesn't interpret another gentleman's data.' I feel strongly that nature is hard enough to understand without inserting artificial barriers. So many theorists refuse to look at experimental facts, on the grounds of some kind of false idea of 'fairness' or of playing science like a game with set rules. Or they insist on using false and sometimes meaningless standards of mathematical rigor to test a theory intended to explain data amassed on fallible instruments or from samples of unknown purity. There is a rigor of *physical* thinking that is necessary but entirely different from these mathematical games.

"Collaborations are, at least now, easy here at Bell, because the presumption and the atmosphere are one of openness. That is encouraged by the fact that our managers manage, not in the sense of telling people what to do but of knowing what people are doing. After the war Peter Debye, who was a consultant here, ran what were known as the Debye sessions. In those, everyone talked about their work in progress in front of Debye and in front of the directors. There was no way not to be open about one's working progress. This kind of working session was continued by Addison White and other managers and is done to this day. Keeping things from other people is one of the rare things on which really negative evaluations at Bell are based. The other pressure is to see to it that the staff member rather than the manager gets the credit for his work. It is looked at very negatively if a member of management gets more credit than he is entitled to. At the very least one can try to make sure that a junior staff member gets his due. Of course, this is the idealized picture; people are not saints.

"If A reveals what he is doing to B, and then B sees that there is something new to be done and does it and writes it up, we put a lot of pressure on B to include A as coauthor. There will always be resentments about who gets to give the invited paper in Gstaad, that kind of thing. But on the whole, we recognize that these problems exist and try to resolve them rationally.

"I spend a lot of my time in universities, and I can see that a university could use more people who are genuinely scientists to administer science in a management capacity. They need people who can administer salaries, for example, perhaps not in the elaborate and detailed way that we do it at Bell but to assure some kind of correlation between salary and merit. Universities could also use administrators who can give detailed advice on all aspects of one's career. Our managers here pay for the high salaries and prestige—usually—of their positions by taking a backseat whenever possible, by providing the technical leadership and then not taking credit for it. Most of them do that."

For over a year Anderson continued to fill his notebooks with various calculations of ferroelectrics. "In the spring of 1950," he told me, "Stan Morgan came and told me what my first raise would be. I came home with it proudly enough, but later I realized that it was a small raise, which should have caused me some concern. I subsequently learned that there were great battles going on in the management as to whether I was worth having on the premises at all, with Shockley taking the negative and Stan Morgan and my colleague Charlie Kittel taking the positive. By this time, I had stopped thinking about ferroelectrics and was working on antiferromagnetism. I had done a couple of bits of quantum mechanics that had impressed Kittel."

If certain substances, such as iron, cobalt, or nickel, are cooled below a critical temperature and brought into the region of a magnetic field, they become magnetic themselves. In these materials are magnetic "domains"—regions in which all the individual atomic magnets line up to produce a large net magnetization. In the presence of an external magnetic field, all these domains line up and the entire material behaves like a magnet. In a "soft" ferromagnet, like iron, these domains lose their orientation when the external field is removed; whereas in some iron alloys they remain. "Permanent" magnets, like those used in a compass or to stick papers on the refrigerator, are usually made of these alloys. In an "antiferromagnet," something very odd happens when the material is cooled below a certain temperature: the magnets of the individual atoms line up in alternating directions to produce a net magnetization of zero.

"I wrote two papers on antiferromagnetism," Anderson told me. "Because of them, somebody—either Kittel or Van Vleck—arranged for me to give an invited paper at a solid-state meeting of the American Physical Society in 1951. At that time in the Bell Labs system, young people rehearsed their papers in front of their seniors before presentation. I was pretty young to be giving an invited paper, and I was thoroughly rehearsed—public speaking has never come easily to me. Even though I don't think management was happy about me—because I obtusely continued to do precisely what my scientific interests and the inner logic of the theory led me to, without any input from my supervisors—at that point my job was presumably secure.

"Although my own motivation and work were basically unrelated to it, our work on magnetism did have a practical side. Jack Galt was doing experiments on antiferromagnets—actually, 'ferrimagnets' where the two opposite spins don't compensate, something that happens in ferrites making them weak ferromagnets—and I was acting as his house theorist. His work led eventually, after all kinds of complicated developments, to the idea of using these materials for fast computer memories, what are known as magnetic bubble memories."

The solid-state theoretical group at Bell Labs is presently organized very much like a university physics department, in the sense that there are postdoctoral fellows, sabbatical leaves, graduate students on loan from leading universities, and summer visitors, as well as subsidized travel for those giving papers at physics meetings all over the world. This is taken for granted now; but, as Anderson explained to me, it came about because of what was essentially a rebellion in the early 1950's. "In 1952," Anderson said, "John Bardeen left. He was followed, in 1953, by Kittel, and, later, by Gregory Wannier. Among other reasons, this was a brief period in which Bell salaries were lower than academic salaries. This had to do with our field, solid-state physics. The transistor had been invented, and this gave several universities the idea that solid-state theory might be a good area to build up. Jobs were opening up and there was a shortage of solid-state physicists. We had the monopoly. If you wanted a good solid-state physicist, you called on

Bell Labs and found some way to offer more money than Bell was paying. John Bardeen was offered a double professorship at the University of Illinois. It finally got to the point where there were only three of us left. Clearly the system about which I have been so enthusiastic wasn't working."

One of the last three was Harold Warren Lewis, a gifted and energetic young theorist whom Anderson refers to as an "organizer, a thinker, and an agitator." Lewis had been an Oppenheimer student and had then gone to the University of California at Berkeley. He refused to sign the special loyalty oath that the state of California required for university professors during the McCarthy period, and he was fired. He went first to the Institute for Advanced Study at Princeton, and then in 1955 he came to Bell Labs. Anderson noted, "Oddly enough, as a private institution, Bell was one of the few places where one would be almost protected from McCarthyism, although a 'security questionnaire' was circulated together with enough pressure from management so that most people went ahead and signed. When Hal got here he realized that the theorists were unhappy. He said, 'Your problem is that nobody in management knows anything about theoretical physics,' which was true, and he provided us with the inspiration for agitating for a theoretical physics department. Not long after, Hal himself left for the University of Wisconsin. (He is now at the University of California at Santa Barbara.)

"So there were, just about then, two rebellions. The first was 'Bob Shulman's List.' (R. G. Shulman is now professor of biophysics at Yale University.) Salaries have always been secret at Bell Laboratories, which had given management an unjustified feeling of power, since everyone here makes almost the same amount of money, and, insofar as they don't, you can guess to within a gnat's eyelash what any given person makes. Bob threatened this power by the simple procedure of saying to a hundred people, 'You can look at my salary list if you will put your own salary on it.' Just about everyone bit, and the usual reaction was, 'I thought *I* was underpaid, but I can see that so and so, who is even better than I am, does even worse.' This happened in 1955, and it worked. Management reacted by picking six people and giving them something like 50 percent raises. The first group included people like Claude Shannon and Conyers Herring. The next year they picked another group, of which I was one. One effect of this was that the top people had salaries that were disgracefully higher than their colleagues', which made it unlikely that they would share their salary information, but in fact it restored people's faith in our merit-raise system and kept people from leaving. In that sense Shulman had actually done management a favor."

Presently the annual starting salaries of research Ph.D.'s are somewhere in the neighborhood of $35,000, and a brilliant young scientist can earn something like $50,000 by the age of thirty. As Anderson explained, salaries at Bell, unlike many university salaries, have kept up with inflation. Most university salaries are now substantially less, although some industrial laboratories reputedly pay more than Bell. One effect of this is that in fields like solid-state physics and computer science, which have industrial applications, it is very hard for universities to compete in the job market. Anderson also feels that some people at Bell Labs would, at some time in their careers, be better off at a university, where they could teach and have graduate students, in addition to doing research. Indeed, universities need them badly. But such people may simply not be able to make the switch without a substantial financial sacrifice.

Anderson's role in the rebellion of 1955 at Bell consisted in creating the Department of Theoretical Physics. "Those of us who were left," he recalled, "went to W. O. Baker, who was the vice-president in charge of research, and asked for a department of theoretical physics and a number of things that we hoped would go with it, like sabbaticals, postdoctoral fellows, and a rotating chairman, preferably to be one of us. Baker said, 'Fine, do it all.' That was in 1956. As I mentioned, the departments had previously been organized around an experimental subject with a house theorist attached. There had never been postdoctoral fellows of any kind. We now have formal postdoc jobs and formalized arrangements for temporary visitors. Ours was the model of what essentially everyone else in research here does now. The present way of doing research is something that we invented in the six months that we were discussing these things with people like Bill Baker and Addison White. Some of the more conservative people around here who thought that 'intellectuals' were destroying the telephone company were sure that the new arrangements would ruin the Lab. They didn't, and now, for example, we have a Theoretical Chemistry Department that runs exactly like ours, along with a number of other research departments that do the same. It was a very imaginative and rather surprising capitulation by management. One of the things it did was keep me here. I felt I had a certain responsibility to hang around and make it work. I think Bill Baker, who eventually became president of the Laboratories, always had an admiration for theoretical physics, which was a powerful force in our favor. The Labs as a whole, however, are even now not very comfortable with theoretical physics, though it has paid off handsomely in terms of fundamental inventions such as the transistor and the laser. Theory always seems somehow less practical. It is the experimental physicist who produces the gadgets and takes out the patents, while the theorist produces the less tangible understanding and conceptualization. Moreover, theorists' working needs—students, travel, communication—often seem like privileges, even though they are much less expensive than experimental equipment. And the whole theoretical process is much harder to show to a visiting executive from an operating company or AT&T."

Solid-state theory is full of what are known as Anderson models. These are mathematical models—generally involving quantum mechanics—which have, at one and the same time, just the right degree of simplicity so that they can be treated mathematically, and just the right degree of complexity so that they adequately describe the essence of some very complex phenomenon involving real materials. Anderson explained to me a bit about models and model-building. "First I decide," he said, "that there is a problem of some interest and that that problem is embodied in a real material like barium titanate—one of Matthias' ferroelectrics. Of course, a material like that is terribly complicated. There are a few very rare examples where, if you are very lucky, you can start with the material and really calculate everything from first principles. I have done that kind of work. My thesis was sort of like that. But normally you can't do that. A real material contains all kinds of junk. There are too many electrons, and so on, so one has to abstract something relevant from the material. The first time I did that was with the ferroelectrics. I did not realize then that I could do it; I just did it. I am told that I have a mind that thinks quantum mechanically. I have always felt that quantum mechanics is a lot easier than classical mechanics. That feeling goes right back to my orals at Harvard—which I almost didn't pass—where they asked me to explain how the top works in classical mechanics, which I couldn't do. I can do at least the simple versions of the top in my head quantum mechanically.

"One of the things I often do," Anderson went on, "is to uncover anomalies. Take glass, for example. It's a great big clashing anomaly right off the bat. It's solid and yet it isn't crystalline. That's anomalous as it is. It has the same structure as a liquid, and yet it is not a liquid. That is the anomaly that I am working on at the moment. An anomaly like that can sit around for a long time, especially if the substance in which it is happening is not fashionable, or if it is something that you have managed to get yourself accustomed to. Chemists, for example, are notorious empiricists, and they are capable of living indefinitely with anomalies that stare them right in the face. People are perfectly capable of ignoring them, or they might puzzle about them for a few years, and if nobody solves them everyone forgets about them. In this sense, they just disappear and get encapsulated. I have seen that encapsulation of anomalies occur again and again in science. They stay there until someone notices them."

During the summer of 1956, while helping to reorganize the solid-state theory group, Anderson began work on one of the discoveries for which he would win the Nobel Prize. This is what solid-state physicists now call "localization." It became an entire "industry" of research. It also happens to be a particularly nice example, both of Anderson's own *modi operandi*, and of the interaction of theorists and experimentalists at Bell. When Anderson began working on these matters, his colleague Gregory Wannier had tried to answer the question of why a diamond is a good electrical insulator. The conventional answer is contained in the concept of the energy bands, discussed on p. 88. In brief, in an ideal diamond—one with no impurities—there is a wide separation in energy between the conduction band and the valence band. It takes a lot of energy to promote an electron to the conduction band, and as long as it remains in the valence band it will not move. It cannot contribute to any electric current in the material, and hence the material acts like an insulator.

This is all very well—and, indeed, correct—for an idealized, completely pure, diamond conductor. The problem is that any *real* diamond is not pure. It contains electrically active materials besides carbon. "In 1956," Anderson recalled, "we were beginning to study diamonds here. We started to realize how incredibly impure diamonds are. They have an impurity atom not for every million or hundred million atoms but for every hundred. These things were massively impure, and yet they had a very large band gap and did not transmit current. They are—impurities and all—incredibly good insulators.

"From a quantum mechanical point of view this did not seem to make any sense at all. In quantum mechanics an electron can tunnel through obstacles as well as diffract around them. The uncertainty principle tells you—at least on the face of it—that if you try to pin down an electron to some local site, you have to give it so much momentum that it is almost sure to move away from that site, something we call 'quantum transport.' In fact the theory of quantum transport, which was just being worked out then, seemed to say that *nothing* could be an insulator since, with high probability, the electrons could hop from site to site. If, for example, there was effective quantum mechanical tunneling of electrons between the impurities in a diamond, it should have been a conductor as good as, or better, than water. You could not use it as an insulator. Its properties wouldn't just be slightly different from what is observed, they would be very, very different. One was confronted by one of those anomalies that are very big and very obvious. Those are the most interesting kind. They are a microcosm of the kind of discovery that Einstein made when, at some point, he suddenly thought to himself that 'inertial' mass is the same as 'gravitational' mass and isn't that strange. It is very strange, and it is a line of thought that eventually led him to his general theory of relativity."

While Anderson was being exercised by this puzzle about diamonds, George Feher, a Czech-born Israeli experimental physicist at Bell, had begun a series of remarkably accurate and ingenious experiments on silicon that presented this localization anomaly in a different setting. Anderson notes, "Feher was responsible for one of these quantum jumps in the quality of equipment and technique in solid-state experimental physics. He was, for example, the first solid-state experimenter to use automatic recording techniques and to digitize a great deal of his measurements. He was just better than most people, and when he did an experiment it was very convincing. Just about this time we also were experiencing a very rapid improvement in the quality of semiconductor materials. When they provided us with a sample of silicon with, say, phosphorous impurities, they could guarantee that the number of impurities per cubic centimeter was, say, $6 \times 10^{+16}$, plus or minus one figure. To see what this means, one has to realize that the material that the transistor was invented on had an impurity content that was uncertain to plus or minus one or two *orders of magnitude*. We were able to provide Feher, and his predecessor Robert Fletcher, with a sequence of samples with controlled impurity concentration. One could take a sample of silicon and dope it with phosphorous so that the phosphorous atoms were a hundred thousandth of a centimeter (a thousand angstroms) apart and then arrange the next sample so that they were eight hundred angstroms apart, the next, four hundred angstroms, and so on. Using some beautiful new techniques, Feher was able to see in detail how the electrons were distributed near the phosphorous atoms, something that we call mapping out the electron's wave function. None of these results made any sense in terms of the existing theory of quantum transport. Feher's experiments should have been a complete and total bust if that theory had been literally correct."

Sir Nevill Mott, who shared the 1977 Nobel Prize in physics with Anderson and Van Vleck, was one of the few physicists besides Anderson to appreciate the sort of dilemmas that these and other experiments suggested. Mott had proposed a localization mechanism that, while distinct from and complementary to the Anderson mechanism, is part of what goes on in an insulator. Mott realized that electrons, which repel each other electrically, can simply get in each other's way. An electron can't move because the place where it would like to go is already occupied by another electron. Anderson's localization mechanism is entirely different and depends essentially on the wave nature of the electron. As Anderson explained:

"If you start an electron off in a certain direction in a substance like silicon doped with phosphorous, various things can happen to it. It can tunnel through obstacles. It can get reflected from them, and it can diffract around them. But a certain amount of the electron wave gets reflected back exactly along the path from which it came. There is a lot of reflection, since there is a whole sequence of reflecting atoms in the solid. A certain amount of what is reflected back from the second obstacle will also get around the first obstacle and come directly back toward you and so on. This back reflective wave can build up and build up, so that it can interfere destructively with the wave that was trying to start off. That eventually destroys the capacity of that wave to go on. The electron finds itself totally frustrated and has to remain in the precise neighborhood of where it started out. This is different from the metallic case, where the back scattering isn't too great. There, the back-scattered wave doesn't build up and the electron manages to get lost—to move around and to follow what we call a diffusive behavior. In a real material the Mott localization mechanism *and* the Anderson localization mechanism can both go on at the same time. One of the things we are quarreling about in the field now is how to determine in particular cases which is which, or whether both are going on. My original paper, which I published in 1958, was very hard to read and probably slightly wrong. It was certainly unnecessarily obscure. We didn't have at the time any of the mechanics for that kind of calculation. The language that we now use just didn't exist. In that paper I made a model that contained what I thought was the physics of the silicon-phosphorous system. There were a number of specific complicating facts about that system that I didn't want to put in since I knew that they were irrelevant. I didn't want to clutter up people's minds with facts. I didn't want to have to argue with people about any one example of this thing. I just wanted to show it as a general mathematical phenomenon. Once I got into it I got fascinated by the mathematics. I didn't want to clutter up the mathematics with a lot of garbage that I didn't understand completely."

Not many physicists were able to follow Anderson's original paper. In his Nobel Prize speech he remarked, ". . . very few believed it at the time, and even fewer saw its importance; among those who failed to fully understand it at first was certainly its author. . . . Only now, and primarily through Sir Nevill Mott's efforts, is it beginning to gain general acceptance." One of the consequences of Mott's interest was that in 1961 Anderson was invited to Cambridge University by Mott. During that visit Brian Josephson, who was then a beginning research student, attended Anderson's lectures. "Josephson claims," Anderson remarked, "that some of the ideas I presented led him to what is now called the 'Josephson effect,' which won him the Nobel Prize. He brought me his paper and asked if it looked right. It looked right to me. I came back to Bell and asked my colleague John Rowell if he had ever seen anything like that. He said that maybe he had, and then we did the first experiments that exhibited what is now called a Josephson junction. This is probably the most important practical gadget that resulted from any of my work in physics; Josephson junctions are used in all kinds of sophisticated measuring equipment, for example, in tracking brain waves and for radio astronomical detectors. They may be the heart of the next generation of computers. Josephson is now a professor at Cambridge, but he has lost interest in physics and spends most of his time on transcendental meditation and what seems to me other dubious causes. The TM people put out a poster showing him 'levitated' several inches above the floor."

While at Cambridge, Anderson had a brief fling with elementary-particle physics. "That was a marvelous time," he recalled, "one of those rare periods when often separated fields of theoretical physics are genuinely exchanging ideas. There was, for example, a new theory of superconductivity that excited the interest of particle physicists and actually served as a model for their ideas about elementary particles. Some of my ideas on superconductivity were taken over by the particle physicists and form a part of particle theory now. Quantum mechanics is all one subject, and a new idea in one area often has very exciting applications in others.

"Five years later," Anderson went on, "Mott was visiting us at Bell and he said to me, 'I have got a professorship. Who would you think I should hire?' He then turned to me and said 'You wouldn't want it would you?' I had just turned down a sequence of offers from universities, one of which I was regretting. I told Mott that it would be a great deal of fun but that I wasn't all that sure about committing myself to a job in England full time. Joyce actually suggested that if he could arrange a part-time job we might do that. And that is what he did."

Beginning in 1967 Anderson spent eight years as visiting professor in Cambridge. "I had always liked England and especially Cambridge," Anderson commented. "I had been there with my parents for three months when I was very young and then again in 1961. I liked the idea that there are all those ancient buildings and customs, and yet in the middle of it there was really an honest-to-God modern, technologically ept, effective, university. I told Bell Labs my plans and they agreed. By that time there were precedents for that kind of arrangement here. The mathematician John Tukey had such an arrangement with Princeton and Bernd Matthias was part-time among Bell Labs, the University of California at La Jolla, and Los Alamos. Matthias maintained three full-time laboratories, and all of them were busy making materials that we were interested in here. I think that if I had not been able to make my arrangement with Cambridge I would have left the Labs. A lot of my friends, my original generation, the gang that had more or less palled around together, were kind of dispersing to the four winds.

"The question of whether or not my visiting professorship at Cambridge carried tenure became something of a cause célèbre. After I had been there for two years they had to have a vote about whether I was really a tenure professor. After the vote I received a telegram here that read 'Praise God for everlasting Grace,' a *grace* being a statute of the University of Cambridge; when you vote, you vote to grace such and such. It was later explained to me that my tenure could not have passed except during vacation and that, at the same time, a second grace was passed saying that there would be no more visiting professorships. I wasn't told *that* in the telegram. In any case, for eight years I spent six months in Cambridge and six months at Bell. While I was there I helped Volker Heine, who is now the group head, to create and run the Condensed Matter Theory Group. We ended up with the entire top floor of the new Cavendish Laboratory. We trained three graduate students a year and eventually had a very large group. It was not a vacation. I used to come back to Bell Labs for a rest. It was certainly a very pleasant life, but by 1975 Joyce and I began to feel like visitors everywhere so we came back. We still have a small cottage in Cornwall, where we spend a month every spring. I now have the same arrangement with Princeton that I had with Cambridge. Like the Cambridge one, this works very well for the young people. Those whom I can bring here to Bell get a much better idea of what research in physics really is about than they could ever get in an academic department alone."

I asked Anderson if the Nobel Prize had changed his life. "It did for a while," he told me. "Now I don't let it. I told myself that I would enjoy it all for a year. I would accept essentially everything that looked interesting; then for a second year I accepted quite a bit. But by the third year I made a rule that I would not give a talk farther than fifty miles from New York unless there was real scientific justification for it. I follow that rule and that essentially takes care of most of the other problems. The other thing is that I'm a pretty obscure Nobel Prizewinner, as they go. I'm not so much better known than I was before; I was, after all, already a councillor of the National Academy of Sciences, for instance. The worst nuisance of winning a prize like that was partly already in place: you become a kind of high-level personnel man or headhunter. Nominations for prizes, letters of recommendation, and so on, could, if one lets it, become a full-time job. I do letters strictly for people I've worked with, and that reduces the pressure somewhat. But I take nominations for major prizes and honors seriously, and that can be time-consuming although it is great when your nominee wins. These things are important because the quality of science depends on keeping the reward system functioning properly; those prizes mustn't be allowed to go to the best logroller or horse trader, or we all lose, and the quality of science loses. Like all Nobelists I signed some autographs for the first year and then made a form letter for autograph collectors."

After returning from Cambridge, Anderson formally directed the Solid-State Laboratory at Bell. Now he functions as a kind of unofficial advisor to the vice-president in charge of research, Arno Penzias. He has given a lot of thought to the future of the laboratories. "There are some things that trouble me," he said. "For the moment they are just symptoms. For example, for the first time in two decades a shipment of physics preprints to the Soviet Union was delayed by Bell; we fought *that* out in the 1960's. We have been wearing identification badges since the fall of 1982—after the divestiture was announced—and visitors are monitored more carefully. The secretaries were having to stamp *Bell Labs Proprietary—Do Not Disclose* on our internal memos, even those which are collaborative papers with outsiders. That also was new. We have been asked to sign a statement affirming, among other things, that we would protect the company's reputation and that the company could control all information acquired as an employee. Of course I didn't and couldn't sign it, and it was not enforced; still it was reminiscent of the McCarthy days. I don't know that I want to go through all that kind of argument again. In those days you kept being asked the same loyalty questions, and it was implied that you had to come up with a new answer each time, since the previous one hadn't indicated acquiescence. It was boring, trying, and counterproductive.

"My attitude on that may suggest that I'm an old-fashioned liberal. I'm not an egghead—scientists aren't considered intellectuals and properly so. They are not in ivory towers. They are very much of this world, since the world pulls them up short when they are wrong. What drives me is an incorrigible curiosity about how things really work. I get very unhappy about unnecessary barriers to the communication and expression of scientific ideas, and I believe they almost always have a negative effect. And of course my primary professional loyalty is to science itself.

"For Bell Labs, my worst fear is that AT&T and Western Electric could begin to treat us the way any other electronics manufacturing lab —say, RCA—is treated. It's possible to think that the courts really wanted that to happen to us.

"For instance, AT&T might insist on a sixty- or ninety-day overview of every preprint that goes out of here in order to decide if it has patent possibilities. We have always had a release procedure, but the problem was to get a patent lawyer to pay attention when you thought something might be patentable. It probably still will be hard to get a patent lawyer to pay attention *and* they may hold up the release. I would worry that, based on things like that, or on a change in atmosphere in general, some of our young people might decide to move out to universities, or other industries, or government labs, and that quality could fall off.

"It appears that the company so far is very sturdily resisting the pressures in that direction. Our budget is maintained at least for several years, most of our personnel will stay, and there is a real sense that Bell Labs are an important asset. Part of my job with Arno has been to watch for such atmospheric changes and to protect against them—for instance, we disposed of those silly *Proprietary* stamps, and I've occasionally exerted some more substantive pressures too. I know that the intention is to maintain us at this level and to keep the research department together for the foreseeable future. I think that the commitment to physics—and especially to solid-state, condensed-matter physics—would be the last to go. It just goes on paying off. But we could lose the great spirit we have here just by mistakes or misunderstandings—by the AT&T management just being too busy to notice."

Aerial view of Bell Labs, Murray Hill, New Jersey.

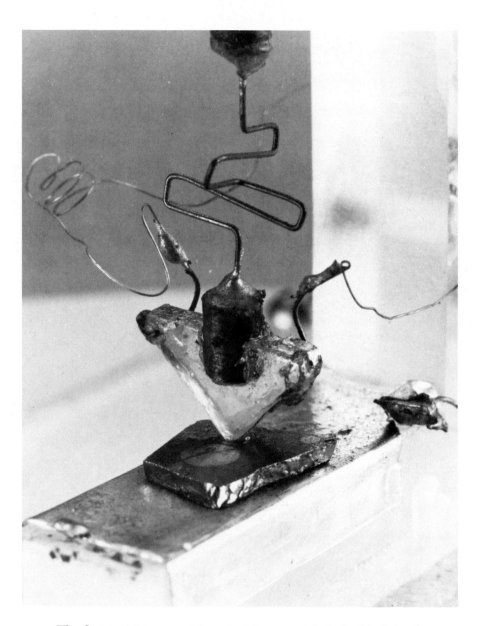

The first transistor, a point-contact type, amplified electrical signals by passing them through a solid semiconductor material, basically the same operation performed by present-day junction transistors.

The inventors of the transistor: William Shockley *(seated);* John Bardeen *(left);* and Walter H. Brattain *(right).* The announcement accompanying this 1948 photo read, "The transistor's potentialities are such that Bell scientists and engineers expect it may have far-reaching significance in the field of electronics and electrical communication."

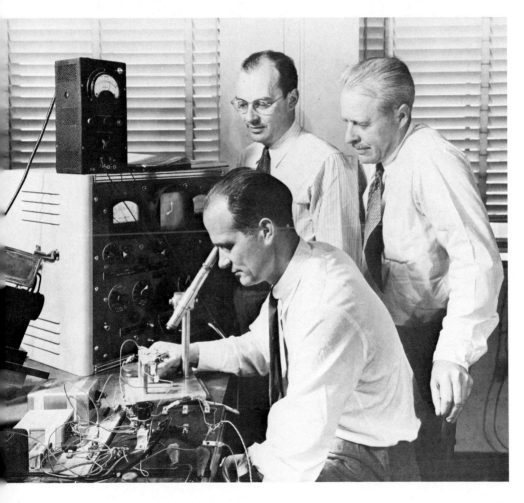

BELLE, the world's computer chess champion *(above)*, with Joe Condon, one of its developers. BELLE analyzes as many as six thousand moves a second and flashes its choices on a terminal, giving new positions for chess pieces. A Bell Laboratories engineer examines a wafer containing microcomputer chips *(above, right)*. Three microprocessor chips shown on a wafer *(below, right)*. Each chip has more computing power than a minicomputer.

Loops of hair-thin glass fiber *(below)*, illuminated by laser light, the medium for lightwave, fiber-optics systems. A fiberguide cable *(above, right)* containing 12 ribbons of glass fibers, each ribbon encapsulating 12 fibers. This cable can carry more than 40,000 voice channels. A laser used to generate light in fiber-optics systems *(below, right)*. The device is shown amid grains of salt.

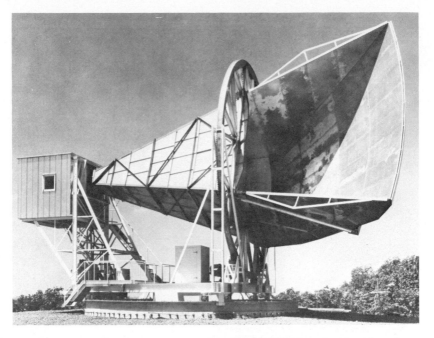

The horn-reflector antenna at Crawford Hill, New Jersey *(above)*, which Robert Wilson *(below, left)* and Arno Penzias *(right)* used to detect the residual cosmic background radiation that permeates the universe.

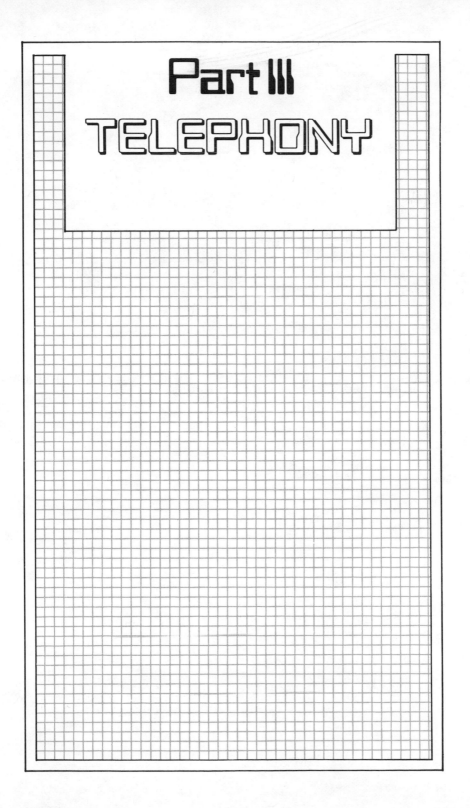

# Part III

# TELEPHONY

# CHAPTER 10

# BORSHT

IN THE TELEPHONE BUSINESS, BORSHT is an acronym for the six basic functions that make a telephone work.

*B* is for battery, which provides the direct current—the basic electric power—that makes a telephone operate.

*O* is for overvoltage protection, that is, the protective devices that prevent high-voltage surges from coming down the line into, say, the telephone user's head. *O* also protects against high sound levels that could cause hearing damage. For home telephones, protective devices are located where the wires come into the house. Equipment in telephone exchanges is also protected. Lightning seldom strikes telephone wires, but storm clouds can cause dramatic changes in the electrical potential near the earth and can result in surges of thousands of volts down a telephone wire, more than enough to electrocute anyone. While the overvoltage protection is designed to keep this from happening, telephone books warn that "absolute protection is impossible" and advise customers not to use the phone during an electrical storm unless absolutely necessary. It is also not a good idea to talk on the phone while in the bathtub.

*R* is for ringing. In order to make the phone ring, a ninety-volt, twenty-cycle-per-second, alternating current is used.

*S* is for supervision. This function enables a telephone exchange, which monitors the line current, to tell if a telephone is on or off the hook. If there are several extension phones, *S* also makes sure that current flows only to those in use.

*H* is for hybrid. A telephone serves as both a transmitter and a receiver. Because we both talk into it and listen to it, there must be a two-way path, one for the transmitted signal, the other for the received signal. At various points these unidirectional signals are joined together in a bidirectional element and are transmitted on a single path —even though they move in opposite directions. The interface between the unidirectional elements and the bidirectional element is called a hybrid. Without these hybrid devices, a transmitted signal could be routed back to the receiver, resulting in unwanted echoes.

*T* is for testing. In addition to the currents that run the telephone, special currents can be sent down the line, for example, voltage surges to test for short circuits. The phone company can also test for illegal extensions. I once discussed this with a Bell Labs engineer, who remarked laconically, "After the divestiture, AT&T Information Systems won't care how many illegal extensions you have, since we are simply going to sell you the phones. AT&T Communications won't care either, so long as you continue to make the same number of long-distance calls. Illegal extensions will be the problem of the Central Services Organization and the seven regional operating companies."

# CHAPTER 11

# Suzanne Nagel

PRIOR TO his work on the telephone, Alexander Graham Bell's primary interest was telegraphy. In this enterprise he had enlisted the help of a young machinist named Thomas A. Watson. The first message sent over a telephone, on 10 March 1876, was the famous "Mr. Watson, come here. I want you." What is not well known is that when Bell transmitted this message he was not kidding. He had just spilled battery acid over his clothes and needed help.

Early in 1875, while the two were working on the telegraph, Bell had explained to Watson what was to become the basic principle of telephony. He said, "Watson, I have another idea I haven't told you about that I think will surprise you. If I can get a mechanism which will make a current of electricity vary in its intensity as the air varies in density when a sound is passing through it, I can telegraph any sound, even the sound of speech." This statement is a perfect capsule description of what is now called the analog transmission of sound by means of varying electrical currents. Indeed, Bell's 1875 "gallows frame" transmitter—named because it sort of looks like a gallows—was an embodiment of exactly this idea.

In essence, Bell's transmitter worked as follows: It had a membrane that sound caused to vibrate. Attached to this membrane was a strip of iron that vibrated when the membrane did. Behind this strip was an electromagnet, in which a varying electric current was set up by the vibrating iron strip. This current propagated along a wire. At the other end was a similar electromagnet with another piece of iron attached to *it.* The current in the magnet would cause the iron to vibrate and this would in turn cause the membrane to which it was attached to vibrate —producing sound. Thus, there was a sequence: sound wave–electromagnetic analog current–sound wave. This was—indeed, until fairly recently—the universal sequence for telephone transmission, although with all sorts of refinements. For example, by the 1890's the vibrating iron had been replaced by granular carbon, which is still used today. Incidentally, all the carbon used by Western Electric in the manufacture of telephones comes from a single mine in Pennsylvania.

As early as 1937, Alec Harley Reeves of International Telephone and Telegraph made the suggestion, which was not, however, implemented until 1962, that fundamentally changed the way in which information is sent along telephone wires. Sending down the wire an electric analog of a sound wave is quite unnecessary; all one needs is the *information*—the complete description—of that sound wave. If that information could be transmitted it could be used at the other end to reconstruct the sound wave. But, if only information needs to be sent, it can be sent *digitally,* in terms of discrete pulses like the 1,0 components of binary mathematics. One great advantage of encoding information in binary form is that a pulse is much easier to keep from attenuating and distorting along a line than is a complicated analog wave form. A repeater has simply to regenerate weakened pulses of a single shape. Indeed, beginning in 1962, the Bell System introduced the first commercial "Pulse-Code Modulation" and began, slowly at first, the continuing program to replace analogue telephone transmission by its digital equivalent. In such a system, the sound waves are first transformed à la Bell into its analogue electrical signal—into electromagnetic waves. It is not necessary, or even possible, to encode all the information in these waves into binary form. These waves are "sampled," 8,000 times a second, and the information in each sample is broken up into units that can be represented by eight binary digits, that is, by a string of eight on-off or 1,0 signals such as 10011101. Each 1 or 0 is known as a "bit" of information, and so information from one such electromagnetic wave is transmitted at a rate of 64,000 bits a second. This is enough to characterize the electromagnetic signal, and hence the original sound wave from which it was derived, with sufficiently great accuracy to ensure good telephone transmission. If Alexander Graham Bell were able to examine what is—or will soon be—sent down the wires connecting telephones, he would no doubt be astounded to discover numbers—a vast array of binary pulses that represent eight-digit numbers. Most telephone calls in the United States are still being transmitted analogically, but this is changing rapidly. The listener cannot tell that a telephone call is being transmitted digitally, since the voice is "re-created" at the receiving end. This digital transmission will probably eliminate part of the hiss that accompanies some long-distance telephone calls, but the quality is limited by the ordinary telephone receiver which, as modern amplifiers go, is of relatively low quality.

If it is possible to send a series of digital pulses that characterize the sound waves down a telephone line and not some electric analog of one's voice, it also follows that, in principle, these pulses can be transmitted by any convenient method—by light, for example. Light waves oscillate at a much higher frequency than, for example, AM radio waves, about a billion times faster. This very rapid oscillation cannot be fully utilized in transmitting information. To do that the light must be bunched into pulses that consist of many individual light waves. Nonetheless, with light pulses, "bit rates"—rates of pulse transmission—can be achieved in the range of billions of bits per second. To get some conception of these astronomical numbers, it is worthwhile to point out that if the information broadcast by an ordinary television transmitter were digitalized, it would result in a bit rate of $10^8$, or about a hundred million, per second. The 1984 Summer Olympics at Los Angeles are going to be transmitted locally over a Bell light-pulse television-transmission system that will operate at a rate of ninety million bits per second. This system will connect widely separated locations to a central control point. After the games, the cables over which the light is transmitted will become part of the Los Angeles telephone system, which illustrates the amazing flexibility of these optical networks.

There were two basic problems in developing optical systems: creating pulses of light and transmitting them. A clue to solving the first question came in 1958, when Charles Hard Townes and Arthur Leonard Schawlow outlined the fundamental principle of the laser. Townes had been at Bell Labs until 1947, when he accepted an appointment at Columbia University (he is now at the University of California, Berkeley). While at Bell he had become interested in microwave spectroscopy. Microwaves are electromagnetic waves with wavelengths of a few centimeters—frequencies of the order of $10^{10}$ per second. At Columbia, Townes and his graduate students invented the *maser*— microwave amplification by stimulated emission of radiation—the practical realization of an idea pointed out by Einstein in 1916. Electrons in excited atomic orbits can be stimulated to emit radiation by being in the presence of radiation. This led to the possibility of radiation *amplification.* An excited atom can be stimulated to radiate, and this radiation can in turn cause neighboring atoms to radiate, creating a kind of avalanche effect. Schawlow, who is now at Stanford, spent two years as a postdoctoral student with Townes, during which they wrote a book about microwave spectroscopy. After coming to Bell Labs in 1953, he continued to work with Townes, who was still a Bell Lab consultant. In their 1958 paper they outlined the general conditions under which stimulated light emission could be amplified—hence the *laser*—"light amplification of stimulated emission of radiation."

In 1959, Ali Javan of Bell Labs suggested what is known as a helium-neon laser. In this device helium atoms collide with neon atoms and the electrons surrounding the neon nuclei are excited, triggering the stimulated-emission process. In 1960 Javan, William R. Bennett, Jr., and D. R. Herriott demonstrated the first continuously operating helium-neon gas laser. (The first laser *ever* to operate was a ruby-crystal laser built by Theodore H. Maiman of the Hughes Research Laboratories in 1960.) It is this laser that probably comes to mind when one thinks of the idea of a laser. Like the ruby-crystal laser, it emits a characteristic red pencil beam and, under suitable conditions, can be used to cut metal. It has been estimated that at least 200,000 lasers are currently in use as teaching tools, measuring systems, scanners, and video-disk readers, as well as "scalpels" for surgery.

Meanwhile, an entirely different kind of laser was being developed, the semiconductor injection laser, which works basically by injecting electrons into a confined region in crystal. The first crystals used for this purpose were made of gallium arsenide. Among the advantages of solid-state lasers is their microscopic size. They have dimensions of the order of a tenth of a millimeter. In addition, solid-state lasers can now be routinely operated to emit more than a billion high-power, extremely narrow pulses a second. Moreover, by changing the materials, it is possible to make lasers that emit pulses at various frequencies, enabling one to transmit two or more sets of independent sources of information at different frequencies. Imagine one set of pulses transmitting tele- phone conversations and television signals and another set operating off a different laser, transmitting its own telephone and television signals —both operations *simultaneously.*

While the development of semiconductor lasers apparently re- solved the question of generating light pulses, there remained the question of transmitting them. A clue was already available in the work of the Irish physicist and mountaineer John Tyndall. In 1870 Tyndall showed that light can be guided in a medium like glass, which has a high index of refraction, when it is surrounded by a medium like air, which has a low index of refraction. The index of refraction is a measure of a medium's ability to bend light rays. Glass bends them more sharply than air. In other words, Tyndall studied the forerunner of the modern optical pipe. While it was well-known—there were even medical ap- plications—that light could be guided in a glass or plastic tube or pipe a few feet, it seemed, until 1966, that there was no prospect that the same technique could be used to propagate it for miles, which is what would be needed to make a "light pipe" effective for the transmission of telephone signals. The unit "decibel per meter" is used in this field to measure how much of the light signal is lost for every meter of transmission. ('Decibel', named after Bell, is conventionally used as a unit to measure the relative intensity of sound but it can also be applied to the intensity of light signals.) To make a viable light pipe, the medium—glass, for example—would need to have a loss of at most about 20 decibels per kilometer. In 1966 K. C. Kao and G. A. Hockman of the Standard Telecommunications Laboratories in England demon- strated theoretically that if glass could be made pure enough and, in particular, water-free, then it could be used to achieve this kind of loss rate. Indeed, they reported measurements on commercially available bulk glasses with losses in the range of a few decibels per kilometer. The first low-loss glass fibers were made by the Corning Glass Works in Corning, New York, in 1970. Their loss rate of 20 decibels per kilometer can be compared to the present, state-of-the-art rate: about .25 decibel per kilometer.

Bell Laboratories began research on optical communications in 1961. Most of the early work, on optical-fiber light propagation was theoretical and was done at the relatively small facility at Crawford Hill, New Jersey, and at Holmdel, under the direction of S. Miller on the overall design of the fiber-optics system. In the early 1970's the main laboratory at Murray Hill began adding personnel, specifically to study the materials aspect: how to make a glass fiber that is extremely strong, free of impurities, and thin enough to be compatible with solid-state lasers. Among those who joined the Laboratory was a very attractive, 27-year-old, auburn-haired, recent Ph.D. named Suzanne Nagel. Of all the people whom I met at Bell Labs, Nagel is one of the busiest. Since July 1982 she has been head of the twenty-seven-member Glass Research and Development Department, which is in the thick of efforts to make optical fibers the standard method of transmitting telephone calls. She is involved in every aspect from pure research to marketing, and she is also somewhat of a rarity at the Laboratories. Her father, an electrical engineer, also worked for Bell Labs.

Suzanne Nagel was born in 1945 in Jersey City, New Jersey, the second of four children and the only one to show any interest in science. "When I was very young, my father worked in the old West Street location in New York City," she told me, "and later moved to Whippany," another Bell Labs facility in New Jersey. "I did not know in any detail what he was doing. I later learned that he was involved in power transmission using pretransistor techniques. Because he is one of the few resident experts left in that field, he still has a valuable role to play. Many of our operating company facilities are in rural areas and still use technology based on things developed thirty or forty years ago. My father was so happy that *one* of his children—me—was interested in a science or engineering career, that it never occurred to him that I might have problems as a woman. I have always thought that his encouragement was very important in terms of my subsequent education. Unlike many of my female colleagues of that era, I did not have a family that discouraged me from going into science."

By the time she entered Rutgers, to study material science, she wanted to become a ceramic engineer. "I must admit I was a little cautious," she recalled. "I actually went into a five-year program in which I got a B.A. in liberal arts as well as a B.S. in ceramic engineering. I wanted to make sure that I could get a job somewhere, even if it wasn't in engineering. I also felt that it was important to get a deeper humanities background. One of the criticisms of engineers was that they didn't know how to relate to people, that they weren't articulate, that they only cared about slide rulers. I wanted to make sure that I was not the stereotypical engineer with a slide ruler on my belt and unable to talk about issues."

Nagel explained what ceramic engineering is. "It could be considered to be high-temperature inorganic chemistry, although it also involves physics. It's definitely a very applied field, aimed at improving the quality of ceramics such as glass, which is the major ceramic material. I got interested in glass as an undergraduate and found it fascinating because so little was known about it. Although it can survive for thousands of years, it is not stable; it is what we call a metastable material. Its preferred state is to be a crystal. To know how to avoid the crystal state, we have to understand it. So when I went on to graduate school that was what I wanted to study." Nagel got her Ph.D. from the School of Engineering of the University of Illinois in 1972. "I did my thesis work with Cliff Bergeron, who is now the head of the Ceramics Department there. It was an experimental thesis in which I verified some of the theories of the crystallization rates of certain glasses."

While Nagel was finishing up her thesis, two recruiters from the Bell Labs "magically appeared at Urbana. I had not signed up for an interview. Those were not especially good economic times and recruiting for jobs was not tremendous, but the Bell Laboratory recruiters were out. I had the opportunity of showing them all of the experiments that I was doing—all my data. It was fairly casual, which worked more favorably for me. Moreover, I was suddenly shocked to find out that Bell Labs had this research effort that went beyond conventional telephone service, that they did research on materials and physics. Somehow that had slipped by me in my earlier years, because I only saw things from my father's rather practical work. I came to Murray Hill for more interviews just when the program for making optical glass for telecommunications was starting. It seemed to present a marvelous opportunity, and I was so excited by it that, quite frankly, I looked very little elsewhere. That was where I wanted to go. I was sold from the start."

When Nagel arrived at Bell, only four other people were working on the production of suitable glass fibers; but the group was rapidly expanding, both through outside recruitment and the redeployment of people within the Labs. The general problem on which she was to work was how to make ultra-high-purity glass. "There was some very specific literature for me to read," she said, "so in that sense I had some direction. I wasn't exactly in a group. We were very loosely structured, all of us working on this general problem. But no one ever said you will work on X or Y.

"I started off doing a lot of crazy things, now that I think back on it. I was trying to develop a technique for making fiber light-guides by evaporation and to make high-purity metallic films and then to oxidize them to form glasses and then to draw these glasses into fibers. Some of my colleagues and I got a patent on that process, but as far as I know it was never put into practice. With those early fibers we were so happy if we could guide light for a few tens of meters. Now we routinely transmit it through kilometers. In those days, even if you made a material that was great in bulk form, you still had to convert it into fibers, and that brought in all the mechanical properties of fibers. We made some fibers that were good optically but poor mechanically, and there was then a mad rush to get them down to our measurement laboratories before they broke up spontaneously into a thousand pieces."

Within a year of Nagel's arrival, two of her colleagues, John B. MacChesney and P. B. O'Connor, invented a process called modified chemical vapor deposition, which transformed the way optical wave guides are made. Basically, such a wave guide consists of a highly transparent core surrounded by, and in optical contact with cladding material. This core usually has a carefully controlled index of refraction that varies across its diameter. This means that light that enters it will be transmitted in just such a way that all the beams, no matter what path they follow in the core, will arrive at the far end of the fiber at the same instant. The light never gets to the surface of the fiber as it is reflected at the boundary between the core and the cladding. In the most recently developed fibers, light is transmitted down a very narrow central core. This is an enormous improvement in economy since it avoids the problems of different beam paths and so provides fibers that can carry enormous quantities of information over long distances. It turns out that the most effective light to use is in the infrared range, which is not quite visible to the human eye.

In the MacChesney-O'Connor process, both the central core and the cladding can be manufactured at the same time. In essence, the materials to be used are vaporized and carried by a stream of oxygen through a silica tube. The tube is rotated and intensely heated, and the vaporized materials are oxidized into fine glass particles that are then deposited as a thin film on the tube. The tube is then collapsed into a rod, which is a short, thick version of the final fiber. This rod is heated to some 2000° C. and drawn into a fine fiber. As a souvenir of my visit Nagel gave me a few turns of the finished product, which is pinkish on the outside and somewhat thicker than a human hair. Its tensile strength exceeds 900,000 pounds per square inch, three times that of steel piano wire. If all of its theoretical capacity for carrying information could be used to transmit telephone light pulses, it has been estimated that it could carry enough information to handle all of the phone calls made at any one time in the United States.

The MacChesney-O'Connor process represented a very significant breakthrough in the manufacture of optical fibers. As Nagel noted, "The important thing was that it was practical. We didn't understand at the time why it worked. We just knew that it did. Its conception was so simple that even small universities could use it to do fiber-optics studies. A fiber-optics device is not a simple piece of glass fiber. It has a very carefully controlled and detailed concentration profile of chemical dopants that affect the light transmission through the light guide. You don't just go into the lab and mix together some materials and make a glass You've got to come up with some very sophisticated way of precisely controlling the chemical composition of a material that is ultimately the size of a human hair. This process allowed us to do that —and to do it two orders of magnitude faster.

"My work," Nagel went on, "was trying to understand the basic physics and chemistry of the process. I was especially concerned with wringing out the last drops of water from the fibers. Very small amounts of water—parts per billion—can cause attenuation of light in the spectral region where the lasers are emitting. That limits how long the fiber can be before virtually all the light is absorbed. Recently, by the way, we transmitted light for a hundred kilometers without the need for reamplification. This was in conjunction with our program to develop fiber-optics cables for undersea systems. The first transatlantic cable is due in 1988. For the land-based lines we have a laser-based repeater system that reamplifies the pulses every ten to twenty kilometers. We could go farther, but there are certain practical constraints. You might have an existing manhole—we now call them splicing chambers—say, fifteen kilometers away from the last one. Why build a new one?

"I guess the most ambitious project is the northeast corridor, which will connect Boston, New York, and Washington. It's what we call a trunking application. There's a lot of traffic on it, and so there's a need for more information-carrying capacity. To give you a feeling for where we are going, the first commercial systems could carry 672 telephone conversations simultaneously over one pair of fibers, with each fiber carrying the call one way. A pair of copper wires might carry twenty-four conversations if you did everything right. The next one we put in carried double that number—1,300 simultaneous phone calls. Then someone said, 'Why should we just send one wavelength of light down? Why don't we multiplex different wavelengths of light, since we have lasers that work at several wavelengths? So a system was designed that was capable of simultaneously putting three different wavelengths down a single fiber, each at a rate of 90 million bits a second. That corresponds to close to 4,000 simultaneous conversations. The systems are still evolving. We're pushing the technology every day to make better fibers, better lasers, and the rest. Because the system is digital, we can imagine putting hundreds of channels of television signals down the fibers, along with the telephone signals. There's an endless number of things we can think of doing."

AT&T is now investing $100 million a year on the fiber business. On 10 February 1983, it inaugurated a 372-mile fiber-optics link between New York and Washington. The cable, which is as thick as a finger, can consist of as many as 144 fibers. Eventually it will carry 240,000 simultaneous telephone conversations. Also that month, using a new laser invented by Won-Tien Tsang of the Solid-State Electronics Group at the Labs, 420 million bits a second were transmitted over about seventy-four miles of fiber. The error rate was one bit per billion. This means, for example, one could have transmitted the entire information content of a 30-volume encyclopedia in *one* second, making a mistake in only a single letter.

# CHAPTER 12

# Loops and Trunks

AN UNTREATED WOODEN POLE, left out of doors, can stand up to insects, fungi, and the weather for only a few years. This vulnerability is of some concern to the Bell System, which has about 22 million telephone poles in the ground. The copper cables that link them, along with the rest of what the telephone companies call the "outside plant," are also of considerable interest. The cables represent, in terms of materials and labor, one of the largest investments of the telephone companies— some $14 billion out of a total of over $50 billion for the entire outside plant. There are nearly a billion miles of copper conducting wires in place, and these provide, at present, most of the connections among the 93 million working telephone lines. To protect such an investment, the Bell System leaves little to chance. So it is not surprising to find an entire branch of the Bell Labs, at Chester, New Jersey, devoted to the outside plant: facilities that have to stand up to rain, wind, sand-storms, lightning, and fires; as well as to such risks, in the case of buried cables, of being cut in two by a farmer's plow. Compared to Murray Hill, with its staff of some 4,000, or the main lab at Holmdel, which has about 5,000 employees, Chester is miniscule, at least in terms of personnel. It has a staff of about forty. This outside facility is located on a 210-acre tract in the farm country of northern New Jersey, about forty miles west of New York City.

Chester has a swamp, which has telephone cables placed in it to see how they do in a swamp and it has one of the highest hills in New Jersey

—a windy 957-foot-high nubbin with telephone wires festooned on top to see how they do in the wind. The wide variety of soil conditions makes it possible to test cable-laying procedures in realistic situations. Certain areas are kept relatively free from electromagnetic interference, such as radio emissions, in order to find out if any of the telephone company's new digital equipment will interfere with television reception. A high-voltage laboratory conducts tests to see how well telephone sets are protected against lightning and also what happens, for example, if a power line falls across a telephone line. There is also a fire-test lab, built, coincidentally, just before the fire of 25 February 1975 in New York City that gutted a telephone exchange and wreaked havoc with service. In this lab a telephone-exchange fire can be simulated and steps taken to minimize its propagation within the building, thus avoiding a repeat of the New York blaze. In Western Electric's automobile lab the interiors of the ubiquitous telephone company repair vans are laid out.

Also at Chester is a large metal-frame structure known as the cable ship *Fantastic.* It has been designed, with the appropriate winches and hoists, to simulate the ship that will lay the major portion of the first transatlantic fiber-optics telephone cable. Machinery for drawing the cable out and laying it over the "stern" is tested in dress rehearsals aboard the landlocked *Fantastic* to ensure that nothing unexpected happens a thousand miles at sea. The real ship will be moving at some 8 knots, and a special winch was developed to lay out cable from the stern at that rate.

At the "tortuous conduit run" telephone cables are tested to determine the frictional strain that they can withstand when they are pulled around bends in underground conduits. These cables are placed down in lengths of thousands of feet. Indeed, for the optical-fiber cables— which are smaller and finer than the copper cables and have considerably less tensile strength—a typical continuous cable length is about 6,000 to 9,000 feet (for the copper cables it is something like 600 feet). The underground tortuous conduit is about 500 feet long and has enough bends to replicate the worst conditions found in the field. At an installation called the "fiber loop," fiber-optics cable is run around the laboratory for about two miles, through every kind of terrain. It is strung from telephone poles. It is buried underground. It runs through the swamp, and it goes over the top of the hill. Cables are often laid underground with a vibratory plow, which churns its way through soil, vibrating rapidly as it advances at a mile an hour or so. As the trench is dug, cable is simultaneously laid from a reel located on the plow. When the plow goes up over a hill, or hits an obstruction, there can be jerks on the cable. Since optical cables can take much less abuse than copper ones, one of the recommendations that came out of Chester was to change the location of the reels in those plows that are used to lay glass fiber and also to supply additional shock absorbers.

At a pond on the site, telephone equipment is tested under water, and in a building in which a dust storm can be simulated, researchers can see how equipment works when it is buried in dust. In the winter, snow and dust combine to form a nasty sludge, and the test equipment is given a chance to perform in a cabinet full of sludge.

Equipment in the Bell System is assembled and repaired by service engineers who, as a rule, are high school graduates and have taken a couple of years of engineering courses. The procedures to be followed in installing and servicing this often complex equipment are spelled out in great detail in manuals and other publications. These, too, are tested. Like any telephone-company customer, the Chester Lab calls up New Jersey Bell and places an order for a new device. While the field representative is installing the equipment, he is watched by members of the Lab to see, as one engineer put it, "If our imaginations differ considerably from that of the typical craftsman. Did we put in too many parts? Did we write too many—or too few—instructions, and can they be readily followed? We do nothing while the New Jersey Bell people are here but stand around and observe. Very quickly they forget that we are there."

One of the first facilities installed at Chester, shortly after its founding in 1928, was the "pole farm," a large field of telephone poles arranged in rows and unconnected to anything. These poles have been treated with various materials designed to lengthen their lifetimes. Most telephone poles are now made of southern pine, treated under pressure with a mixture of coal tar, creosote, and pentachlorophenol. They should last for at least forty years.

My tour through the Chester facility was conducted by two extremely articulate and helpful engineers. Duncan Hutchings Looney is director of the Loop Plant Construction Installation and Protection Laboratory. He goes by the name of "Hutch" and it was something of a surprise to have a message on my answering service "to call 'Hutch Looney.' "

His wife is a psychotherapist who uses her maiden name. Like many of the management personnel, Looney first came to Bell as a research scientist—in his case physics. Norwood G. Long, an electrical engineer, is director of the Loop Transmission Systems Engineering Center. Both men work out of the Whippany branch of Bell Labs, about fifteen miles from Chester. The Chester Lab was assembled in pieces, with Bell buying a small parcel of land in 1928 and then increasing it over the years to its present 210 acres. One of the facilities missing there is a cafeteria. As Looney put it, "There are no food facilities on the Chester site. It is what we call a brown bag place—a very informal atmosphere." As in all the development areas at Bell Labs, as opposed to the pure research area, people are hired to fit in with a group that has a rather well defined project in hand. Presumably because of the uncertainties caused by the divestiture, there has been a general slowdown of hiring throughout the Labs. This has affected Chester as well, even though much of the work there is related to fiber-optics communication, which is becoming a large Western Electric product line. For a while there was a serious question as to what would happen to Chester after the divestiture. It was such a valuable facility that it was finally split between Bell Labs and Bell Communications Research, Inc.

Looney and Long explained some of the complications involved in repairing fiber-optics cables. As Looney put it, "When we put a lightguide cable into the ground, we think it's going to be there forever and that we have buried it very securely. But unfortunately for us the cable TV people, or the water people, or someone else will come along and sooner or later accidentally cut our cable. When that happens we lose thousands of conversations. The phones are out of service. One of the things we worry about at Chester is how to restore service when a light-guide cable is cut. We have to consider various ways that a cable might be cut. For example, if a plow cuts it, does it do so when the cable is in a duct or when it is directly buried, and what are the characteristics of the break in each case? We have a 'bogey' in the Bell system that is set up by Long Lines: any cable repair ought to be accomplished in no more than eight hours. We can complete the repair in eight hours—that's not the problem. The real problem is finding the break and getting the right people to the right spot with the right equipment.

"With the fiber cables," Looney went on, "the recommended technique is not to splice the broken ends together but to replace the section." Part of the reason for this is the problem of aligning the strands in a fiber cable. When two sections are joined, the strands must be aligned to a few thousandths of a millimeter in order to keep the propagating light from leaking out. Bell Labs has developed a linking device that does this when two undamaged cable sections are joined. But, for a fiber system, the sections from one manhole to the next are a mile long or more, and the Labs are also exploring ways of splicing without replacing the entire section.

Long, who is responsible for such things, told me that the buried cables have shown no natural deterioration. "You must keep in mind that these cables have more than glass in them. The glass itself has an extraordinarily long lifetime. If you put the proper material around the glass and are careful about stresses and strains and plastic cracking— that sort of thing, it looks at least as durable as our copper cables, which have an average lifetime of forty years. The fiber cables may last even longer. We may be putting down stuff that has a material lifetime of a hundred years."

"With the copper cables," Looney added, "the major source of deterioration is people." The pair of copper wires that connects a telephone to the central exchange is called a "loop." A connection is closed when a telephone call is made, and a loop of flowing electric current registers in the central office by closing a relay. These wires are constantly being spliced and respliced when telephones are brought into service and taken out of it. This manipulating of the "pairs" of wire by craftsmen, according to Looney, is the main cause of troubles in the copper plant. "If, with a light-guide cable," he added, "we're successful in introducing a technology for which that kind of splicing is no longer done, then once we have put in our cable, there is almost no reason ever to touch it again. That is very important to us. Once we put something into service, particularly in the loop network, it goes out in tremendous quantities. Since it gets buried in the ground, it is often very difficult to do anything about it after the fact. So any disaster that occurs tends to be a large one."

We arrived at Chester and drove up to a neat wooden building that serves as the laboratory's headquarters. A slide projector and screen had been set up in the main conference room so that Looney could show me what to expect at the "fiber loop," which has been set up to simulate almost every obstacle—natural and otherwise—that can confront a fiber-optics cable in the field. We were joined by David Setzer, another young engineer and supervisor of the Fiber-SLC Design Group. In the Bell System jargon, SLC—pronounced "slick"—stands for Subscriber Loop Carrier. It is the state-of-the-art system for bringing the digitization of telephone transmission either by glass fiber or copper wire to consumers. "Digits to the Customer" is the motto. Fiber SLC ("fiber slick") makes use of fiber-glass transmission as well as digitization. Long promised to show me a fiber SLC installation and to explain a bit about how it works.

We then drove around a dirt track following the glass run. To my eye, at least, there was no discernible difference between the telephone poles that carry a fiber cable and the garden variety, which carry copper cables. For perhaps a mile, the cable runs above ground, meandering up the 957-foot hill. Even though it was a warm spring day, there was a stiff breeze on top of the hill, and during the winter the experimental telephone lines there must get quite a workout. For the rest of the run, the cable is buried underground, its location virtually indetectable.

Having finished the run, we pulled up at a trim, one-story, wooden structure, which houses the fiber SLC. With its delphic array of flashing lights and clonelike structures, the SLC is as agitated and confusing to the untutored eye as an ant colony. Long proceeded to explain its role in the telephone system. "The telephone used to be a simple gadget. It had a carbon transmitter that modulated current, a little electromagnetic receiver, and a bell. That's what it *was,* and for that kind of system a pair of wires works very well. The problem is that they are very labor-intensive, more so by far than any other part of the telephone business. Even though the price of copper hasn't been going up all that much, the cost of building the loop plant has gone up rapidly —faster in some areas than inflation. The first reason we started looking for an alternative to copper pairs was just cost."

There is a story about the copper pairs that is probably as old as the Bell System itself. Many years ago a Bell serviceman went to connect the telephone line of a farmer in New Jersey. After he had connected the wire pair, the farmer asked "Can I speak Italian over this phone?" The Bell service man is said to have replied, "Italian? Why didn't you tell me before? Now I will have to hook up a third wire, and that will be an extra fifty dollars."

For many years telephone systems have been using a technique called multiplexing, in which a copper pair carries more than one telephone circuit. In the present loop system, two pairs of copper wires can be made to handle twenty-four simultaneous digital circuits multiplexed together. In the SLC 96, the standard "slick", four such two-pair units are conjoined, making it possible to handle the telephone conversations of ninety-six customers. An additional pair is used for fail-safe protection. Thus, instead of adding new pairs for each customer, ten pairs, plus the SLC 96, in the central-office system are used. "We put this equipment in the central office and close to the customer," Long continued. "Although we originally used it because it was cheaper, it really is different in a transmission sense. It is digital and there is no transmission loss. The reason it saves money is kind of interesting. Its hardware cost is actually a lot more than a pair of wires, but it takes about a quarter of the labor. It's the labor that has had the high inflation rate, about 10 percent a year. With a multipair cable, each pair has to be drawn in through a conduit and put up on the poles, and each pair is separately spliced. The labor content of planning where the pairs go, of splicing and rearranging them, is very high.

"With this thing," Long said, pointing to the SLC 96, "all you have to do when you want to provide a new circuit is to plug in one of these." Long then pulled out a small module from the SLC 96—a sort of temporary lobotomy. It made a kind of "choonk" sound when he replaced it in the SLC, thereby reinstating the hypothetical circuit. "Until you need it," Long went on, "you don't even have to plug it in. You build the frame, the digital line, and the housing, which, say, take an equivalent amount of labor as an original copper installation. But when you need more pairs what do you do? You walk out there and you go, "choonk," like that. The average cost of this and of copper is now about the same, although this will come down as our large-scale integrations increase. With copper, more than half the cost is labor, however. In this case, less than a quarter of it is labor. So this stuff is going in at a great rate in the Bell System."

The state of the art—the system undergoing intensive testing at Chester—is the mixture of fiber-optics transmission and the SLC. There are two distinct types of fiber-optics transmission: the trunk, which links central offices, and the loop, which connects a central office to the customer. It is a fiber trunk that AT&T inaugurated on 10 February 1983 between New York and Washington. The light pulses in a trunk are generated by lasers and are reamplified every ten miles or so by relay-station repeaters. In the loop applications, the pulses are generated by a "light-emitting diode"—an LED, that gives off light with a wavelength of 1,300 angstrom units, just outside the visible range. These near-infrared wavelengths maximize the transmission down a glass fiber, and, indeed, the lasers used in optical transmission also work at these wavelengths.

As Long put it, "An LED is not nearly as finicky as a laser. It hasn't got the current density of a laser, but it lasts for a hell of a long time. We have been making them for twenty years, and the ones that we make as optical transmitters aren't basically all that different from the ones that you find, for example, giving off red and green lights on the instrument panel of a slick. The LEDs we use for optical communication have to be able to form very precise light pulses, and they have to be coupled to the integrated circuits that drive them at 12.6 million pulses a second, which will soon be upped to 45 million. It's been a very successful technology. An LED has enough power to generate pulses that can travel some twenty kilometers without reamplification. That is adequate for essentially all of the loop applications."

The fiber SLC system was first assembled at the Chester Lab in February 1980. It took a year before the test system was running and another year before the first operational system was installed in Chester Heights, Pennsylvania. Long explained the choice.

"Chester Heights is a sort of rural area that is expected to grow rapidly. So Pennsylvania Bell is betting that by putting fiber in along this whole route, they're going to be able to withstand whatever the developers, or the economy, or anything else, can throw at them. If that area suddenly blossoms and gets enormously big, they will already have the necessary outside plant built in. All they would have to do is supplement the electronics. The other thing about optical fiber, once you put it in, is that it can also carry television transmission. None of our copper pairs will do this, but our fibers can carry 90 million bits a second, which is enough for a TV picture. The telephone companies are extremely interested in that. Now that we are in a competitive era, the telephone companies may be able to compete with the cable TV people. They are talking about providing telephone service, and burglar alarms, and everything, and the telephone company wants to say, 'Well, gosh, we've always been able to do that over our copper pairs, and now we can also provide video.' So we'll at least have a capability standoff.

"Also, the phone companies have begun to get interested in fiber for their large business customers. If you look at the profile of a typical telephone-user population, you will find that between 1 and 2 percent of the customers provide half the revenues. These are the large businesses like Exxon or Xerox. One would like to be able to say to them, 'Do you want to move data from computer to computer? Do you want to have video teleconferences so you can avoid trips? Do you want to have access to minicomputers for your engineers?' Those people will work with you to see if we can get together. For example, a very intensive commercial section in Miami called Brickell Avenue has hundreds of small, largely South American banking concerns. There is also a rapidly growing industrial section there and large condominiums. So Southern Bell feels that by placing a fiber overlay over this entire section, they'll be able to go to these large business customers with all kinds of services that they could not have offered had they left their old copper plant in place. Soon, we're probably going to be involved in a dozen installations of this kind. For example, we're looking at a leading engineering school in Pittsburgh that wants to have an extended network linking students and computers. We've looked at big cities in the Midwest as well.

"We're working both sides of the street," Long concluded. "We are still trying to figure out what this stuff does for the ordinary telephone user. It's higher quality and lower maintenance. If the customer doesn't want to pay for a lot of extra services then you have got to make your money on that—the bread-and-butter side of the business—what many people here call the plain old 'vanilla loop.' A lot of telephone companies want to get used to fiber for the conventional user. But I think that we are going to have copper pairs in this business at least through the year 2000 or even 2100. There are so many of them out there and they have a lot of capability. One possible scenario is that you put more and more fiber in but never rearrange the old copper pairs. That will extend their lifetime. So you will have copper pairs where they are useful—for telephone service and low-speed data—and fiber for video and high-speed data."

When Long finished, he offered to let me make a phone call over the Chester fiber-glass loop to see if I could detect any difference in acoustical and transmission quality between this state-of-the-art technology and existing facilities. The loop is hooked into New Jersey Bell, so I could call anywhere in the world. I called a friend in New York. The line was busy.

# CHAPTER 13

# David Thomas

THE MAIN LABORATORY of Bell Labs at Holmdel, New Jersey, is a striking contrast to Chester in every way. It is housed in a gigantic, very modern-looking structure designed by Eero Saarinen. Nearly 5,000 people work in it. As seems to be typical now of such buildings, there is an atrium with plants and shrubs of various kinds in circular planters suspended from the ceiling. I was told that Rudolf Kompfner, who was director of the Radio Research Laboratory at nearby Crawford Hill in the 1960's, took an active dislike to the aerial greenery and dropped weeds of various kinds into the planters. The plants that fill them now are plastic.

With its gigantic dining room, serving simple, inexpensive food, Holmdel is definitely not a brown bag place. As in the dining room at Murray Hill, a signboard displays the latest price of AT&T stock. Holmdel also houses the office of the president of Bell Labs, Ian M. Ross, who took over from William O. Baker in 1979. Ross follows the general tradition of Bell Labs presidents in having a strong background in research and development. He was one of the people who made the modern field-effect transistor work.

Just as Murray Hill specializes in research, the 8 percent or so of the activity for which the Labs is probably best known, Holmdel specializes mainly in development. One of the most significant areas deals with transmission, which includes the field of fiber-optics transmission. I was fortunate to learn about this activity from David G. Thomas, the British-born chemist who has been, since 1976, executive director of the

Transmission Systems Division. Prior to that, Thomas and his collaborators played a key role in both the research and development that led to the introduction of light-emitting diodes into the Bell System. LEDs are now commonplace—they are used on office telephones and as the numerical displays on pocket calculators. When a high-tech device like this is really successful, it is almost taken for granted, as a sort of birthright. We really notice it only if it breaks down.

In his present activity, Thomas has a staff of about 550 and an annual budget of approximately $87 million. He is concerned with transmission-related activities that range from communications satellites to underwater fiber-optics cables. AT&T has been back in the domestic satellite business since 1976, although, until recently, the Federal Communications Commission allowed the company to transmit only voice messages—telephone service. It is now permitted to transmit television and other special data. Some of the people who work for Thomas spend their time at the Hughes Aircraft Corporation in Los Angeles overseeing the $127-million Telstar 3 satellite program. The old satellites were launched in 1976 and are beginning to wear out. Thomas explained to me that to get the satellite up, "You 'rent' a rocket. Our first one is going off a Delta rocket from NASA, and the second one will probably go off the space shuttle. We also negotiated with a European consortium that was going to launch from near Devil's Island. You get the best deal you can." Because Thomas' people are watching over the construction of the new Telstars, AT&T got a favorable insurance rate.

Thomas is also responsible for the development of many of the terrestrial fiber-optics telephone systems and the proposed transatlantic cable. On 16 November 1983 AT&T was awarded a $250-million contract to design and develop a major portion of it, in a competition decided by the postal, telephone, and telegraph authorities of the Atlantic basin countries. In September 1982, Thomas' group laid and retrieved a section of submarine cable with a repeater, at a depth of 18,000 feet, a thousand miles off Cape Hatteras. As Thomas explained, the fact that it was laid successfully at such an enormous depth, a record for fiber-optics submarine cables, was very important. As he remarked, "Sometimes you have to pull the cable back up—without breaking the fibers." Thomas' division was also responsible for the development that led to the fiber link between New York and Washington. Fiber cables will soon connect New York with Boston, Washington with Richmond, Virginia, and San Francisco with Los Angeles.

Thomas' division is also responsible for the development of TASI —Time Assignment Speech Interpolation—first used in 1959. In any conversation there are pauses; in telephone transmission, pauses can be utilized to transmit other conversations along the same cable. This is something like computer 'time sharing,' in which a computer can simultaneously service several users by taking advantage of pauses in the computer's activities. With digital systems, TASI increases the capacity of the cable by a factor of as much as five, and this ability will be an important feature of the submarine-cable system.

David Gilbert Thomas was born in London on 4 August 1928. His father, Alan, had been an infantry officer in World War I, and his grandfather, a successful banker. There was no scientific or technical background on either side of the Thomas family. At the age of eight, Thomas was sent to boarding school, which he intensely disliked.

"And then the war came in 1940," he recalled, "and there was threat in England of bombing and of invasion. So with my brother and a large part of the school we went to Ottawa, Canada, while my parents remained in London. I think that the Canadian school, which I didn't like very much, was on the verge of bankruptcy but that this infusion of English children kept it going."

Thomas then attended the Putney School, in Vermont, until 1943, "by which time the threat of a German invasion of Britain had passed, and we had the opportunity to go home. My brother and I landed in Lisbon," he said. "Then we flew to London, just two weeks before Leslie Howard was shot down on one of those flights. The Germans knew Leslie Howard was on the flight. They didn't like him so they shot the airplane down."

Thomas had his first contact with physics and chemistry at Harrow. "The physics teacher," Thomas recalled, "was also the chaplain of the school. At the time I leaned towards physics as being a sort of cleaner thing than chemistry. I thought one ought to be able to do it more precisely, but the teacher did not have much time for any additional activities beyond the classroom, since he was involved in tending to the pupils' spiritual well-being. The chemistry people, on the other hand, were more devoted to their science. There were two of them, Lockett and Barrett. They were prepared to let me work in the lab after hours.

The great thing in the English public school, of course, was to be good at cricket and soccer. I wasn't particularly good at games, and I didn't really want to do them. I preferred working in the laboratory. Whereas in Putney one had considerable freedom—unstructured library periods and the like—in Harrow School you had a homework assignment which had forty-five minutes devoted to it and thirty minutes to another subject; everything was structured. I have always felt that I benefited from the freedom I had had at Putney. I had the intelligence to understand that if one didn't understand the Latin terribly well—in which I was totally idiotic—one should spend more time on that, and if one could do the chemistry one should spend less time on that. The mixture of the freedom I had had at Putney helped at Harrow although, at the time, it certainly led to some inner turmoil."

At the age of sixteen, Thomas took the school certificate examination, and for the next two years he was allowed to specialize. "I just did chemistry and math—a little bit of mathematics—and some physics. Because I was not old enough, I was not conscripted into the armed forces, and by the time I graduated I was excused to continue my scientific education. In 1946 I got a scholarship to Oxford, where I took up chemistry completely. I had three undergraduate years where I studied nothing but chemistry and a little technical German, quite literally, without any exams. Then, after three years you had about a week of exams upon which rested your whole career. During those first three years you had a tutorial once a week with your tutor, but one was sort of left on one's own. I think that there were a hell of a lot of things I should have known which, to this day, I don't know, but still, I guess, it was a pretty good education. After that, in order to get your B.A. in chemistry, you had one year to do a thesis—original research—followed by a *viva voce* examination on that work, which was sort of a nonevent. Then, if you had pretty good marks, you could take a 'D. Phil.', as we called it, which occupied another two years and was just research work. At the time Irving Langmuir and David Turnbull were engaged in experiments to make rain by seeding clouds. I did the same sort of thing with liquids other than water. I made clouds in a special apparatus and found the temperatures at which they froze spontaneously.

"I think my D. Phil. was sort of useless, but I took some pleasure in reading the literature and in the feeling that I could, at least, give some sort of phenomenological explanation of what was going on in these rather mysterious changes. During that time I had a Harmsworth Fellowship to Merton College—the great press lord, Lord Harmsworth, funded fellowships—and I hoped after my D. Phil. that I could become an academic scientist. I had become a friend of Professor H.W. Garrod at Merton, who was one of the leading authorities on English literature. He edited *The Oxford Book of English Verse.* He told me about a junior fellowship at Merton and suggested that I apply for it. I did, and I was not chosen. I don't think that it was because of my academic record, but I think that when I had my interview with the fellows of the college it became apparent that I was not really cut out for that life. I am not truly an academic person. I don't have that talent. I don't rejoice in teaching; I rather rejoice in doing things. I just haven't the patience for teaching. I had done well at Oxford. I had gotten First-Class honors and this Harmsworth Fellowship, so I decided to apply to the National Research Council in Ottawa. But I hadn't bothered to prepare the way. I think my application might not have gotten there in time, and they didn't know who I was, so they didn't take me either. But then someone else said, 'There is a fellowship you can have at the Royal Military College in Kingston, Ontario'; and I said, 'Well, okay, I'll go there.' "

Thomas arrived at the Royal Military College, which he said was rather like West Point, in the fall of 1952 and spent the next year and a half there. He felt that he almost had the "duty" of providing a contrasting "academic" atmosphere to the military ambience, which was the norm. "As a sort of academic fellow I had an obligation to walk across the parade grounds with my hands in my pockets and generally create a slovenly appearance. It was quite fun. They had a proper chemistry lab, and they had funded research. I did work on the adsorption of gases onto charcoal. We discovered that a certain plastic could be decomposed in charcoal and acted like a molecular sieve. It would absorb flat molecules but not spherical ones—benzene but not pentane. The commandant used to bring people around and say, 'Do you see that chap over there? He is working on a form of charcoal which will mean that you can put a gas mask into a cigarette box.' It wasn't true but it was, I suppose, a rationale for supporting the kind of work that I was doing, since charcoal is used in gas masks. I published some papers, but by that time I wanted to get out of there."

What happened next was a matter of pure serendipity. During a school vacation he visited a friend and her family in East Orange, New Jersey, who took him to a dinner party. After dinner, he recalls, "People began to sing madrigals. As Professor Garrod used to say, art had been left out of my soul. I don't have much love for madrigals. So I was sitting at the back of this room and wondering what might happen next when somebody turned to me and said, 'What do you do?' I told him I was in chemistry. He said, 'Have you ever visited Bell Laboratories?' and I said that I had never *heard* of Bell Laboratories. It turned out that it was Richard M. Bozorth, one of the world's greatest authorities on magnetism and author of the article on magnetism in the *Encyclopedia Brittanica*. "He didn't seem to know exactly what to make of me," Thomas said, "but the next day he arranged a visit to Bell Labs, in Murray Hill. They somehow or other thought I was looking for a job and had me go to the employment center, where I was kept waiting for a couple of hours. Finally I was shuffled off to meet several people, including Addison White, who was then laboratory director in chemical physics. I recall saying to him, 'Mr. White, I have to tell you in all candor that I am not a mathematical wizard. I have other qualities, but that's one I don't have.' He said, 'Okay,' and they offered me a job. But it was very difficult to get a visa. I applied in Toronto and didn't get it for an entire year."

In 1956, AT&T laid the first transatlantic submarine cable for voice. (The first transatlantic cables had been laid in the last century, but these carried only telegraph messages.) This was a copper-cable system with vacuum-tube repeaters for reamplifying the signals every ten miles or so. Since these cables were hard to pull up and therefore expensive to repair, the repeater tubes had to be made as long-lived as possible. The shortest-lived element of these tubes is the cathode, which during its operation is heated so as to emit electrons. With a new recruit from M.I.T., Thomas was "put off in a little corner of the research department to work on barium-oxide cathodes for these repeaters, to see if we could extend their lives. This was not mainstream research, which in those days was in silicon and germanium, with the transistor just being developed. It was very funny that I worked on that as my first job, since I am now engaged in building the next generation of submarine cable across the Atlantic with fibers." It rapidly became clear, even in 1956, that vacuum tubes were about to be replaced by solid-state devices, so that the whole matter of the cathodes was largely academic. Hence Thomas soon found himself involved in semiconductors, especially in their optical properties.

As discussed previously, in 1939 Russel Ohl had accidentally discovered the photovoltaic effect in silicon. Vagaries in the preparation of the silicon crystal that he was using had caused it to act like an $n$–$p$ junction diode. When Ohl's laboratory bench light shone on the silicon, the light quanta gave up their energies to the electrons in the valence band of the silicon and promoted them up into the conduction band. When Ohl applied an electric potential across the illuminated silicon sample, electrons flowed from the $n$-region across the boundary into the $p$-region. It was this photo-induced current that Ohl measured. All photovoltaic devices function in essentially this way.

But with this picture in mind it becomes clear that, under the appropriate conditions, such a diode can also emit light as well as absorb it. If an electron can be induced to flow from the $n$-region, where electrons are in a majority, to the $p$-region, where the holes are in a majority, it can lose its energy by simply filling up a hole. A hole is simply the absence of an electron, a place in the semiconductor lattice where there is room for an electron. When the electron loses its energy by recombining with a hole, that energy must go somewhere. Indeed, what happens is that electromagnetic radiation is given off. This capturing process is a sort of inverse reaction to the photo-effect reaction, in which the radiation is absorbed to provide the energy to promote the electron into the conduction band. All of this was well understood by the 1950's.

It was also understood that if such a semiconductor diode could be made to emit usable quantities of light—*visible* light—one would have a kind of ideal lamp. In terms of longevity, economical use of power, and size such a lamp would be to conventional lamps what the transistor had become to vacuum tubes. When Thomas began his research, the electromagnetic radiation given off in the materials being used was infrared, invisible radiation. Also the energy generated by the hole–electron recombination did not appear as light of any sort but simply heated the crystal since the crystal absorbed the light quanta. (There are applications, such as in fiber-optics communications, where light-emitting diodes in the infrared are actually used.) The characteristic of a semiconductor that determines what kind of light will be emitted when an electron and a hole recombine is called the energy gap. This is just the energy that separates the conduction and valence bands, represented by the same diagram that appeared in our discussion of the transistor:

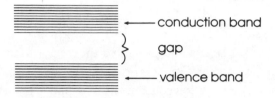

This energy gap is conveniently measured in electron volts. One electron volt is about $10^{-20}$ thermal calories, a very tiny unit of energy. Semiconductors have energy gaps ranging from 2.5 electron volts down to 0.1 electron volts. Green light consists of photons—quanta—with energies of about 2.4 electron volts, while red-light photons have energies of about 1.8 electron volts. In contrast, the infrared photons produced by the light-emitting diodes used in fiber-optics telephone transmission have an energy of about 1 electron volt—somewhat below the visible red.

To produce a device that emits visible light, one should therefore look for semiconductors with band gaps of at least 1.8 electron volts. From his work on cathodes, Thomas knew that zinc oxide had a suitable band gap, and he tried, unsuccessfully, to make a light-emitting diode out of it. He then turned his attention to various alloys of gallium, in particular gallium phosphide. With its band gap of 2.3 electron volts, this semiconductor should potentially be able to emit light over a range of the spectrum from green to red. When Thomas studied the light emitted by gallium phosphide, which had been cooled to liquid-helium temperatures ($-268°C.$), he discovered that the spectrum was incredibly complex. It consisted, in part, of about a hundred sharp green lines corresponding to energies near the 2.3-electron-volt band gap. At this point he enlisted the help of John Hopfield, a young Bell Labs theoretician who, after a distinguished career in solid-state physics, is now doing brain research at Cal Tech. Hopfield had an inspired idea of how these green lines were being produced in gallium phosphide.

As it turns out, gallium phosphide belongs to a class of semiconductors in which light is not emitted simply by an electron directly recombining with a hole: such "indirect-gap" semiconductors produce light through the agency of something else. While the gallium-phosphide samples that Thomas was working with were considered pure by the standards of the day, they contained impurities, in particular, nitrogen. Hopfield realized that these nitrogen atoms quite unexpectedly acted as "traps," capturing electrons in such a way as to give off a certain amount of green light. The fact that the presence of such an impurity led to visible-light emission, in a given region of the spectrum, turned out to be the key to making useful light-emitting diodes. In particular, it was discovered that zinc and oxygen added to gallium phosphide produced a trap that gave off red light. As Thomas put it, "Those discoveries are at the root of making gallium phosphide emit reasonably efficiently in the red and green region of the spectrum. Today if you pick up a modern office telephone made by AT&T you will see it will have red and green lights—light-emitting diodes—that derive from some of the work that John and I did. A lot of the old telephones have incandescent light buttons—a keyset we call them. Before we had LEDs those were tungsten lights, which required a massive amount of wiring—a great thick cable. Now we can use a very thin cord but with an enormous functionality going over it, along with the power to run those lights. That is what solid-state lights enable you to do. If you lift up a Princess telephone at night, you will see a beautiful green glow. Those are our diodes made with isoelectronic nitrogen traps replacing phosphorous in gallium phosphide."

Thomas also explained how AT&T makes these light-emitting diodes. "We grow light-emitting diodes by a process called liquid-phase epitaxy. [The integrated circuits are made by vapor-phase epitaxy, in which the crystal substrate is brought in contact with a gas or by molecular-beam epitaxy, in which the surface is bombarded by a beam of molecules.] You start with a single crystal of gallium phosphide, which is going to serve as the crystal substrate. Then you take some gallium, a liquid metal, and dissolve into it some gallium phosphide and whatever impurities you want, like nitrogen. You heat this up to something like 800° C. Then you tip it so that some of this liquid gallium with its controlled impurities flows onto the surface of the crystal substrate. As it cools it will grow as a single crystal—now doped—of gallium phosphide. You can then grow another layer in the same way but differently doped so that you can get a *p–n* junction. If you are lucky you can get the crystal perfection good, so that recombinations of electrons that *don't* produce radiation are *de minimus*. It is a very delicate business. After you cool the liquid, you can remove it and cut the resulting solid slice into hundreds and hundreds of little pieces which, when you attach wires to them, will glow red or green when hooked up to a current and can go into telephones. As far as I know, that activity is still going on at a fairly good clip. We haven't lost all that business to the Japanese. Our diodes are still being used in telephones."

In 1969 Thomas moved from research to development, as executive director in charge of device development, which included work on the light-emitting diodes. That year he and Hopfield were awarded the prestigious Oliver E. Buckley solid-state physics prize by the American Physical Society. In 1976 he became executive director in charge of transmissions. Much of his time is now spent supervising the development of fiber-optics transmission systems, especially for trunk applications, from one central office to another. The loop systems that were developed in a sister division headed by Norwood Long's boss, Jess Chernak, and which I had seen at Chester, have differences from the trunk applications. For the trunk transmission, the light pulses are produced by gallium-arsenide, solid-state lasers that generate light pulses in the infra-red. The loop-transmission pulses, on the other hand, are generated by diodes that are a complicated alloy of indium, gallium, and arsenide-phosphide. One characteristic of light-emitting diodes is that the infrared radiation is concentrated in a very small region near the boundary of the *n* and *p* regions. A lens is used to focus the light from this spot and beam it into the glass fiber, which has the thickness of a human hair.

Part of Thomas' responsibility is to function as a liaison between Bell Labs, where the development goes on, and the factories, where the manufacturing is done. With computerized, high-tech manufacturing this means something quite different from what it might mean in a classical smokestack industry. Speaking of Bell Labs, Thomas said, "For all intents and purposes, the only product that we have is paper, hardware designs and also software. In the case of software, once you have written a program, if you have gotten it right, you have done a large part of the manufacturing business. That presents AT&T a problem, because how do you earn money on that software? It's a problem that technology forces on us and that we have got to solve. We have solved it in part by licensing the right to use this softwear. It is probably true that 40 percent of the people, the technical people at Bell Laboratories, now work on software. Software is a product in the sense that, for example, a telephone switching machine, these days, is totally useless unless it has a computer program behind it. In that sense Bell Labs manufactures, but not in a hardware sense. You can compare the old and the new kinds of manufacturing at the Cable and Wire Division of AT&T in Atlanta. The part of the factory that makes metal cable is noisy and dirty and has heavy machinery, and big people. In a different section of the same building they make this glass fiber. It's like going into a hospital. It is clean and white and quiet and full of lasers and computers. It is an industry that is just starting up, and it is something to see."

One of the things that Thomas wanted me to see at Holmdel was the "artificial ocean." Housed in a long chamber near the main laboratory building, the "ocean" is filled with saltwater kept at deep-sea temperature and pressure. Fiber cables in it are maintained under those conditions to see how they bear up. Joining us for this visit was Jack Stauffer, head of the Lightwave System Development Department, that wing of Thomas' operation that has to do with fiber-optics communication. Stauffer came directly to Bell Labs after graduating from Purdue University in 1962. He continued his education at Bell, receiving an M.S. under a program in which (in this instance) instructors from New York University taught at Murray Hill. Such classes are common at the Laboratories, and many staff members receive advanced degrees from nearby universities. Stauffer worked on conventional undersea-transmission systems before switching to the fiber system in 1979.

"I was looking at fiber-optics transmission from a developer's point of view," he explained. "We had heard a lot about it from the research area. The appropriate lasers had been demonstrated about seven years earlier. But was fiber communication really more economical than pursuing another generation of the old cables? What would the fibers really cost? Would the devices be reliable, and what was the supporting data for that view? For example, in its early stages, most of the laser testing done in the research area was strictly what we call light bulb testing. Namely, does light actually come out of the laser? That is certainly something that is useful to know in the early development of that technology, but if you are actually going to use a laser in a transmission system you have to know much more. The demands go way beyond simply generating light. For example, you have to make sure that the laser doesn't oscillate at some unwanted frequency. A developer who was thinking of using that device in a system would have a whole string of requirements. So a dialogue begins between research and development, and you go back and forth until you start to converge. When you have competing technologies, as in the cable business, there is a built-in mechanism for keeping people honest. If, for example, you are making unreasonable estimates—perhaps overly optimistic—that a new technology will wipe out the current one, then those people who are the champions of the current technology will make sure that your ledger sheet is kept fair. So there is a kind of cross-check. There are a lot of great-sounding technical ideas that are never developed, because there is no market for the product. We have to worry not only about engineering excellence but also about the needs of the marketplace. With the divestiture, the research people are really looking for their products to get into the marketplace."

Stauffer was speaking while he, and I, and David Thomas were on a tour of the laboratories that Stauffer oversees. One of them had the latest fiber-optics, central-office-circuit apparatus—an entire wall of electronic equipment. One could see the exact place on the fiber where the beam of light stopped and was converted back into electric current. The fiber cable came into the board and the light was converted into a current of electricity, which can run a telephone.

We then went into a lab where the cable that had been lowered 18,000 feet into the ocean is now stored in a tank under the floor. Then we went to the artificial ocean where a similar cable was under high pressure. If all goes according to plan, in 1988 one will be able to call Europe over a cable just like this one. It's immediate predecessor, a classical copper cable of a design first installed in 1976, went under the ocean in July 1983. It can handle 10,000 simultaneous transatlantic calls, a stunning improvement over the first copper transatlantic voice cable—the 1956 version—which could handle only fifty-one calls. The 1988 fiber cable will be the eighth transatlantic cable. It will transmit 560 million bits of information per second, which translates into 40,000 simultaneous telephone calls.

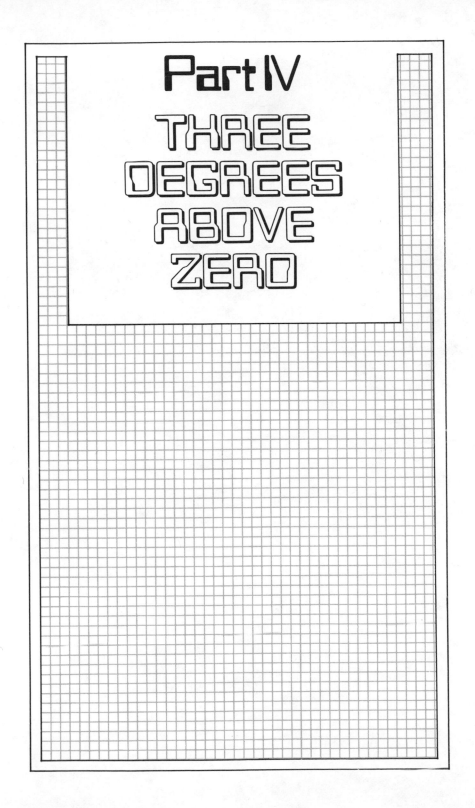

# Part IV

# THREE DEGREES ABOVE ZERO

# CHAPTER 14

# Robert Wilson

EACH FALL, in New York City, the Swedish consul hosts a dinner and reception for Nobel laureates in the area. At the dinner a couple of years ago, Isaac Bashevis Singer, who won the Nobel Prize in literature for 1978, happened to be talking to Robert W. Wilson and Arno A. Penzias, who, along with the Russian physicist Peter L. Kapitza, shared the Nobel Prize in physics that year. Kapitza was awarded the prize for work in various branches of experimental physics; Penzias and Wilson won it for their joint discovery, published in 1965, of what has become known as cosmic black-body radiation. This discovery—as it is now interpreted—found that in every cubic centimeter of the universe there are, on the average, something like 400 very low-energy photons, or light quanta, that originated in the so-called Big Bang. According to present ideas, the universe began in this cosmic explosion, which occurred some 12 to 15 billion years ago. Since then, the universe has been expanding and cooling, and now has an average temperature of some 3° above absolute zero. This is the temperature of the "fossil" photons that Penzias and Wilson discovered. Singer wanted to know if it was possible to listen to these photons and so, in effect, to hear the residual noise of the Big Bang.

The radio antenna on which the discovery was made is located on a wooded promontory just above the Crawford Hill, New Jersey, facility of Bell Labs. The antenna, which looks like a large horn, is in apparently reasonably good repair but is not being used. When I visited there, Wilson, a soft-spoken Texan, told me, "Singer asked me again, on two or three occasions, if he could hear the hiss from the Big Bang. About a year ago, when we were about to reactivate the antenna, I made a cassette. You can hook the antenna to an audio amplifier and listen to the signal. We did this when we were doing the original experiments in 1964, so that we could listen for radar. Radar makes an audio tone that ranges from a few hundred to about a thousand pulses a second, and we wanted to make sure that we were not picking up radar, which would have been, for us, unwanted background noise. It turned out, actually, that, on the next hill over, there was one of the radars that was then associated with a Nike surface-to-air missile. But they were cooperative about telling us when they were running. Anyway, eventually I made the cassette for him. I made a couple of copies and asked our publicity people if they wanted to hand them out to people. But they didn't know what to do with them, so they sent them back to me. Would you like to hear it?"

I wanted to very much, so Wilson found one of the copies in his office and we put it into my tape recorder. Wilson briefly describes, over a gently hissing background, how the recording was made. When his commentary is finished, one hears only the hiss—something like the flowing of the sea. About a tenth of the noise can be attributed to photons that are as old as the universe itself, the rest, to noise from the receiver used to detect them.

Radio astronomy, as the name suggests, is the study and detection of radio waves from astronomical sources. Like all waves, they can be characterized by a wavelength—the distance between two adjacent places on the wave where it is at the maximum of its oscillation. A visible lightwave is typically half a millionth of a meter long. AM radio waves can be six hundred meters long. FM waves are about three meters long, and microwaves, characteristic of both radar and radio astronomy, are a few centimeters. These are signals, then, that cannot be seen in any direct optical sense. Until the advent of radio astronomy many of the sources of these signals were completely invisible.

Radio astronomy has been a curiously serendipitous science. One celebrated example was the discovery, in 1968, by Jocelyn Bell and Anthony Hewish, of Cambridge University, of "pulsars"—rapidly pulsing radio sources attributed to spinning neutron stars that are the remnants of supernova explosions. In fact, the creation of the entire field was serendipitous. Karl G. Jansky, its founder, had come to work at the Bell Telephone Laboratories in Holmdel, New Jersey, in 1928, when he was twenty-two. Overseas shortwave-radio telephone service had been inaugurated by AT&T a year or so earlier, and Jansky's job was to record and measure shortwave radio static. Short waves meant in this case wavelengths of a meter and a half, a few million times longer than visible light. Jansky used a large radio antenna mounted on a turntable that rotated three times an hour. Because the antenna was directional, he could tell from which direction the static originated. A chart recorder made a tracing of the strength of the arriving signals, and Jansky also listened to them on a shortwave receiver to try to determine the character of the noise. After four years, he was confident enough of his results to publish them as "Directional Studies of Atmospherics at High Frequencies" in the *Proceedings of the Institute of Radio Engineers.* The noise, he reported, came from three major sources: nearby thunderstorms, distant thunderstorms, and an unidentifiable source, which provided a continuous hiss. He noted that this hiss varied in intensity throughout the day, reaching its maximum four minutes earlier each day. A.M. Skellett, a Ph.D. astronomy student from Princeton working at the Bell Labs, explained to Jansky that this variation is what would be expected if fixed stars were the source of the hiss. The wave cycle that Jansky had observed lasted 23 hours, 56 minutes and, 4.091 seconds—the length of a sidereal day. The difference between a sidereal day and the twenty-four-hour solar day is due to the earth's moving in an orbit around the sun. If one calls sidereal noon the time at which a certain star is directly overhead, this time, it turns out, is four minutes earlier per day than the time at which the *sun* is directly overhead, since the apparent position of the sun shifts a little each day. Jansky's effect was maximized when the stars in question were directly overhead. In 1933, Jansky published, in the same journal, "Electrical Disturbances Apparently of Extraterrestrial Origin" and, the next year, again in the same journal, "A Note on the Source of Interstellar Interference." He had been able to show that most of the noise came from the center of the Milky Way, our own galaxy.

While these papers constituted the very foundation of radio astronomy, they were almost completely ignored at the time. One reason may have been that Jansky did not publish them in an astronomical journal. More important, by presenting his results in units that were unfamiliar to astronomers, he concealed the potentially exciting fact that the processes producing these radio waves were extremely energetic. We now know that they are caused by highly energetic electrons that, when they get trapped in magnetic fields, spiral around the field lines and emit synchrotron radiation—one of many sources of radio waves from outer space. Indeed, the next work in radio astronomy was done in 1941 by Grote Reber, an enthusiastic radio amateur who built, in the garden of his house in Wheaton, Illinois, a thirty-foot paraboloidal bowl antenna. (This is now one of the most familiar shapes of radio-telescope antennas; Reber's original antenna is preserved, as a museum piece, at the entrance to the United States National Radio Observatory at Green Bank, West Virginia, facing a full-size copy of Jansky's original antenna.) Using his antenna, Reber was able to confirm Jansky's results and to make the first radio maps of the sky. He also tried to detect radio waves from the sun but was unsuccessful because the sun was relatively quiescent and was not emitting a detectable signal. Considering that he was not a professional scientist, this work was altogether remarkable.

During World War II, Jansky's and Reber's work finally surfaced, because the cosmic hiss set a practical limit to the sensitivity of radar detectors. In *The Story of Jodrell Bank,* the distinguished British radio astronomer Sir Bernard Lovell described his experience.

Reber's work was published in an American scientific journal and his observations, together with those of Jansky, constituted almost our total knowledge of the radio waves from space when the war ended. At that time I knew about these observations in a circuitous manner and had no conception that their further pursuit was to occupy so much of my post-war career. I remember precisely the occasion on which I first heard about the existence of this cosmic static. We were engaged in a desperate attempt to increase the sensitivity of some of our airborne radars in order to detect enemy submarines and other land targets of greater range. There were three avenues open to us: increase the transmitter power, increase the size of the aerial, or improve the sensitivity of the receiver. The first was at the limit of current techniques and, in the case of the second, we had already caused consternation amongst the aircraft designers by our demands for large aerials. The improvement of receiver sensitivity seemed the easiest and most obvious course. Alas! This easy optimism was punctured by a member of my group who respectfully informed us about the existence of cosmic static which must inevitably set a limit to the receiver sensitivity which could be realized in practice, and in due course he produced copies of the papers by Jansky and Reber.

After his paper of 1934, Jansky seems to have put aside radio astronomy, as did Bell Labs, until well after the war. Bell had become heavily involved during the war in radar research and, in particular, with the problem of transmitting and receiving centimeter-wavelength radio transmissions. In 1942, the distinguished Bell radio engineer Harald T. Friis, in collaboration with A.C. Beck, designed the horn-reflector antenna. (Friis had been Jansky's group leader and had worked with Jansky in designing the antenna that Jansky used.) The horn-reflector antenna is a rectangular cone with a parabolic reflector at the smaller end or base. At the wider end, or mouth, the microwave signals enter. It is in common use today as the microwave radio relay that carries most of the country's long-distance telephone and television signals. Penzias and Wilson's discovery of cosmic blackbody radiation was made with such an antenna.

The unlikely series of events that led to that discovery included the invention of the communications satellite. The first suggestion of a communications satellite—a relay station that hovers over a fixed point 22,000 miles above the earth—was made in 1945 by Arthur C. Clarke. Clarke was a flight lieutenant in the Royal Air Force when he thought up the idea, which he described in a paper published in the British journal, *Wireless World.* Later he ruefully described his idea in an essay entitled "A Short Pre-History of Comsats; or, How I Lost a Billion Dollars in My Spare Time," a reference to his failure to patent it, although it is not clear that it could have been patented. The idea was resuscitated by the noted Bell engineer and science-fiction writer, John R. Pierce, in 1954, for an address to a meeting of the Institute of Radio Engineers in Princeton. Pierce became the guiding force behind the realization of Clarke's fantasy. In putting together the technical design, he was able to take advantage of NASA's program for launching a giant plastic balloon, *Echo,* to measure the density of the atmosphere at high altitudes. Pierce proposed bouncing radio signals off *Echo,* and in 1960 radio signals were transmitted between New Jersey and California using the balloon. In 1960 A Bell Labs engineer named A.B. Crawford built a twenty-foot horn-reflector antenna on Crawford Hill expressly to receive the weak signals returning to the earth from *Echo.* Four years later, Penzias and Wilson used it to detect the cosmic photons.

Robert Wilson was born on 10 January 1936 in Houston. His father, Ralph, had been raised on a farm in north Texas and was a chemical engineer for a company that serviced oil wells. As Wilson recalls, "My father was sort of managing an operation in which they looked to see what was coming up with the cuttings while a well was being drilled. They looked for evidence that the drillers were passing through an interesting formation. When I was a kid I used to go around with him to the oil fields, and sometimes we would go into the shop on Saturday mornings and I would tinker around. My mother and father had been raised on small subsistence farms in the Dallas–Fort Worth area, but both sets of grandparents had the definite idea that their children should be educated—that that was the way forward— so both my mother and father went to college. My father fixed radios around the house, and when I was very young I learned some electronics from him, and then I started reading some things about electronics. By the time I was in high school I fixed radio sets for people, and later, when TV was around, I fixed their television sets. I could take one and mess around with it, analyzing its misbehavior until I found the bad part, and then replace it."

Wilson was educated in the Houston public school system. He enjoyed high school science and mathematics but was not an outstanding student. "I graduated a third down from the top of my class—in the 67th percentile. Then, in 1953, I went to Rice, where I started making all A's in physics and math. I am told that when I was quite young I used to go around saying that I was going to the Rice Institute, where my father had gone. I actually went to Rice to become an electrical engineer, but early in my freshman year I switched to physics. I didn't like the electrical engineering curriculum, which dealt with power engineering and things like that, which didn't seem to me to be very forward-looking. In junior high school there was a wood-shop teacher whom I used to talk to about electronics and radio, rather than doing wood shop. He was interested in building radios. When I went to Rice I lived at home, only a few miles away from the campus, so I didn't go and talk with the professors much. My freshman physics professor, Harold Rorschach, who was fairly new at the time—he is still there—said later that I made quite an impression on him, although I don't remember spending much time talking to him. Since I had straight A's in all my science courses, I guess I got decent recommendations to graduate schools, and I was accepted at both M.I.T. and Caltech."

In 1957 Wilson went to Caltech, with no clear idea of what kind of physics he wanted to specialize in. He considered working in low-temperature experimental physics, a subject on which he had done his senior thesis at Rice, but that laboratory at Caltech did not have room for him, so he spent the first year and a half at Caltech taking basic graduate courses. "I had not done," he noted, "what I've seen many other students do—take graduate courses as an undergraduate. When I got to Caltech I took, for example, a quantum mechanics course with Murray Gell-Mann [the inventor of the quark]. I missed H.P. Robertson's course on general relativity somehow. I have always regretted that, because it was the last chance to have taken it." Robertson was a great American cosmologist who died in 1963. Ironically the cosmology course Wilson did take was given by British astrophysicist Fred Hoyle, one of the principal architects of steady-state cosmology. This theory argued that the universe had no beginning and that it was continually evolving in a steady state. Wilson and Penzias made this theory essentially untenable when they provided the decisive evidence that the present universe began at a finite time in a cosmic explosion.

The graduate school at Caltech has traditionally admitted each year about twenty extremely brilliant physics students, and the atmosphere is rather competitive. "I think I liked a certain amount of competitiveness just for its own sake," Wilson recalls. "I remember that I had a couple of friends there who were more theoretically inclined than I was, and I can remember a few triumphs when I beat them in some quantum-mechanics tests. Partly this was because I had, I think, a better practical insight into the problems than they did. I don't think I understood the theory as well, but I was able to think, for example, of a pendulum as a real-world object as well as a quantum-mechanical object. For the first year I lived in a place called the Athenaeum. That's the faculty club, but they rent a few rooms out to students. There was a British astronomer named David Dewhirst there—he was some sort of visiting fellow—and I told him that I was looking around for a project to do at the end of my first year. It was expected that at about that time one would begin thinking in terms of a thesis field. He told me about a radio astronomer named John Bolton, who had come to Caltech from Australia to set up a new group. Dewhirst sent me over to see him and that, from the beginning, seemed like a good match." In 1958, after his first year at Caltech, he married Elizabeth Sawin who is also from Houston. In 1960 their first child, Philip, was born. They have two other children—Suzanne born in 1963 and Randall in 1967.

In Sydney, Bolton had used a radio telescope to detect signals coming from what he correctly identified as a remnant of the supernova explosion of A.D. 1054, which produced the Crab Nebula. Bolton had in mind to build an interferometer—two radio telescopes working conjointly—in the Owens Valley, some 250 miles north of Los Angeles. "The Owens Valley is fairly dry, and Los Angeles owns the water supply," Wilson told me. "They own a lot of land out there, so Caltech was able to get a big piece of it with the assurance that there would be no development around it. It was a good place to put a radio observatory. When I got there, the heavy construction had been done, and one of the antennas was beginning to operate, although it had only the first approximation of a receiver on it. Originally, the idea had been to use the interferometer to observe the microwave radiation from interstellar hydrogen. That was a very good idea, but the trouble was that there was a slip in the development of things. To pass the time, John and I did a survey of the Milky Way. We made a picture of its radio radiation at a wavelength of thirty-one centimeters by doing a series of drift observations. We would set the antenna to the west of the Milky Way and let the galaxy drift by in the sky as the earth rotated. This technique allowed us to separate terrestrial sources, which remained constant, from celestial ones. At thirty centimeters there are two important sources of radio waves from the Milky Way: the synchroton radiation, which Jansky had observed, and thermal sources.

We were able to make a radio map that matched a map made at a longer wavelength by a group in Australia. That, as it turned out, became my thesis project. Frankly, I don't think much ever came out of the thesis scientifically, although it was a very good learning experience, and I did get a chance to meet most of the world's radio astronomers, who would come through Caltech to visit."

Wilson finished his thesis in the spring of 1962 and remained at Caltech for a year as a postdoctoral fellow. Unlike most of his contemporaries, he never had any intention of going into academic life. "From childhood on, most of my experience had been with industrial people, not academic people," he said. "I didn't have—and still don't have—the feeling that I compare to someone like a Gell-Mann or Richard Feynman. I don't have that kind of theoretical insight. I had seen people get in over their heads in academic research. I get along very well with experimental things, and that is what I wanted to do. Anyway, when it came time to look for a job, the best of possibilities happened. Bell Labs was looking for somebody to do radio astronomy. By 1962 I had talked to Warren Danielson, who was doing military research for Bell at Whippany at that time. He was a Caltech graduate and was the Bell Labs recruiter assigned to Caltech. Also, Bill Jakes from Crawford Hill had been through. He told us about the new horn reflector. He was visiting radio astronomy groups to try to find out what sort of work Bell could do with this instrument. If they were going to be doing radio research and had a large antenna, they figured they ought to do some radio astronomy to remain in the field a little bit. The interviews were fairly informal. They would show up and just come around and talk to people. When I decided not to continue as a postdoc I called Warren Danielson and said, 'I am interested in coming for an interview,' and he said, 'Fine, when can you come?' "

In the spring of 1963 Wilson came to Crawford Hill, where Arno Penzias had been working for a year. "When I came into the radio research group at Crawford Hill it was clear that Arno and I were going to work together," Wilson told me. "I suppose we might have done separate things, but that didn't make much sense. The instrument we were going to use was clearly the new horn reflector. The question was what sort of science we were going to do with it. We discussed that with our group leader, Rudy Kompfner, but the decision as to what to do was ours. After all, we knew more about radio astronomy than any one else around. The people here had put in a lot of effort making the horn for the *Echo* project; they felt that it had something to offer to astronomy, and they wanted to see the instrument used that way. It's nice that that sort of thing happens at the Labs. Rudy had the vision to see that he wanted to have some radio astronomers around, because our discipline was close enough to satellite communication to be relevant to what others at Bell Labs were trying to do. By the way, I had taken my degree at Caltech from the physics department, not the astronomy department, although I had taken many of the graduate courses in astronomy. Caltech is pretty good about having interdisciplinary people. There were, for example, geologists doing astronomy. However, I actually found that the interdisciplinary cooperation was much better at Bell Labs. At Caltech our group had some discussions with electrical engineers, but in a fairly formal way; most of the time we never saw them. One of the things that has made Bell Labs such a good place to be is that if someone comes up with a new idea—with a new way of doing something—and if you have a new application for it—he is delighted to cooperate. That is encouraged. People get a lot of credit for it, so they're happy to do it."

The horn used to communicate with the *Echo* balloon had been left in place to use with Telstar, the Bell-designed, first actively powered communications satellite, which was launched in July 1962. *Echo* had been simply a passive reflector of signals—a kind of mirror. Telstar relayed both speech and television signals to Europe and demonstrated the feasibility of long-distance communication. "The horn was available in case the Europeans did not get their earth station going, but they did get it going. So the group was willing to let Arno and me dismantle the communications receiver and make a radio telescope out of the thing. That took us about a year. One of Arno's first activities was to get a cab put in so that we would have a little more room for equipment."

In the summer of 1963 Penzias constructed what is known to radio astronomers as a cold load, a device that provides a precise amount of low-level radio noise. Any object can be a source of radio noise, because all objects consist, in part, of electrons, which move around in thermal motion and inevitably emit electromagnetic waves. In a container with opaque walls—a "blackbody cavity"—the walls will emit electromagnetic waves, or radio noise, that will be trapped in the box. Remarkably, the intensity of this noise depends not on what the walls are made of, but only on their temperature. The higher the temperature, the more intense the noise. One can select a given wavelength of blackbody radiation and study its intensity at that wavelength. If one does this for all wavelengths and plots them on a graph, a characteristic curve results (see below). Its shape depends on the *temperature* of the walls, and essentially nothing else. The discovery of this curve, around 1900, led the great German physicist Max Planck to introduce the quantum. This curve cannot be explained by classical physics, as Planck found out after trying for well over a decade to do so.

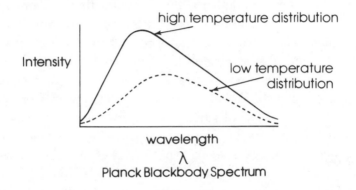

Planck Blackbody Spectrum

Now, radio astronomers find it convenient to describe the intensity of the noise received on a radio antenna in terms of temperature. In doing this they imagine that their telescope is placed inside an imaginary box whose walls are giving off the same noise profile as the one that they are actually observing. It is a convenient way to normalize the results, and in the case of cosmic radiation, it is more than simply convenient, since the universe is, from this point of view, an immense box with photons trapped inside it. To use this idea in practice, Wilson and Penzias intended to provide the horn with a test case. They wanted to prove that the horn would introduce no noise of its own, so they made their measurements at a wavelength at which no celestial radiation was expected. By studying what was actually measured, they would be able to calibrate their telescope and could then go on to measure signals from the Milky Way at longer wavelengths. As things turned out, they never got to this part of their program.

"There was a maser already in place that the Telstar people had been using," said Wilson. "But they had been using the antenna as a communications receiver, and it had been connected to some apparatus that made things very unstable. The total noise was just sort of wandering up and down continuously. We threw most of that stuff out, and I made a stable amplification system to replace it. We put in a chart recorder to register the signals. Before I got here, Arno had already started to build the cold load, which was a helium-cooled source. When I got here, I made a good switch to connect the receiver alternately to the antenna and this reference-noise source. I had had a lot of experience making receivers, while Arno's main experience was with masers. He understood how to make them work. And he could talk to the people at Bell who had designed the maser for the horn in the first place. Actually, Arno had had a good deal to do with recruiting me. We met first when I came to Crawford Hill for my interview, and shortly afterward, at a meeting of the American Astronomical Society, we talked for several days. He realized that we had complementary skills and experience. During 1963 we put more and more pieces together, and in 1964 we decided to try everything out by measuring radio signals from Cass A. [Cassiopeia A is the brightest radio source in Cassiopeia; it subtends about five minutes of arc when measured from the earth.] Cass A is a supernova remnant," Wilson continued, "and we intended to write a definitive paper on the intensity of seven-centimeter radiation from it. We picked that wavelength because that was what the maser we had in place detected. The measurement we finally made is still about the most accurate one ever done. We also wanted to measure the intensity of the radio noise from the halo of the Milky Way and Arno and I both wanted to redo our theses. We had a list of projects that we were going to do—nothing, we thought, that was going to get a tremendous amount of attention from the world."

From the outset, it was clear that something was terribly wrong. As Wilson put it, "The results didn't fit together too well. The antenna temperature was too high"—that is, there was too much static. In a certain sense, three-degree cosmic radiation had already been discovered. From the time the Bell Labs engineers began working with the horn for *Echo,* they realized that it was too hot, that is, it put out a little more noise than expected when pointed at the empty sky. One of them, E.A. Ohm, in an article in the *Bell System Technical*

*Journal* in 1961, said that the excess in the noise output over what he expected corresponded to roughly three degrees. In other words, it responded as if it were in a box filled with three-degree radiation. At that time, the instrument was being used not for radio astronomy but for communications, and because Ohm's system did not have the reference-noise source, the accuracy was not high enough to establish the result—the experimental error was itself of the order of three degrees—so nothing was done about this odd fact. Since it did not interfere with the communications work it was more or less ignored. But Wilson and Penzias could not ignore it. If they could not understand all the sources of noise in the antenna, they simply could not proceed with their program.

As Wilson said, "If we were missing three degrees at seven centimeters, how were we ever going to be able to see a one-degree halo at twenty-one centimeters—one of the next things we wanted to do. We are inside the halo of the galaxy," Wilson continued, "and when we look out through it, it adds a small amount of noise—one degree—at twenty-one centimeters. The only way we could measure that was to measure the total noise received by the antenna and then subtract the terrestrial sources. We expected to see nothing from the halo at seven centimeters, and we were actually doing the experiment at that wavelength to verify that this was true when we discovered the unexpected noise. Later on we actually built a twenty-one-centimeter receiver. The *Echo* people had had a very practical thing to get done. The big emphasis was on that, and we had the fortune to come along at a more relaxed time. Also, our effect was more definite. We had a liquid-helium-cooled noise source, which we expected to be at about 5 degrees, and the antenna was putting out more noise than *it* was. The antenna was at about 7 degrees, whereas it should have been at only about 3.3 degrees; 2.3 degrees coming from noise in the atmosphere, and about a degree from the radiation from the walls of the antenna. Radiation from the ground should have contributed almost nothing. That would have meant that the antenna should have been about 2 degrees colder than the load; but instead it was 2 degrees hotter. There had been a tradition around here—the work of a man named D.C. Hogg—of understanding microwave propagation through the atmosphere. You can measure that directly with the horn by pointing it straight up and then pointing it 10 degrees above the horizon to measure the difference. That sort of thing had been done, so we knew how much noise to expect from the atmosphere."

For a while, Wilson and Penzias continued to measure the radio signals from Cassiopeia A, hoping that the buzzing in their antenna would somehow go away. It didn't. As Wilson put it, "We decided that we had to face up to it, and so what we started doing was to really go to work on the antenna." One of their first discoveries was that a pair of pigeons were nesting in the antenna horn, depositing what Penzias once referred to as "white dielectric material." The pigeons were sent to the Bell Laboratory site at Whippanny, New Jersey, but flew back to the horn. Eventually, they were moved out permanently. The antenna horn had been assembled with aluminum rivets, and Wilson and Penzias worried that this might have changed its expected characteristics. They sealed the joints with an aluminum tape using an electrically conductive glue. None of this had much effect on the noise. At one time, they thought that some of the noise might be coming from New York City, which is less than fifty miles from Crawford Hill. Wilson said, "Here we were on a hill that overlooks New York City, so how could we claim that we were making very sensitive radio-astronomy measurements with all that manmade stuff around? We turned the antenna in the direction of New York to see how bright it was at our wavelength. It was reasonable—a little hotter than thermal, but not much. We even considered the possibility that we were detecting radiation from the 1962 high-altitude nuclear explosion that filled the Van Allen belts with charged particles. But that source would have diminished with time, while, in fact, our effect remained constant."

By this time, nearly a year had passed since Wilson and Penzias began working with the radio telescope. The noise had continued unabated during one entire revolution of the earth around the sun— during all four seasons, night and day. Then, in January 1965, Penzias made a phone call to a friend at M.I.T., which is described by Nobel physicist Steven Weinberg in *The First Three Minutes*.

The meaning of the mysterious microwave noise began to be clarified through the operation of the "invisible college" of astrophysicists. Penzias happened to telephone a fellow radio astronomer, Bernard Burke of

M.I.T., about other matters. Burke had just heard from yet another colleague, Ken Turner of the Carnegie Institution, of a talk that Turner had in turn heard at Johns Hopkins, given by a young theorist from Princeton, P.J.E. Peebles. In this talk Peebles argued that there ought to be a background of radio noise left over from the early universe with a present equivalent temperature of roughly 10°K. [In the absolute temperature scale, absolute zero corresponds to $-273.15$°C. This scale is usually called the Kelvin scale, after the nineteenth-century British physicist Lord Kelvin]. Burke already knew that Penzias was measuring radio noises with the Bell Laboratories horn antenna, so he took the occasion of the telephone conversation to ask how the measurements were going. Penzias said that the measurements were going fine, but that there was something about the results that he didn't understand. Burke suggested to Penzias that the physicists at Princeton might have some interesting ideas on what it was that his antenna was receiving.

At this point, the scene shifts to Princeton. Robert Dicke, who is now a senior professor of physics at Princeton, had worked on radar during World War II. He has a reputation as one of the most imaginative physicists in the business. After the war he put in a stint as a staff member at the radiation laboratory at M.I.T., where he had been during the war. In 1946 he led a radio-physics group there that, while measuring the radiation from the earth's atmosphere, was able to set an upper limit on just the kind of noise that Wilson and Penzias were receiving. They found that it could not correspond to a temperature greater than 20°K. Since they had no particular cosmology in mind, they did not have a theoretical context in which to put this observation. Indeed, as Weinberg reports, by 1965 Dicke had forgotten that he had done this experiment and that he had found this upper limit. Soon after Dicke's experiment, however, a theoretical context was developed by George Gamow and his collaborators, but it had no influence on subsequent events, since neither Dicke nor Wilson and Penzias were aware that it existed. In 1964 Dicke began thinking about cosmology, this time in terms of an oscillating model, in which the universe undergoes alternate phases of expansion and contraction. At present, the universe is expanding, according to this idea, but it may once again, in the far future, start to contract, and another Big Bang could occur. Dicke was led to speculate that the last Big Bang might have left traces of cosmological radiation. He suggested that Peebles try to calculate its temperature, and Peebles had estimated that it should be something like 10° K. This first calculation was an overestimate—it is now known to be about 3°K.—but Peebles and others soon refined these early calculations. Dicke had two other graduate students, P.G. Roll and D.T. Wilkinson, and he suggested that they construct a small, low-noise, radio antenna on the roof of Palmer Laboratory at Princeton, some forty miles away from Crawford Hill, to search for the very radio noise that Wilson and Penzias had been studying for nearly a year. Before Dicke, Roll, and Wilkinson could complete their observations, Dicke received an entirely unexpected phone call from Penzias.

"By that time," Wilson recalled, "we knew that the effect did not change with the temperature of the atmosphere during a complete year. We knew that it was not connected to the phases of the moon. We had looked over a sizable fraction of the sky and always had this effect. We weren't hiding it, but I don't remember talking much about it to anybody. Obviously, Arno was talking to people when he called Bernie Burke. Bernie said we should get in touch with the Princeton group, although at that point neither of us understood why. Anyway, Arno called up Dicke and Dicke said, 'That sounds very interesting,' and shortly afterward, the Princeton group came over to Crawford Hill for a visit—all four of them. We showed them the horn and the measurements we had been making—what we had been seeing. Then they came down to the conference room and told us the cosmology."

This meeting sounds like an extraordinary occasion in the history of science, but Wilson's feelings at the time do not suggest that. "Although we were pleased to have *some* sort of answer, both of us at first felt a little distant from the cosmology. I had taken my cosmology from Hoyle at Caltech, and I very much liked the steady-state universe. Philosophically, I still sort of like it. I think Arno and I both felt that it was nice to have one explanation but that there may well have been others."

In retrospect, it is easy to see the relevance of Wilson and Penzias' discovery to the Big Bang cosmology. But, at the time, without a distinct theoretical bias, it was not evident that the results were connected. In particular, the Big Bang cosmology predicted not only that there should be cosmic photons but also that their spectral distribution (see the curve above) should have the blackbody shape. Wilson and Penzias had measured this curve at one wavelength—seven centimeters —and from that observation it was not even certain that their result lay on such a curve at all. In *Gravitation and Cosmology* (1972) Weinberg presented a list of every experiment done, at various wavelengths, on the cosmic spectrum. Measurements had been performed by over twenty different sets of observers at fifteen different wavelengths, ranging from 73.5 centimeters down to .002 centimeters. Below 3 centimeters, the earth's atmosphere interferes with cosmic radiation, so some of these observations are made from mountains and balloons. The curve that results by plotting the experimental points from all wavelengths fits a blackbody spectral curve, with a temperature of about 3 degrees, extremely well. Recently, some small deviations have turned up, one of which reflects the fact that our entire galaxy is moving like a great ship through this sea of cosmic photons. This shows up in the data as a Doppler shift of the photons' wavelengths in certain preferred directions in the sky—the direction of galactic motion. The other deviations may be experimental error or may reflect something subtle about the cosmological description.

Since Wilson and Penzias did not know any of this in 1965, they wrote a very low-key article, "A Measurement of Excess Antenna Temperature at 4,080 Mc/s," for the July 1965 *Astrophysical Journal.* (Their telescope was tuned to radiation of 4,080 million cycles per second in frequency, or 7.35 centimeters.) Almost the only mention of the cosmology was this laconic reference: "A possible explanation for the observed excess noise temperature is the one given by Dicke, Peebles, Roll and Wilkinson in a companion letter in this issue." "I guess we wrote a very understated article," Wilson told me. "Some of the steady-state people were pleased by the way we had gone about things. We felt that, at least until they had had a chance to think about our results, we shouldn't go out on a theoretical limb that we couldn't support. For me, the last nail in the coffin of the steady-state theory wasn't driven in for quite a while—not until the blackbody curve was really verified. That's the point when I stopped worrying about it."

Another sidelight to this story is worth discussing. In the late 1940's, while teaching at George Washington University, the Russian-born physicist George Gamow began to explore the Big Bang model of cosmology with two young colleagues, Ralph Alpher and Robert Herman. Their early model differs in many essential respects from the present standard cosmology, but the spirit is there. In 1948 Alpher and Herman made the specific prediction that there should be a background cosmic radiation with an average temperature of 5° K., reiterating this conjecture in 1953 in collaboration with J.W. Follin, Jr. During this period, Alpher and Herman asked several groups of radio astronomers whether it was possible to measure this radiation. They were told that it was not. Wilson now believes that the measurement could have been done with World War II receivers, provided that the antenna and the cold load were correctly connected. In any event, by the time the Princeton and Bell Labs groups got around to writing up and interpreting their discoveries, in 1965, the earlier work had been all but forgotten; indeed, there is no reference to it in the two 1965 papers.

There is another ironic twist to this story. In 1964 two Russian scientists, A. G. Doroshkevich and I. D. Novikov, published a paper entitled "Mean Density of Radiation in the Metagalaxy and Certain Problems in Relativistic Cosmology," which was translated into English but largely ignored. This paper suggested detecting Planck distribution of the cosmic radiation with a microwave receiver. It said that the ideal detector for this would be the horn at Bell Labs and refers to Ohm's paper, which the Russian authors misread. They somehow came to the incorrect conclusion that Ohm's result ruled out Gamow's prediction of cosmic radiation. Meanwhile, totally unaware of both papers, Wilson and Penzias were observing the very radiation that the Russian paper said had been ruled out.

In *The First Three Minutes*, Weinberg makes an important point about the significance of the Wilson and Penzias discovery. Prior to 1965 there was so little data of any apparent relevance to cosmology that, as a discipline, it seemed to have little connection to physics. It was thus possible to entertain both the steady-state-universe and the Big Bang cosmologies, which completely contradicted each other. Each was more or less pure speculation. When a field is in such a state, it is difficult for many scientists to take it entirely seriously. For theorists, speculations waste only time—not money. But for an experimental physicist or astronomer they might involve a commitment of hundreds of thousands of dollars in equipment and years of work. Their reluctance to chase down what may well be a fantasy is quite understandable. Weinberg sees another lesson to be learned from this story—the reluctance of theorists to attach enough significance to their own work. "Our mistake," he says, "is not that we take our theories too seriously, but that we do not take them seriously enough. It is always hard to realize that these numbers and equations have something to do with the real world. Even worse there often seems to be a general agreement that certain phenomena are just not fit subjects for respectable theoretical and experimental effort. Gamow, Alpher, and Herman deserve tremendous credit above all for being willing to take the early universe seriously, for working out what known physical laws have to say about the first three minutes. . . . The most important thing accomplished by the ultimate discovery of the 3° K. radiation background in 1965 was to force us all to take seriously the idea that there *was* an early universe."

Cosmology today is one of the most active branches of both physics and astronomy. Because of its high temperatures, the early universe was a kind of ideal laboratory in which both the familiar elementary particles, such as the neutron, proton, the electron and positron, the various neutrinos, and the light quanta—the photons—and the unfamiliar ones, such as the quarks, played a role. The earliest time that theorists now discuss is the Planck time, $10^{-43}$ seconds after the Big Bang. There is considerable uncertainty as to when the Big Bang itself took place, but a reasonable estimate places it about 12 to 15 billion years ago. Most scientists agree that it is probably meaningless to discuss space and time prior to the Big Bang. In some sense, space and time were created by the Big Bang, and it is likely that the laws of physics, as we know them, may have to be altered before they can be applied to the period prior to the Planck time. The quantum mechanics of gravity has not been fully worked out, and it may require entirely new ideas. However, the first instant after the explosion was also an epoch when the universe was expanding and cooling extremely rapidly.

At about $10^{-35}$ seconds the original chaos of the explosion began to smooth itself out. When the temperature had dropped to about 100 billion degrees K., after about $10^{-2}$ seconds, the particles that were present were in thermal equilibrium. They were in a very dense gas, consisting mostly of electrons, positrons, neutrinos, and photons. Scat-

tered throughout this gas were also a small number—one in a billion
—of neutrons and protons and their antiparticles. It was from these
particles that the light nuclei, such as helium and deuterium, were
eventually synthesized. (Elements heavier than iron did not appear
until billions of years later, after stars had been formed, since they arise
from the explosions of supernovas.) The temperatures were much too
high for atoms or atomic nuclei to exist. Any nucleus that formed was
ripped apart by a collision with X rays—very energetic light quanta.
Only after about three minutes, when the temperature had dropped to
a billion degrees K., could atomic nuclei, once formed, stick together.
Another 700,000 years would pass before the temperature had fallen
enough so that atoms with electrons bound to nuclei could be formed.
This is an important cosmological date, because before that time, the
primordial photons were trapped by collisions with free electrons. After
the electrons were attached to nuclei, the universe became transparent
to radiation. This newly free gas of radiation continued to cool as the
universe expanded, and it is this cooled radiation that Penzias and
Wilson discovered, as "static," in their antenna on Crawford Hill. This
brief scenario, given in detail in *The First Three Minutes,* is based on
the most solid science we have. It can be made quantitative as well as
qualitative. It has predictive power, and the predictions that it has
yielded can be—and have been—tested. Speculation has been turned
into science.

After publishing their article, Wilson and Penzias continued to
work on cosmic radiation for another year. They got a military-surplus
maser that had been built for one of the Nike radar systems, and with
it as a detector they used the horn to measure the background radiation
at 21 centimeters. At about the same time, Roll and Wilkinson measured it at 3.2 centimeters; the blackbody curve was beginning to fill
itself in. After he and Penzias had done their work on cosmic radiation,
Wilson recalls, "The local management here decided that we had had
our fun doing astronomy and that now we really ought to contribute
something to the telephone company too." This kind of alternation of
practical and pure research has been characteristic of the Crawford Hill
branch of Bell Labs. Indeed, after having founded the science of radio
astronomy thirty years earlier, Jansky too had been encouraged to
return to company business. Wilson and Penzias set up a laser on top

of Crawford Hill, with the idea that the laser beam might propagate through ground fog and would therefore be useful for communications. It didn't. "We did the wrong measurement," Wilson said. "If you go into New York City, say, to the third floor of some building, and send the beam to the third floor of another building, it will propagate fine, since fog doesn't usually form there. But fog in the suburbs immediately wipes it out. Next, I built a thing called a Sun Tracker. It did just that. It was programmed with data from an ephemeris and pointed at the sun all day. It could measure the sun's brightness at wavelengths of one and two centimeters. Since the sun's output is essentially constant there, the measurements told us about transmission through the earth's atmosphere—an interesting question since our boss, Roy Tillotson, had proposed using these bands for satellite communication."

In the late 1960's Wilson and Penzias returned to radio astronomy. A group at Crawford Hill had become interested in transmitting microwave radiation through two-inch pipes. Their interest was a practical one. These wave guides, it was envisioned, could be used for digital telephone communication and might carry half a million simultaneous telephone calls. Charles Burrus, a physicist who occupies an office only a few doors from Wilson's, invented what Wilson said were the world's best millimeter-wave receivers. Coincidentally, at about the same time, the National Radio Astronomy Observatory, which has its telescope at Kitt Peak, Arizona, had constructed a millimeter radio-telescope antenna. Using some of Burrus' equipment and literally bolting the wave guides together, Wilson and Penzias made their own millimeter receiver, which they then transported to Kitt Peak in the company of Keith Jefferts, who was then an atomic physicist at Murray Hill and now runs an enterprise that makes sophisticated equipment for tagging and counting fish. "Keith is the same sort of person as I am as far as electronics is concerned," Wilson commented. "We're both very happy to pile in with our own hands, so he and I ended up actually putting the receiver together and taking it out to Kitt Peak a few days before Arno got there. Sandy Weinreb, the head of the electronics section of the observatory, was tremendously helpful in getting together the rest of the spectrometer. At that time something else was going on here that helps to explain why our millimeter research got supported. In 1963, about six months before I got here, Comsat was created, and AT&T was legislated out of the overseas-satellite business. But by 1970 it seemed as if domestic communications satellites might be useful. It wasn't clear whether, under the rules that applied then, AT&T would be allowed in that business, but it seemed interesting enough for Bell Labs to do research on it. One of the things they wanted to find out was how close together in orbit one could put two communications satellites. They were also worried about rain. Water droplets absorb and scatter millimeter waves, and that would affect the signals from a satellite. A few years later, we built a millimeter telescope here for this research. It went into operation in 1977, and even though it was set up with satellites in mind, it turns out to be a very good instrument for radio astronomy. It has a clean beam and makes clean spectra.

"In any case, the first time we hooked up our receiver to the Kitt Peak telescope and pointed it toward the Orion Nebula, in 1970, the carbon-monoxide line just popped out." Wilson was referring to its appearance on a monitor display of the receiver output. "That was the most 'Aha!' discovery I've ever made. They just pointed the thing and it was there, and when I told them to move the telescope it went away. Our receiver worked on a wavelength that was just short of 3 millimeters, and this line was at 2.6 millimeters. We thought we might have to observe for a long time to see something interesting, but it was just suddenly there. After that, there was an intense period at Kitt Peak since, for a while, we 'owned' that part of the spectrum. It was an entirely new way of looking at our galaxy—the gas clouds in the galaxy. They have a very rich molecular chemistry that until then had not been appreciated. That frontier is gone now. Most of the easy observations have been made."

In 1978 Wilson and Penzias shared the Nobel Prize in physics with Kapitza. Had the Nobel Prize substantially affected Wilson's life? "I think so," he replied. "It certainly brings many more invitations to talk than before, and ceremonial, or functional, things to do. I have certainly felt more hassled than before. It causes people to expect me to do things that I can't or am not going to do. People listen to me a lot more than they used to. Maybe they shouldn't. They want me to be an expert on anything. I am not. It has probably assured that the remainder of my life will be comfortable. And I am doing something

now in which it actually helps. I am trying to organize the community
of radio astronomers who work with millimeter wavelengths. We are
working toward building a new national millimeter instrument, and
having a little bit of clout doesn't hurt in something like that."

Asked if he had ever thought of moving to a university, Wilson
replied, "Oh, occasionally I have that idea. But I am so well fixed up
here that it is a little hard to jump off, especially in these days of
scrimpy government funding. I am a little worried about Bell Labs'
changing with the divestiture. I do not think that is what the owners
of the company want. I suppose that it could be that, when it comes
down to meeting the bottom line, the owners are going to have less
interest in basic research than they have had in the past. But from
everything they say, they seem to understand the value of basic research, and they appear to realize how much Bell Labs has contributed
over the years. Basic research is a small fraction of the whole financially,
but it has paid off handsomely. So assuming our owners understand and
mean what they say, they are not going to want to get rid of basic
research. But I see the people in research react to all the talk about
competition, and they worry about the future of the company. A lot
of people are getting interested in fairly practical projects. I have an
idea for making cordless telephones, although I haven't gotten around
to doing much with it yet."

Wilson is now head of the Radio Research Department at Crawford Hill. Besides himself, there are two other full-time Ph.D. radio
astronomers, and Penzias also continues to use the new millimeter
telescope. There are also several graduate students, some from Princeton, where Penzias has been an adjunct professor for many years. The
rest of the department—the larger part—concentrates on designing
microwave devices for communications, which has been the traditional
mission of the Radio Research Laboratory. When he is not musing
about cordless telephones, Wilson uses the radio telescope to study
regions in the Milky Way where stars are still being formed, regions
like the Orion Nebula. "The galaxy," he remarked, "is much more
dynamic than most people think."

The day of my visit was a warm, sunny, early spring day. Wilson
suggested that we have a look at the new telescope, and we drove to
the top of Crawford Hill. Although not much of a hill, it does dominate

the surrounding, flat countryside. Some of the staff members were getting ready to play a lunchtime game of volleyball; the atmosphere seemed very relaxed. The telescope is housed in a building that looks something like a Cape Cod cottage. Inside is an impressive collection of electronic instrumentation. Wilson studied the readings on a few of the instruments and spoke to the graduate student who was running the telescope. Then Wilson and I went outside and climbed up a small, somewhat precarious-looking metal ladder to the roof. Wilson crawled into the telescope and I followed. No sooner were we inside than the telescope began to move. It was like riding a gentle roller coaster. Wilson explained that the student was moving the telescope back and forth across some radio source in the Milky Way—perhaps in the Orion Nebula. The signals coming into the telescope had begun their journey about a thousand years before the Florentine explorer Giovanni da Verrazano touched the New Jersey coast in 1524.

# CHAPTER 15

# Arno Penzias

SOME YEARS AGO a top research director at Bell Labs gave an address at a meeting in which he attempted to describe the special balance between research and development that then existed at the Laboratories. At that time, AT&T had the main responsibility for providing telephone communication for the United States, and it appeared that this state of affairs would endure indefinitely. The Laboratories thus had to be concerned with any scientific development that might affect telecommunications and, consequently, *had* to be committed to a vigorous program of pure research. Following the talk, the research director of a chemical company declared that the purpose of research in *his* company was to make money. As the Bell Labs executive told me, "That, of course, was also the purpose of research at Bell, but the difference was that the chemist didn't know what business he was going to be in in twenty years, and I did—or I thought I did. Now I don't know what business AT&T and this laboratory are going to be in in twenty years, and that is what worries me".

This uncertainty is widely shared. On 24 August 1982 the consent decree that split up AT&T was approved, although not in final form, by Federal District Court Judge Harold H. Greene. The final form was agreed to on 3 August 1983. Under this decree, on 1 January 1984, the twenty-two telephone operating companies were reorganized into seven regional organizations that split off from AT&T. The new AT&T retained Western Electric (the manufacturing arm of the company); Long Lines, to provide long-distance service; an international company to provide products and services overseas; an entity originally called American Bell but then changed, under court order, to AT&T Information Systems, intended, according to a stockholders' report, to provide "enhanced communications and information services and equipment for businesses, government, and residence customers"; and Bell Laboratories. As for the Laboratories, the same stockholders' report comments:

> Most of Bell Laboratories activities will be focused on specific product lines of business and guided by the demands and opportunities of the marketplace.
>
> However, the need to continue an extensive program of basic research —the source of new knowledge vital to tomorrow's information systems and services—remains a high priority. Accordingly, the management of A.T.&T. has pledged to continue support of fundamental research at Bell Laboratories.
>
> This will continue to assure A.T.&T. its place among America's most innovative business enterprises and America its place as a world leader in science and technology.

Shortly before this report was written, 4,000 employees of Bell Labs were transferred to AT&T Information Systems; 3,000 more are being transferred to the Central Services Organization, which will do for the twenty-two regional companies what Bell Labs traditionally did for the old operating companies: provide them with technical support, in the way of research and development and testing, that is closely connected to actual telephony. This means that nearly a third of the 25,000 members of Bell Labs before the divestiture have been transferred to the new entities. As someone at the Labs said to me, "It is like watching the breakup of a family." To be sure, the vast majority of the Bell Labs "family" has never been occupied with basic research—the kind of activity common in universities. But in terms of financial investment, AT&T's commitment to basic research has been extraordinary.

Some feeling for it can be gotten from the figures for 1981, the last full year before the divestiture decision. The total cost to the parent company—AT&T—of the Bell Labs that year was $1.63 billion; about half this staggering amount went into product design. In this respect, it is important to realize that in high-technology industries like Western Electric, much of what is manufactured—at least in terms of cost —are computer programs—software—which, in turn, run the highly automated telecommunications business. Bell Labs is responsible for this software as well as for the software that runs the telephone switching system, which, taken as a whole, is the world's most complex computer network. It involves tens of millions of lines of programming, a substantial fraction of the Bell Labs budget. In 1981 about 8.3 percent—$135 million—went for basic research. This covered a spectrum of activity ranging from neurophysiology to materials science. It is instructive to note that the National Science Foundation, the federal entity that supports most of the nation's pure research, had a 1983 budget of $1.1 billion. The Bell Labs budget for basic research is, depending on the year, somewhere between 10 and 15 percent of the *entire* budget of the National Science Foundation. No one at Bell is directly supported by the National Science Foundation; all the money comes from AT&T. As a distinguished physicist at Bell said, "If, because of lack of support from the company, the people at Bell were forced to apply for government contracts in our fields, we would saturate the National Science Foundation budget in the relevant fields. In much of what we do, we are the best and would get most of the contracts."

If Bell Laboratories is to preserve anything like its predivestiture shape, two things are necessary. The parent company must continue to have the wherewithal to support research, and must be committed to it—must want to spend its resources on research. No one can guarantee the former, but if the present vice-president in charge of research, Arno A. Penzias, has anything to do with it, the future of research would be assured. Penzias, who was born in Munich on 26 April 1933, has spent essentially all of his professional life in research at Bell. He and Robert Wilson shared the 1978 Nobel Prize in physics for their joint discovery of the cosmic background radiation—the fossil radiation—that is a remnant of the cosmic fireball, the Big Bang, in which the universe began. Any applications of this discovery to telephony have yet to be revealed. A lanky, spare man of clearly boundless energy, Penzias took on his present job in December 1981, just a few weeks before the divestiture plan was first accepted by AT&T. In that sense, he and the new Bell Laboratories start off together.

Penzias' office, the largest I saw at the Labs, is hardly luxurious by American corporate standards. As one might imagine, there are various state-of-the-art office systems, and on one of my visits, two Bell engineers were showing him a new, homegrown one. Since he is still actively doing radio astronomy, he has a computer terminal that ties in to his research activity. A wall cabinet houses various mementos, including a metal casting of a bagel. Penzias gives almost weekly bagel breakfasts, inviting a few people at a time in order to discuss what is going on and to listen to their problems.

Arno Penzias was born, as he remarked, "the same day that the Gestapo was formed. I've lasted a little longer fortunately. My father, although born in Germany, was a Polish citizen. The place where the Penziases come from has belonged to three different countries in three generations. My mother and her family were German, going back generations, although she converted to Judaism when she married my father. My father had a small leather business, a little loft somewhere, where he bought hides and then sold them to shoemakers."

As a child, Penzias had no realization that there was anything abnormal about being a Jew in Nazi Germany. "Things were not especially bad for me and my brother, who is a year younger. We were sent to a Jewish school, so I didn't feel the anti-Semitism directly. During that period Jews were forbidden to go to stores except during certain hours. So, as I learned later, the wife of an S.S. sergeant who lived in our building would go shopping for my mother. She said, 'We —the S.S.—don't want to hurt small children.' It seemed that then people felt that the Jews they knew were fine. It was the *other* Jews they read about who were the 'bad' ones. The only incident I remember from that time was once when we were on a trolley car and I was showing off. When you are the adored eldest son, you sort of get the feeling that you should show off all the time. I said something that made it clear to the other people there that I was Jewish, and that so changed the atmosphere of the trolley car that my mother had to take us off and wait for the next one. From that incident I learned that I was not supposed to talk about being Jewish in public and that, if you did, you put your family in danger. It was a big shock for me."

In the fall of 1938 the Germans began deporting people like the Penziases, who did not have German passports. However, as Penzias put it, "The Polish government agreed with the Nazis on only one thing, and that was their dislike for Jews. So they declared that as of 1 November 1938 all Polish passports would be invalid except those that were renewed at a local consulate. At the same time they instructed the consulates not to renew any passports belonging to Jews. Since the Germans wanted to get rid of as many Jews as possible, in October all the Polish Jews in Germany were rounded up. They were trying to beat the November 1st deadline, after which our Polish passports were no longer valid and they couldn't push us over the Polish border. First we were put in a prison cell. I remember the cell as being a great big room with bunks up one side, and my cousins and I all scrambled up and down and had a great time. We were then put on a train—a normal passenger train. I was five, and the whole idea of being on a train then seemed like a circus. People from other Jewish communities along the way would line up at each one of the stops and give us food. They gave the kids candy. I remember stuffing myself with chocolate."

On 7 November 1938, a seventeen-year-old boy named Herschel Grynszpan assassinated a junior counsellor in the German embassy in Paris. Grynszpan's elderly parents had been deported on a transport train that was just ahead of the one that the Penziases were on. They were taken off the train at the Polish border and kept in an open field, where they died of exposure. To avenge his parents, Gryszpan shot the first German in uniform he could find. This episode resulted on 9 November in *Kristallnacht*—crystal night—when Jewish homes and shops throughout Germany were attacked. The "crystal" refers to the sound of breaking windows. More than 30,000 Jews were arrested, and thousands were sent to concentration camps. By 23 November the Nazis had enforced a set of decrees that eliminated Jews from German economic life.

"We got to the border," Penzias said "an hour or so after the November 1st deadline. We were allowed to return to Munich because we couldn't be deported. The Poles were filling up their field only until midnight. After midnight, forget it—they weren't taking any more. As soon as we got back to Munich, my father was given six months to get out of Germany, after which he was going to be arrested. My parents knew what that meant, because Dachau was already in operation. When they arrested people during the *Kristalnacht* they sent them to Dachau, which was the first concentration camp. It was in a suburb of Munich. My father and my uncle were among the young men who would go down to the railroad station to pick up people who had been released from Dachau and sent back. In those days the Nazis killed a few in Dachau, but it was not yet a factory. It was a prison. It was a place to torture people, not to kill them. Many were sent back. In the 1970's, my uncle met somebody in Queens, where he now lives, whom he had picked off a train back from Dachau at that time.

"*Affidavit,*" Penzias went on, "was the first English word I ever learned. I didn't even know then that it was an English word. Everybody was talking about an *affidavit,* but to me it was just a word." In order to immigrate to the United States, it was necessary to have someone claim you as a relative and guarantee that you would not become a public charge. With this affidavit, one could apply for a visa for the United States; with the visa it was possible to get an exit permit from Germany.

"Children at that time had no trouble getting out," Penzias recalled. "There were even trains running to England. But my parents weren't willing to let us go until at least one of them could get out as well. There were people in the United States who were willing to say that they were related to you, but often their own financial resources were strained because they were trying to bring their own families over. So people would knock on doors until they found someone who would help rescue a family that they didn't know. In our case somebody said yes with about a month to spare. My father is a great worrier anyway, so I can imagine what strain he must have been under. My parents concealed all of that from the children very effectively. Finally, in the late spring of 1939, my brother and I were put on the train for England —I was six—and they said, 'Look, you are the grown-up one. You take care of your brother, and take care of these two little suitcases. Don't eat too much candy, don't go with strangers'—a whole set of instructions. They were giving me all these instructions. It was a nightmare. My father got out a few days later. At that point my mother did not have an exit permit, and so she was not sure that she would ever see us again. But a few months later she joined us. By September the war was on and no one could get out anymore, so we made it with very little to spare."

While he was still in Germany, Penzias' father had bought steamship tickets for the family from England to New York, and in December 1939 they sailed for America. "We arrived in New York the first week of January 1940. I remember the month, because on the ship, a Cunard liner, we had both a Christmas and a New Year's party. Here we were, refugees fleeing for our lives, and they had parties with balloons. You could eat yourself sick. Somehow, while I was in England, I had learned some English—I am not sure how. I even learned to read in the few weeks I was at school there. I still remember the two-room schoolhouse. One day I looked at a book and it all made sense. My father couldn't speak English terribly well, and he could only get a job doing some kind of manual labor. The unspoken agreement with the person who signed your affidavit was that you were not supposed to bother them once you got here. You were supposed to be on your own. You had a moral obligation to feed yourself and not use your sponsor as a resource. Anyway, we first lived in a furnished room in the Bronx and then an apartment on the Grand Concourse that we couldn't afford, and finally my father became a superintendant—a super as they called them—in various apartment buildings in the Bronx. He collected garbage out of the dumbwaiters, stoked coal for the furnace, and the like; and then a few years later, my mother went to work in the garment district."

Penzias recalls attending about half a dozen New York elementary public schools and then a junior high school in the Bronx. "I suppose everybody is unhappy in junior high school, but I started out not being able to speak English, so I had a foreign accent. I never really learned kids' ways. By the time I could speak English well, I could not play the games well. I thought the teachers in junior high school were sometimes destructive. I still remember one time we were shown a siphon, and the teacher asked us to write down the principle of the siphon. The class said it worked because of air pressure. Somehow I intuitively realized that that couldn't be right, since the air pressure was higher in the lower of the two beakers. Air pressure works in the wrong direction. I said that, and the teacher asked me how I thought it did work, and when I tried to explain, the class totally broke up. They thought that it was incredibly stupid that I didn't understand that the thing worked by air pressure. The teacher was, I guess, not a bad fellow, but there was not much guidance there."

In February 1947, Penzias entered Brooklyn Technical High School. "Once I got there, I didn't feel so strange and isolated any more. There were more kids like myself. I made friends for the first time. It was a fairly elite school from which the kids went to college. At home, my father had always talked up chemistry. Like most German Jews, he was a big German patriot. Everything done in Germany was better. He knew about I.G. Farben and German chemistry. So at Brooklyn Tech I sort of drifted into chemistry. I was more interested in electronics actually, but I talked myself out of it. I had some friends who were radio hams, and I sort of figured that they knew so much more electronics than I did that I couldn't possibly compete with them. I didn't do well in the high school physics courses that I took. By this time I was sort of moving toward technology as a way to make a living. I didn't think I could make a living on my social skills, and once you eliminate social skills what else is there? The thing I wanted to make absolutely sure of was that I wasn't going to be poor. Writers and artists were poor. I didn't have the eyesight to be a pilot, so the only kind of job I could imagine that would work had to do with technology. It was clear to me that I wanted to go to college because people who went to college seemed to dress better and to eat more regularly. It was also clear to me that I wanted to do something 'real.' So it seemed that the way to go to college and get a job doing something real at the end was to study engineering, or something like that."

In the fall of 1951, Penzias entered the tuition-free City College of New York. "The price was right," he remarked. "I realized," he noted, "that after about one semester in that place I was sick of chemistry. I had taken so much in high school that college chemistry was a real nuisance. It involved a lot of memorization of stuff that I already knew. I also took elementary physics, which was taught by a very nice teacher named Hardy. I went to see Professor Hardy and I asked him, 'Can physicists make a living?' That's what I asked him. He said that physicists think they can do anything that an engineer can do, and if they can do that they can at least make a living as engineers. I said 'fine' and switched majors to physics.

"I took the standard physics courses and the required math courses as well. I never really enjoyed the math courses much. I suppose, compared to the average person one meets in the supermarket, I'm very good at math, but compared to a mathematician I'm very primitive. I don't think of myself as a very mathematical person. To the extent that I use math at all it's more on intuition than any real mathematical skills. I graduated maybe sixteenth in a class of a hundred and seventy, but of the fifteen or so kids who were ahead of me, half of them were physics majors. So I was well back in the pack of good physics majors. In those days, the physics majors were the curve busters. They were the odd, bright kids who didn't fit in. Physics was unglamorous then. This was before Sputnik. The number of physics majors was small, and nobody was led into it. The top bright kids seemed to be attracted to it for aesthetic reasons. I didn't get into it, at first, for those reasons, but I found, as I studied it, that it was something I liked. The competition was extraordinarily tough. I had a feeling at that time of not being terribly good . . . of being only a barely adequate physicist."

When the Penziases came to the United States, the family acquired American first names. His brother Gunter became Jim, and Arno became Allen, adding it as a middle name when he took out citizenship papers in 1946. While at City College, he met his future wife, Anne. They were married in 1954. "When I met her she was dating an Al. So to keep from being confused, she alone among all the people in the world called me Arno. So I got Arno back. Recently someone said to me, 'You're not an Al,' although I may have tried to be for a while. I sign my name Arno A. Penzias. It is a vestige of my attempt to Americanize myself."

Another vestige was a two-year stint in the Army Signal Corps after Penzias graduated from City College in 1954. While in college, Penzias had joined the Reserve Officer Training Corps. By being able to receive five words a minute in Morse code, Penzias managed to get a ham radio license, which was enough to qualify him for the Signal Corps. "I was stationed at Fort Devens in Massachusetts. It was a clear waste of two years of my life," he said. "I haven't touched Morse since."

Near the end of this period, Penzias went back to City College to ask advice from his former professors about getting into graduate school. "Given my record, I didn't know what kind of graduate school I could get into. One of the professors gave me a list which unfortunately included M.I.T. I say 'unfortunately,' because M.I.T. turned me down. I had a few choices, but at the last minute my wife said that she was really sick of living outside New York. At the end of our teenage years, we had both wanted to move somewhere else, but I guess the biggest single thing the army did for me was to show me what life was like outside of New York. I decided that I didn't like it. The only thing to do was try to get into Columbia. Well, Columbia was willing to take me but not willing to give me a teaching assistantship. So I went over there, and on the basis of my Signal Corps experience and a little fast talking, they were willing to give me a research assistantship. The people in the Physics Department office called the Columbia Radiation Laboratory upstairs, and they, it turned out, had plenty of money. They were willing to pay me $180 a month, provided I paid my own tuition. That seemed like so much money. I also had G.I. Bill money, and my wife worked for a couple of years as an elementary school teacher. We moved back to the Bronx and got a little apartment, and I commuted down from the Bronx to Columbia everyday."

The Columbia Physics Department that Penzias entered in the fall of 1956 was a maelstrom of scientific activity. I.I. Rabi had won the Nobel Prize in 1944 and Polykarp Kusch in 1955. Tsung Dao Lee would win it in 1957 and Charles Townes in 1964. Townes had come to Columbia from Bell Labs in 1947, and just prior to Penzias' arrival, he and his students had invented the maser (microwave amplification by stimulated emission of radiation). The department had a reputation for being tough on graduate students, and Penzias did not have an entirely happy time at Columbia. "They let just about anybody in," he recalled. "People came in with degrees in English. Then they failed half the class for the first three or four semesters. They just flunked people out like mad. It never seemed to occur to anyone that they were ruining people's lives. It seemed to me to be a sort of mechanical, mindless grinding of human beings.

"I just got through Columbia by the skin of my teeth," Penzias told me. "I didn't actually flunk any courses, but I got a couple of incompletes and had to take the exams over. I will never forget my first exam, in an optics course I took from Townes. It was an open-book exam with five questions. I couldn't do any of them. By the time I got to number five I was in a cold sweat. I was sitting in this room, and I had just gone through the first four questions. None of them could I answer—not any one. I got to number five, and I looked around and saw that everybody else was working. I asked myself, 'What are the odds that I am the dumbest person in this room?' The rest of them seemed to be able to do the exam—at least they were working—so I decided to try number five. I got it wrong. But then I went back and worked on the rest of them. I got a 54, which, it turned out, was the second highest mark in the class. Townes, it turned out, was just beginning to think about lasers. So he had wanted to learn about optics, and on the exam he asked about things that *he* was interested in."

In 1957, Penzias asked Townes if he could do a thesis with him, and Townes agreed. Townes had just gotten two students to build a maser that would detect radiation with a three-centimeter wavelength. It was the first operating maser receiver. Penzias built the second maser, designed to work at a wavelength of twenty-one centimeters. (These early masers were fussy laboratory devices; the first practical maser was built at the Bell Labs in 1957—following ideas of N. Bloembergen at Harvard—by G. Feher, D. Scovil and H. Seidel in connection with the Telstar project.) The choice of this wavelength was not accidental. The hydrogen atom emits radio waves at twenty-one centimeters, and Penzias hoped to use his maser in conjunction with a large radio antenna to detect hydrogen in outer space—indeed, the hydrogen then thought to be present in the gas between galaxies. Penzias brought his maser to the Naval Research Laboratory at Maryland Point, Maryland, which had a large antenna suitable for detecting astronomical radio signals.

Penzias told me, "I had read an article in a journal where some fellow had reported that he had found hydrogen in the galactic gas in several clusters of galaxies. So it seemed like it would be an easy thing to do to use my maser, which was very sensitive, and make a tremendous catalog of intergalactic hydrogen. I went to the antenna and pointed it to where I thought I should see something, and saw nothing. So I called the guy up, and he said, 'Oh, yes, all my results were wrong. All my hydrogen signals were spurious.' At that point I figured that the best thing to do was to place an upper limit on the amount of hydrogen in a few clusters of galaxies. I did see a signal, but it was not hydrogen-line radiation. Later in my career I did some more intergalactic-hydro-

gen work because it has cosmological significance; but that was the idea
of the thesis. It was a dreadful thesis, and I felt that I had just barely
gotten through with it. It was something I felt I had to live down or,
at least, do over, better. There were two things that I was good at. One
was an ability to organize things in mechanical terms—to build things
—and the other was that I had, and have, a great ability to endure pain.
These were the two things that got me through Columbia."

Penzias got his doctorate in 1961. A year earlier, Townes had taken
him and a few other students to visit Bell Labs' Radio Research Laboratory at Crawford Hill. Bell was getting into the communications satellite business at this time but got out of it when the Communications
Satellite Corporation was founded in 1963. The *Echo* balloon, which
was simply a passive reflector of electromagnetic radiation, was
launched in 1960, and a new antenna had just been constructed at
Crawford Hill to receive signals from it. Later that year, Penzias got
the notion that he might use a maser—either his or one built at the
Labs—to redo his thesis. He asked the then director of the Radio
Research Lab, Rudolf Kompfner, if it would be possible to have a
temporary appointment, just long enough to carry out his project.
"Rudy said," Penzias recalled, " 'Why not take a permanent job that
you can always quit? We have permanent jobs here in the sense that
there is no particular time attached to them where the job is automatically reviewed. We don't really have a tenure system. We have a
continuing review. If the quality of someone's work goes below a
certain level, then some kinds of separations can be effected. We have
a standard that we adhere to, but we don't assume that some fraction
of what one might call our assistant professors will not become associate
professors. The normal assumption is that, given satisfactory work,
everybody stays. We don't have—the way you do in a university—some
number of tenure slots that is smaller than the number of people we
hire. But a small fraction of people who have been here for five years
will not make it to ten, and some smaller fraction will not make it to
fifteen, and so forth. But by and large, unsuitable people are weeded
out—usually by mutual agreement—within the first few years.' In any
case, he offered, and I accepted the job and came to Crawford Hill in
1961. I had always thought, even before I came, that Bell Labs would
be a great place to work. I liked the connection between the work done

here and useful things. I have always wanted to do something practical."

A part of the first project that Penzias worked on had to do with the "antenna pointing committee," organized to set up a system to help point an antenna accurately. Penzias explained, "The antenna at Crawford Hill was fairly small, so it wasn't all that hard to know where it was pointing. But the one at Andover, Maine was substantially larger. It was used to communicate with Telstar—the first active communications satellite—which was designed at Bell Labs. These antennas are made of steel. Steel bends under gravity, under wind load, the sun, temperature, what have you. The gears are not perfect. The foundation is not cast exactly horizontal and so forth. These errors are very hard to find and can even vary with the time of day. So to solve this problem, Bell Labs had created the committee, which had about thirty members. I came to the first meeting and said that I knew how to solve the problem."

In essence what Penzias proposed was to put a second receiver in the antenna, which he could then point at some known natural source of radiation, such as the remnants of an exploded star. By comparing the star's position—according to the telescope's instruments—with the position as given by an astronomical table, he could then tell by how much the telescope was mispointing. "The committee," Penzias noted, "immediately dissolved itself and gave me the job, and I went off and did it."

Penzias then decided that he had had enough of the communications-satellite business and returned to radio astronomy. "They offered me the opportunity to use the horn antenna—the one that Wilson and I used later to discover the cosmic background radiation—at Crawford Hill for some satellite communication work on the Telstar project. I said, 'No, I'd rather do radio astronomy.' In those days, as now, the Laboratories funded a number of disinterested experiments. That way we're not just a sink of information, but a source as well. We want to be coupled to the basic scientific community because we get information from them. The only way we *get* information is to give some back. In any case I took a little antenna of my own on a corner of the Hill and did my own experiment. By that time—1963—only the twenty-one-centimeter hydrogen line from interstellar space had been discovered. I thought that it would be nice to look for the hydroxyl molecule, the oxygen-hydrogen molecule, — OH. It had a line at eighteen centimeters. My antenna had a very broad beam, so that if OH had been distributed across the sky the way hydrogen is, I could have found it. But OH, it turns out, is much more concentrated. What I needed was a much larger antenna with a tinier beam. So some Australians, with a large antenna, were the first to find it. After that, I joined a project at Harvard that had a large antenna, and I used my own receiver to do some additional OH work for a little while. It was an OK project but not a roaring success, since these other people, with the right kind of antenna, had beat me out."

In 1963 Robert Wilson came to Bell Labs. There was only one radio astronomy position, so he and Penzias split it, with each working half-time on other projects. Because Bell got out of the communications satellite business that year, the horn antenna that had been used to communicate with the Telstar satellites became available for full-time radio astronomy. Thus began the remarkable series of events that led to their joint discovery in 1965 of the cosmic background radiation —the whispers of radiation that permeate all space and are as old as the universe itself. I asked Penzias to describe the effect of this discovery on him. He said, "I was a late starter. My first refereed paper came out in 1964, not all that much before my thirty-second birthday. That was the work on the hydroxyl molecules. But in 1965 our cosmic background radiation work had burst upon the scene. It made me think of a farmer in Egypt who finds one of those famous tombs. If I were that farmer, the first thing I would do is to cover the tomb and go off to archaeology school to get my archaeologist's license, because the first person to make a discovery like that should be an archeologist, not just a person.

"So I felt that I needed my astronomer's license, and for the next few years I proceeded to get it. Wilson and I opened up an entirely new field. I put together a group to work on the millimeter-wavelength portion of the radiation spectrum produced by interstellar molecules. We used Bell Labs technology to make a receiver that we used in conjunction with a large antenna in the National Radio Astronomy Laboratory in Arizona. Along with Keith B. Jefferts we discovered, in 1970, carbon monoxide in the Orion Nebula. Then we found some of the dozens of interstellar molecules, ranging from ethyl alcohol to hydrocyanic acid, that everybody knows about now. The millimeter portion of the spectrum is so rich that it is hard to take an antenna and point it at certain sources in the sky and not find new lines. When we opened up this field it was a tremendous step forward, and it was very profitable both professionally and scientifically."

In 1972, Arthur B. Crawford, who had been the head of the Radio Research Department at Crawford Hill during the eleven years that Penzias had worked there, retired. Having put together the millimeter-wavelength astronomy project, Penzias had made a favorable impression as a scientific organizer and was offered the job. "I had already turned down a couple of department-head offers, because I was happy doing what I was doing, and I wasn't really sure that I wanted to manage anybody. The thought of sitting in meetings all day and taking stuff from my in basket and putting it into my out basket sounded dreadful. And Crawford, although he liked the recognition of having been promoted, regarded the job itself as a burden. I was happy to be working for him so long as he was there, but once he retired I didn't feel like working for anyone else so I took the job. It was a department of about a dozen people."

In the Bell Labs organization a department is run by a department head, a laboratory is run by a director, a division is run by an executive director, and an area is run by a vice-president. The technical areas include Electronic Technology, Operations Systems and Network Planning, Switching Systems, Research, Computer Technologies, Military Systems, and Transmission Systems. In less than ten years, Penzias went from being a member of the Radio Research Department to the vice-president in charge of research, an advance that he regards as "nothing short of miraculous."

"The nice thing about each of the administrative jobs that I have had," he added, "is that the previous occupant had retired, so that I was able to redefine the job. In each case I became convinced that I had the best conceivable job, not just in Bell Laboratories but probably in the world of science. But when I said to my wife that I didn't want the next job because it was a terrible job, and that the job I had was the last *good* job, she said just what Rudi Kompfner told me, 'Take it. You can always quit.' But I never wanted to, because each new job turned out to be marvelous."

In 1978 Penzias and Wilson were awarded the Nobel Prize in

physics. Asked to tell a little about it, Penzias replied, "I can now, after six years, say 'Nobel Prize' without stammering. A Nobel Prize can make one feel intimidated. One sort of feels that the people around you are sharper and perhaps a little bit smarter; that they get things faster and don't have all the doubts and questions that you have; that they really understand the stuff that they are talking about and that the stuff that you understand is, maybe, simpler. I think that's a general feeling among scientists. I don't know about other fields. But I think around here the really good people do have a certain amount of anxiety. Also, when you win the Nobel Prize you get into the same company with people like Hans Bethe and Charles Townes, and one can have the feeling that those people are really more deserving. I have sort of finessed that by saying that I don't want to be judged by how much I deserved the prize but rather on what use I have put it to. I have tried to use it in positive ways. For example, the first thing I did when I won it was to go from Stockholm to Moscow, where I delivered my Nobel lecture in Brailovsky's apartment. [Viktor Brailovsky is a distinguished Soviet computer scientist and dissident. He and his wife, Irina, had a tiny three-room apartment where about thirty dissident scientists held regular seminars to keep up with their professions. In November 1980 Brailovsky was arrested and imprisoned for "defamation of the Soviet state."] I try to use the visibility that comes with such recognition in ways that I think are helpful to society, the society that has nurtured and benefited me. That makes me feel a little better about it. Basically I am glad that I won it. Among other things, you tend to meet a hell of a lot of interesting people. It is, as the sociologist Robert Merton put it, a 'haunting presence.' If I go to a party with people I don't know, sometimes I think I am having this great time with all these people chuckling at my jokes. And then, after it is all over, people come and say, 'It was an honor to meet you'—as if they weren't listening to me at all. So it's a haunting presence you carry with you, but it's not terrible."

I had heard that there was a story connected with the tuxedo that Penzias wore for the Nobel ceremonies. "Well," Penzias said, "it was a Jewish story. I wanted, if I can call it that, a Jewish tuxedo, something made in the garment district. My mother worked there, and a whole generation of Jewish immigrants put the next generation through college by working there. I didn't want to buy a tuxedo in Princeton, or in a fancy New York store, where it might be sold to you by someone who would make you ashamed of the clothes you were wearing when you came in to buy it. I wanted the tuxedo to be me and not some sort of costume. I did not want to change. I still have the same friends and live in the same house that I did before I won the prize. So I went to a loft on lower Fifth Avenue where I had bought clothes in the past. My secretary called them up and found that they had tuxedos in stock, very good quality stuff but more in keeping. Those were the hectic days before the actual award, and I needed the tuxedo for a banquet that was a couple of days away.

"But this is a loft where things don't work that way. Although they are set up for the retail trade, it is really a clothing factory where the tailor is in charge. You get your suit off of a pipe rack, and then you go to the tailor to discuss alterations. He has been there for twenty or thirty years and has a measuring tape around his neck. The first thing he says to you is 'Go and try on the pants, but don't get them dirty.' —that kind of a place. So I picked my tuxedo off the rack and went to the tailor and showed it to him. He said, 'That's fine. Just go pay for it.' I said, 'I have a problem. I have to have it altered, and I need it back this afternoon.' He looked at me in disbelief and said, 'If you want it this afternoon you don't get it altered.' I then started telling him a few things. I said, 'Look I need it for a banquet for Israel.' I thought that might soften him up. 'It's a very important banquet, and then I have to go on a television show.' He was weakening, but not much. He said, 'All right, you can come back a week from Saturday.' Finally there was nothing else to do so I said, 'Look I didn't want to tell you, but my name has been in the papers. You may have even heard of me. I just won the Nobel Prize.' And he looks at me and says, '*You're* Isaac Singer?' I had to tell him that I had won a different prize, but finally he did the tuxedo."

In December 1981, Penzias took on his present job and moved to Murray Hill, New Jersey. "I had one week to get over here from Holmdel and put my furniture in my office before the Christmas holidays. Then I got back from Christmas and was all set to start working, when they broke up the telephone company. I didn't believe that the case would ever be settled out of court, but I was wrong. It was a jolt, and it made me even busier than I was. I had a student from

Princeton who just finished a thesis with me, and he got a good deal less attention than he might have if I had been less busy; and my own research sort of got squeezed out. I've had an amazing amount of freedom in this job. Nobody tells me how to do my job, but there is a tremendous pressure to do a good job. Everybody from the chairman of AT&T on down says that they think research is a good thing. It's like supporting motherhood. But they say it almost on faith. It is part of my job to show this in a quantitative way. I have given myself a twofold charter. The inside of this place has to look the same as it was to the people working here, and the outside has to look different to our owners. We have to make sure that the people who are paying for the research get value for their money. We have to provide the foundation and understanding for the people who are responsible for products and services. Nobody gives me a quota that tells me I have to turn out so many patents. But there is pressure all over. Pressure from the Japanese, who are competing with us and pressure from within to help the lightwave people, help the terminal people, help the switching people —help every single group as fast as we can. One of our strengths, and one of the unique things about our research, is that we are tied very closely to development and manufacture. The new laboratory that is being set up for the Central Services Organization, that will serve the operating phone companies, will have a much smaller research operation than we do. They will not have the responsibility of inventing products that can be produced by Western Electric. We at Bell Labs keep that responsibility. Some of our people will go to the new laboratory, but eventually they will be replaced here.

"Our research role is to provide an understanding of the broad range of technologies that will support what we call 'the information age.' The fields that are needed in this range all the way from graph theory to surface science. It requires essentially the same number of people and the same mix of skills as before. So the mission of the Laboratories has not really changed. What has changed is that the mechanism by which we can transfer concepts into products has become clearer. Before, some of the products that arose because of our knowledge could not be produced here. The 1956 decrees [which settled AT&T's earlier antitrust case] would not allow it. Now, for example, we can get into medical electronics. We can certainly get into computers, and we are certainly going to. This is not to say that we are going to stop doing and publishing pure research or that we are, in any way, going to change our ethics or standards. But the focus of the research and the goals are very clear. We've got competitive AT&T Communications. We've got Western Electric. We've got an international company. We've got AT&T Information Systems, and each of those outfits has a product line. The most important of our customers will still be the telephone companies. We don't want the flow of equipment that comes from our science to result in products from some Japanese manufacturer or to be made in South Korea, or Taiwan, or West Germany, or somewhere. We are going to lose some business I expect, but basically we want to maintain the flow, which means our products had better be the best. We want to use American labor, which is more expensive. Our only advantage is knowledge.

"We *have* streamlined. We are working harder than we used to. We have a sense of urgency. With respect to the development departments, some people say we used to have a kind of Tarzan complex, as if we were going to teach the 'apes' how to read or something. We are now working much closer to development. But I am not doing this just to make money for some stockholders. I am doing it because I think it is good for the country, good for science, as well as being good for Bell Labs. If we have a financially healthy organization here, then we can afford to do fundamental research—the kind of stuff that I do in my own radio astronomy. I have just sent a paper to a journal on interstellar isotopic abundances. I think that was worthwhile doing. There are other people here working in fields that range from cognitive psychology to the structure of polymeric molecules. We have fundamental research all through this organization. But fundamental research is always under pressure here. We are going to fund only the best stuff. We are a tighter and leaner organization than we used to be. For example, we don't tolerate run-of-the-mill physics as much as we might have done in the past. Partly that is my own doing. Long before the divestiture, when I became a head of a division, the number of people who left it dramatically increased. It is as much my personality as anything else. I demand a certain standard of myself and of everybody else. Keeping someone here has to be weighed against the cost to the people who are outside. To have somebody here in a secure job when there is somebody on the outside who is far more deserving, scientifically, is not necessarily fair. We have to be sensitive, of course, but if people aren't doing their jobs well, then we have to question whether they ought to be doing that job. Somebody who spends twenty years grinding paper after paper out of the same piece of apparatus, just because nobody else is interested in doing the work, doesn't, in my view, qualify as doing top-notch science. But we also have to understand, and I think our owners do, that it can take years and years before someone may be able to make something useful out of a piece of pure research. That we understand this is one of the unique strengths of this place. I have compared us to all of our competitors. We go through this all the time. The few competitors we have, who hire people as good as we do, and who fund them at least as well as we do, do not do as well as we do because they manage too closely. There is too much short-term management. One of the things that people are constantly amazed at in this place is just how little short-term management there really is, just how little short-term management I get. People don't believe that nobody tells me what to do on a daily, weekly, or even a monthly basis. Occasionally I get a little bit of 'fatherly' advice, but in the past year I do not think I have spent as much as four hours with my boss, discussing how I should be doing my job. Instead we focus on our long-range objectives.

"If people are doing an outstanding job," Penzias summed up, "we let them alone, and we're going to continue to do that. But if Western Electric turns belly up and we close all our factories because we can't afford American workers, then all bets are off. As long as there is a healthy Bell Laboratories we need fundamental research desperately. Fundamental research is our window to the universities, to the scientific community. This year, for example, we are wooing theoretical physicists as if they are movie stars. These are not people who are going to make us better light bulbs or better word processors. If I hire the fifth-best theoretical physics student in this country I can get away with it, but if I hire the fifteenth-best I am wasting my time. We are looking for number two or number three, and we want to compete with the best universities for number one. That is where we are. I am a high-pressure guy, and I didn't take this job to conduct a going-out-of-business sale."

# Selected
# Bibliography

Philip W. Anderson, "Absence of Diffusion in Certain Random Lattices," in *Physical Review,* 109 (1958), 1492–1505.

———. "Local Moments and Localized States," in *Les Prix Nobel 1977* (Stockholm, 1978), 83–105.

AT&T Annual Report, 1982.

Bell Telephone Laboratories, *Facts About Bell Labs,* 12th ed. (Murray Hill, N.J., 1982).

———. *A History of Engineering and Science in the Bell System: The Early Years (1875–1925),* M.D. Fagen, ed. (Murray Hill, N.J., 1975).

Ernest Braun and Stuart Macdonald, *Revolution in Miniature,* 2nd ed. (Cambridge–New York, 1983).

John Brooks, *Telephone: The First Hundred Years* (New York, 1975).

M. R. B. Clarke, ed., *Advances in Computer Chess 3* (Oxford, 1982).

D. A. Fraser, *The Physics of Semiconductor Devices,* 3rd ed. (Oxford, 1983).

John Frisby, *Seeing: Illusion, Brain, and Mind* (Oxford, 1980).

Norman Hannay, ed., *Semiconductors* (New York, 1959).

Lillian Hartmann Hoddeson, "The Roots of Solid-State Research at Bell Labs," in *Physics Today,* 30 (March 1977), 23–30.

———. *Multidisciplinary Research in Mission-Oriented Laboratories: The Evolution of Bell Laboratories' Program in Basic Solid-State Physics Culminating in the Discovery of the Transistor 1935–1948* (Urbana, Ill., 1978).

———. "The Entry of the Quantum Theory of Solids into the Bell Telephone Laboratories, 1925–40: A Case-Study of the Industrial Application of Fundamental Science," in *Minerva,* 18 (Autumn 1980), 422–447.

————. "The Emergence of Basic Research in the Bell Telephone System, 1875–1915," in *Technology and Culture,* 22 (July 1981), 512–544.

Bela Julesz, *Foundations of Cyclopean Perception* (Chicago, 1971).

————. "Textons, the Elements of Texture Perception, and Their Interactions," in *Nature,* 290 (12 March 1981), 91–97.

Alfred Charles Bernard Lovell, *The Story of Jodrell Bank* (London–Oxford, 1968).

Prescott C. Mabon, *Mission Communications: The Story of Bell Laboratories* (Murray Hill, N.J., 1975).

Mitchell Paul Marcus, *A Theory of Syntactic Recognition for Natural Language* (Cambridge, Mass.–London, 1980).

David Marr, *Vision* (San Francisco, 1982).

Arno A. Penzias, "The Origin of the Elements," in *Reviews of Modern Physics,* 51 (July 1979), 425–431.

Phillip F. Schewe, ed., *Condensed Matter Glossary* (New York, 1983).

Steven Weinberg, *The First Three Minutes* (New York, 1977).

Robert W. Wilson, "The Cosmic Microwave Background Radiation," in *Les Prix Nobel 1978* (Stockholm, 1979), 113–133.

# Index